Trends in Corrections

With a fresh set of interviews exploring cross-cultural differences and similarities, Volume Three of this book includes lessons from practitioners in a diverse array of countries including Honduras, Japan, Lithuania, the Philippines, Thailand, the Slovak Republic, South Africa, and the United States. This book series is based on the premise that comparing countries around the world and getting 'inside' information about each country's correctional system can be best derived by having people who are seasoned practitioners in each country share their views, experiences, philosophies and ideas.

Since most correctional practitioners do not have the time or inclination to encapsulate their experiences into a book chapter, the insight of the practitioner can be best captured by a revealing interview with a researcher given the questions and interview guidelines associated with each chapter. Researchers selected are scholars in corrections, will possibly have conducted original research on the topic, and will have access to the corrections officials in his or her country. Additionally, the researcher exhibits a deep understanding and knowledge of his or her country's correctional system, and questions will be derived specifically from the laws and conditions present. Any current crises or solutions will be able to have focused questions crafted by each researcher, while still having each interviewer stay within the topic areas that the general questions probe. Each researcher explains any esoteric or unusual terminology used by the corrections official, and defines any current issues necessary for the reader's knowledge.

While there are many books written on corrections management, ethics and practices, there is great value in approaching international corrections practices and policies from this unique vantage point and as a result this book will be of interest to academics, researchers, practitioners and both undergraduate and postgraduate students with an interest in corrections and comparative criminal justice studies.

Dilip K. Das has years of experience in police practice, research, writing, and education. Dr Das is a professor of criminal justice, a former police chief, and a human rights consultant to the United Nations. He is the founding president of the International Police Executive Symposium (IPES), where he manages the affairs of the organisation in cooperation with an appointed group of police practitioners, academia members, and individuals from around the world. Dr Das is also the founding editor in chief of *Police Practice and Research: An International Journal*. He is the author, editor or co-editor of more than 30 books and numerous articles and has received several faculty excellence awards.

Philip Birch is a Senior Lecturer in Criminology at the Centre for Law and Justice, Charles Sturt University, Australia. His research interests include offender rehabilitation and management as well as wider criminal justice practice and professions. Philip is currently the editor in chief for the peer review journal *Salus*, an international journal for law enforcement and public safety (2018–present) and he also sits on the editorial board for the *Journal of Aggression, Conflict and Peace Research*.

Interviews with Global Leaders in Policing, Courts, and Prisons Series
International Police Executive Symposium Co-Publications

Dilip K. Das, Founding President-IPES

PUBLISHED

Trends in the Judiciary: Interviews with Judges Across the Globe, Volume One
By Dilip K. Das and Cliff Roberson with Michael Berlin
ISBN: 978-1-4200-9978-2

Trends in Policing: Interviews with Police Leaders Across the Globe, Volume Four
By Bruce F. Baker and Dilip K. Das
ISBN: 978-1-4398-8073-9

Trends in Policing: Interviews with Police Leaders Across the Globe, Volume Three
By Otwin Marenin and Dilip K. Das
ISBN: 978-1-4398-1924-1

Trends in Policing: Interviews with Police Leaders Across the Globe
By Dilip K. Das and Otwin Marenin
ISBN: 978-1-4200-7520-5

Trends in Corrections: Interviews with Corrections Leaders Around the World
By Jennie K. Singer, Dilip K. Das, and Eileen Ahlin
ISBN: 978-1-4398-3578-4

Trends in Corrections: Interviews with Corrections Leaders Around the World, Volume Two
By Martha Henderson Hurley and Dilip K. Das
ISBN: 978-1-4665-9156-1

Trends in the Judiciary: Interviews with Judges Across the Globe, Volume Two
By David Lowe and Dilip K. Das
ISBN: 978-1-4822-1916-6

Trends in Corrections

Interviews with Corrections Leaders Around the World

Volume Three

Edited by Dilip K. Das and Philip Birch

NEW YORK AND LONDON

First published 2020
by Routledge
52 Vanderbilt Avenue, New York, NY 10017

and by Routledge
2 Park Square, Milton Park, Abingdon, Oxon, OX14 4RN

Routledge is an imprint of the Taylor & Francis Group, an informa business

© 2020 Taylor & Francis

The right of Dilip K. Das and Philip Birch to be identified as the authors of the editorial material, and of the authors for their individual chapters, has been asserted in accordance with sections 77 and 78 of the Copyright, Designs and Patents Act 1988.

All rights reserved. No part of this book may be reprinted or reproduced or utilised in any form or by any electronic, mechanical, or other means, now known or hereafter invented, including photocopying and recording, or in any information storage or retrieval system, without permission in writing from the publishers.

Trademark notice: Product or corporate names may be trademarks or registered trademarks, and are used only for identification and explanation without intent to infringe.

Library of Congress Cataloging-in-Publication Data
A catalog record for this title has been requested

ISBN: 978-0-367-27142-8 (hbk)
ISBN: 978-0-367-34510-5 (pbk)
ISBN: 978-0-429-29506-5 (ebk)

Typeset in Sabon
by Swales & Willis Ltd, Exeter, Devon, UK

Contents

Series Editor's Preface — viii
Acknowledgements — x
About the Editors — xi
About the Contributors — xiii
About the Interviewees — xviii

1 Contextualising the Issue: Leadership in Corrections — 1
   MARK A. NOLAN, MARTHA HENDERSON HURLEY,
   DILIP K. DAS AND PHILIP BIRCH

SECTION I
Europe — 7

2 Živilė Mikėnaitė, Director General of the Prison
   Department of Lithuania — 9
   ILONA LAURINAITYTĖ (ČĖSNIENĖ)

3 Martin Lulei, Project Manager, Ministry of Labour,
   Social Affairs and Family, Slovak Republic — 23
   PAVOL KOPINEC

SECTION II
North America — 39

4 Danny W. Pirtle, Deputy Director of Executive and
   Administrative Services (former), Dallas County
   Juvenile Justice Department — 41
   DAVID C. HURLEY

5   Adonay Davila, Senior Warden (retired), Texas
    Department of Criminal Justice   61
    MICHAEL SANCHEZ

6   Stephen Anderson, Major for Cherokee County Sheriff's
    Office, and Director of Cherokee County Detention
    Facility Gaffney, SC, USA   85
    FRED LUX

SECTION III
South America   103

7   Orlando Garcia Maradiaga, Director, National
    Penitentiary Institute of Honduras   105
    BRIAN NORRIS

SECTION IV
Asia   125

8   Satoshi Tomiyama, Director-General of the Japanese
    Correction Bureau   127
    CAROL LAWSON

9   Randel Latoza, Jail Superintendent, Quezon City
    Jail Male Dormitory, Philippines   149
    RAYMUND NARAG

10 Nathee Jitsawang, Ex-General Director of Department
    of Corrections, Thailand   166
    DITTITA TITITAMPRUK

SECTION V
South Africa   179

11 Mr Johan Ellis Le Grange, Prison Leader – South African
    Department of Correctional Service   181
    ANNI HESSELINK

12 **Reflecting on Leaders in Corrections** PHILIP BIRCH, MARK A. NOLAN, MARTHA HENDERSON HURLEY AND DILIP K. DAS	213
International Police Executive Symposium (IPES) *Call for Authors Guidelines for Interviewers: Trends in*	224
Corrections, Volume 4	226
References	234
Index	241

Series Editor's Preface

The International Police Executive Symposium (IPES) has launched a book series entitled, *Interviews with Global Leaders in Policing, Courts, and Corrections*. The objective is to produce high-quality books aimed at bringing the voice of leading criminal justice practitioners to the forefront of scholarship and research. These books, based on interviews with leaders in Criminal Justice, are intended to present the perspectives of high-ranking officials throughout the world by examining their careers, insights, vision, experiences, challenges, perceived future of the field and the related issues of interest.

Arguably, the literature is replete with scholarship and research that provides academic interpretation of the field, its practices and future. However, these publications are often difficult to access journals and are written from the perspective of the academic, with little interpretation or feasible action items for professionals working in the field. A comprehensive literature discussing an on-the-ground, day-to-day understanding of how police, courts and prison systems work and do not work, along with examining the need to improve, is lacking. This series provides 'inside' information about the systems as told to respected scholars and researchers by seasoned professionals. In this series, the dialogue between scholar/researcher and practitioner is opened as a guided, yet candid, discussion between two professionals, providing the opportunity for academics to learn from practitioners, while practitioners also learn from the outlet of expression in terms of their experiences, challenges, skills and knowledge.

Throughout the world, the criminal justice field is at juxtaposition and the time is ripe for change and improvements. Many countries throughout the world have long-standing policies that have been successful for their culture and political climate, or they are in need of serious revamping due to budgetary concerns or corruption. Other countries are at a precipice and are beginning to establish new systems. In all of these situations, the international criminal justice field stands to benefit from an accessible, engaging and enlightening series of frank discussions of the leaders' personal views and experiences in the field.

The current volume, *Trends in Corrections: Interviews with Corrections Leaders Around the World, Volume Three*, sets the stage to enhance the readers' understanding of correctional programming and management styles used throughout the world from an insider's perspective. The correctional leaders interviewed in this volume represent a variety of cultures, political environments, and economic systems. Representatives from the Americas, Asia, Europe and South Africa are interviewed. The introductory chapter introduces the reader to the issue of international corrections and the need for a forum to discuss corrections from the perspective of noted corrections officials. Chapters 1–11 each provide the transcribed interview of the corrections leader as conducted by the scholar/researcher. A brief portrait of the corrections system in that jurisdiction is also provided. The final chapter is a reflection on the interviews and summary of common themes evident throughout the book.

Thus, *Trends in Corrections: Interviews with Corrections Leaders Around the World, Volume Three*, continues the work of the IPES and its series *Interviews with Global Leaders in Policing, Courts, and Corrections* by advancing knowledge about the corrections system, examining comparative corrections from the perspective of correctional leaders in a variety of countries, and opening a dialogue between scholars/researchers and practitioners. It is anticipated that this addition to the series will facilitate discussions within and between countries' correctional systems to add value to their current operations and future directions. It is hoped that this series will also bridge the gap of knowledge that exists between scholars and researchers in academia and practitioners in the field. I invite correctional scholars and researchers and practitioners across the world to join in this venture.

Dilip K. Das, PhD
President
International Police Executive Symposium

Acknowledgements

The publication of this volume could not have occurred without the support of numerous individuals, institutions and agencies who contributed time and effort in the spirit of openness and mutual learning. The fact that such a volume can be published with such cooperation is so important for the future of comparative corrections practice and scholarship.

We would like to thank the interviewers and authors, Ilona Laurinaityté (Česnienė), Pavol Kopinec, David C. Hurley, Michael Sanchez, Fred Lux, Brian Norris, Carol Lawson, Raymund Narag, Dittita Tititampruk and Anni Hesselink for their submission of chapters to this volume. Thanks is also offered to both Mark A. Nolan and Martha Henderson Hurley for their contribution to this volume, in particular to Chapters 1 and 12 that support the contextualising of leadership in corrections.

We also want to express our sincere thanks to the correctional leaders who graciously gave of their time in interviews conducted around the world, in Europe, North America, South America, and Asia: Živilė Mikėnaitė, Martin Lulei, Danny W. Pirtle, Adonay Davila, Steven Anderson, Garcia Maradiaga, Satoshi Tomiyama, Randel Latoza, Nathee Jitsawang and Johan Ellis Le Grange. This book could not have been completed without their taking time out of their very busy lives to have conversations about their life experiences and perceptions. Special mention can also be made of those from within the Correction Bureau of Japan, within the Japanese Ministry of Justice, who facilitated the interview with Satoshi Tomiyama.

The editors, authors, and interviewees wish to express our thanks and appreciation to Ellen Boyne and Kate Taylor from the Taylor & Francis Group for their unwavering editorial support for this series.

About the Editors

Dilip K. Das has years of experience in criminal justice practice, research, writing, and education. After obtaining his master's degree in English literature, Dr Das joined the Indian Police Service, an elite national service with a distinguished tradition. Dr Das is a professor of criminal justice, a former police chief, and a human rights consultant to the United Nations. He is the founding president of the International Police Executive Symposium (IPES), managing the affairs of the organisation in cooperation with an appointed group of police practitioners and academics from around the world. He is also the founding editor in chief of *Police Practice and Research: An International Journal*. He is author, editor, or co-editor of more than 30 books and numerous articles. Dr Das has received several faculty excellence awards and was a distinguished faculty lecturer.

Philip Birch, BSocSci (Hons); PG Cert (HEP); PG Cert (SSRM); PG Dip (SocSci); MSc; PhD, is a Senior Lecturer in Criminology in the Centre for Law and Justice at Charles Sturt University, Australia. He has previously held posts at the University of Western Sydney, the University of New South Wales, Sydney, Australia and the University of Huddersfield, in the UK. Prior to entering academia, Philip worked as a criminologist in the field, holding posts in the UK prison service as well as in the crime and disorder field, which involved managing a specialist crime unit. Philip has published internationally, including books, book chapters, peer reviewed articles and government reports in his main areas of research – offender management and rehabilitation; police, prisons and probation practices; gender symmetry violence with a particular focus on domestic family violence and sex work. He has secured over $830,000 in research funding and support grants, which has addressed at a variety of themes within his areas of expertise and, in May 2017, he was invited to represent Australia at the United Nations, presenting on his research. Philip holds an honorary research fellowship in the School of Psychology, University of Central Lancashire, UK, as well as a Senior Research Associate in the Ashworth Research Centre, Mersey Health Care, National Health Services, UK. He is also a fellow of the Higher Education Academy. Philip was the co-founder and inaugural editor in chief of the *Journal of Criminological Research, Policy and Practice* (*JCRPP*, 2014–2017) and is currently the editor in chief of *Salus*, an international journal for law enforcement and public safety (2018–Present); he also sits on the editorial board of the *Journal of Aggression, Conflict and Peace Research*.

About the Contributors

Anni Hesselink is a professor employed at the University of South Africa (UNISA) at the Department of Criminology and Security Science. She is a criminologist and an NRF-Rated researcher who has been actively involved in volunteer expert criminological offender assessments (needs and risks) for the Department of Correctional Service for over 24 years. During this period, Hesselink has worked with all types and categories of offenders. She has published widely in numerous national and internal scientific journals on issues pertaining to offending behaviour, including males, females, and juvenile and youth offenders and victims.

David C. Hurley is an adjunct professor at Angelo State University, St Angelo, Texas. He received his doctorate in Criminal Justice from the University of Cincinnati in 2003 and has broad experience as both a researcher and a practitioner. He has experience as a juvenile caseworker, working with emotionally disturbed and delinquent children at the Children's Home of Cincinnati and St Joseph Orphanage, both located in Cincinnati, OH. He is also a former police officer and has developed curriculum and conducted on-site training for other police departments in Ohio, Kentucky, and Indiana. Dr Hurley is an experienced instructor with over 20 years' teaching experience. Currently, his focus is intelligence, terrorism, policing, crime prevention, homeland security and criminal justice administration.

Martha Henderson Hurley is a professor and the Director of the Criminal Justice Studies Program at the University of Dayton, Ohio, USA. Before her current appointment, Dr Hurley was Department Head and professor in the Department of Sociology and Criminal Justice at Texas A&M University, Commerce, USA. Dr Hurley was born in South Carolina and received her undergraduate arts degree from Furman University. Following her Master of Arts degree at the University of Cincinnati, Dr Hurley earned her PhD in criminal justice from the same university. Her specific areas of research and teaching experience include criminal justice ethics, risk assessment and classification, analysis of performance measures, organisational change, prisoner re-entry, special populations, and implementation of evidence-based practices in corrections. She has also worked as a senior researcher for the Ohio Department of Rehabilitation and Correction and served as a research analyst and facilitator of group sessions in a community-based juvenile programme. Dr Hurley published *Correctional Administration and Change Management* with CRC Press, and her most recent book, *Aging in Prison: The Integration of Research and Practice*, was released by Carolina Academic Press in November 2013.

Pavol Kopinec is a doctoral graduate and researcher at the Institute of Social Studies and Curative Education at the Comenius University in Bratislava. His main subject of interest is migration and the human rights protection of vulnerable groups. He has worked as a programme manager for refugee camps in Slovakia and with the UNHCR (Separated Children in Europe Programme) as a coordinator of support to unaccompanied children coming to the Slovak Republic. He has participated in international teams monitoring the living and care conditions of children in the asylum process and detention centres in various European countries. From 2011, he worked as a consultant for the International Organisation for Migration in the capacity building field. He has published two books on working standards and provision of high quality services to refugees and vulnerable groups.

Ilona Laurinaitytė (formerly Čėsnienė) is an associate professor of psychology at Vilnius University. She teaches postgraduate courses in forensic psychological assessment and counselling, undertakes research, supervises probationary and police psychologists. Her particular research interests are centred on the assessment, theoretical understanding and treatment of violent offenders and sex offenders. Laurinaitytė was the principal researcher of a research project 'The relationship between personality traits and criminal risk factors in a sample of incarcerated violent offenders'. She was the first representative of Lithuania and MC member in the COST Action IS1302 'Towards an EU research framework on forensic psychiatric care'.

Carol Lawson is a researcher at the Australian National University College of Law in the Australian Capital Territory (ACT). Her current research interest is the regulation of criminal justice systems. In 2015–2016, she used mixed methods to collect empirical data from around 2,500 key actors in the Penal Institution Visiting Committee system at over 50 Japanese prisons: senior corrections officers, Visiting Committee members and inmates. She is undertaking similar research at the ACT prison, with data to be fed into policy preparations for OPCAT compliance in the ACT, and contributing to the first empirical research project investigating the lifeworld of Japan's mature-age women offenders. In 2015, she published a book chapter on the origins of Japan's 2005–2006 penal reforms, the first substantive reforms in 97 years. She was an adjunct associate professor at the Nagoya University Graduate School of Law Leading Graduate Schools Program in Cross-Border Legal Institution Design across 2012–2014. Ms Lawson is literate and fluent in Japanese, and a veteran legal translator. She served as the Chair of JATLAW, the legal translation chapter of the Japan Association of Translators during 2010–2016, and on the Japanese Examiner Panel, National Accreditation for the Accreditation of Translators and Interpreters (NAATI) across 2011–2015.

Fred Lux is recently retired from the law enforcement field, having worked the majority of his career for the Spartanburg County Sheriff's Office in Spartanburg, SC, USA. During his time in law enforcement, he served in capacities as a patrol officer, investigator, and administrative command. He culminated his career as the lead investigator for the agency's fire and arson investigation unit. He is a graduate of the University of South Carolina Upstate and Anderson University, with degrees in the academic disciplines of experimental psychology and criminal justice. He is currently pursuing his criminal justice doctoral degree from Saint Leo University. Having left law enforcement as a practitioner, he now teaches for Limestone College in Gaffney, SC, USA. There he instructs baccalaureate courses in criminal justice, related theories, and research methods.

Raymund Narag is an assistant professor in the Department of Criminology and Criminal Justice at Southern Illinois University Carbondale. Dr Narag's area of research includes comparative criminology and criminal justice with a special focus on the Philippine criminal justice and correctional systems. He regularly conducts training programmes for officers of the Bureau of Jail Management and Penology (BJMP) and the Bureau of Corrections (BuCor) and other Philippine criminal justice agencies. Prior to being a member of academia, Dr Narag was once an inmate in the Quezon City Jail for almost seven years (1995–2002), falsely accused of a crime he did not commit. Upon acquittal of all the criminal charges, he wrote a book detailing the lives of inmates behind bars. That incarceration experience also inspired him to work for the improvement of the Philippine criminal justice and correctional systems.

Mark A. Nolan is a professor in the ANU College of Law, School of Law, at the Australian National University (ANU) in Canberra, Australia, having worked there since 2002, and is currently the Director of the JD programme. Dr Nolan was born in Kempsey in New South Wales, Australia, a small country town with a large prison. He has volunteered to teach legal literacy programmes to detainees at the local prison in Canberra, the Alexander Maconochie Centre, since 2010. Dr Nolan teaches and researches in criminal law and procedure (including federal criminal law and military discipline law), and legal psychology. Research and teaching interests include criminal defences, investigative interviewing, expert psychological and psychiatric evidence, human rights law, citizenship law, identity and intergroup relations psychology, social justice perceptions, counter-terrorism law, and law regulating human trafficking. Dr Nolan's PhD in social psychology from the ANU, and his Masters degree in Thai language and Asian Studies, in addition to his law qualifications, has also led to him being a guest lecturer in psychology and Asian Studies courses at ANU, a presenter at many national and international conferences, and a supervisor of research projects with interdisciplinary links between law, psychology and Asian studies. Recent law reform work has included parliamentary submissions on post-sentence detention for terrorists and commissioned research on memory for the Australian Royal Commission into Institutional Responses to Child Sexual Abuse. He also works with professional associations, such as the Australian and New Zealand Association of Psychiatry, Psychology and Law and the National Judicial College of Australia, to bring comparative and interdisciplinary perspectives to bear on law reform questions and criminal law scholarship. Together with co-author Professor Jane Goodman-Delahunty, Dr Nolan published the interdisciplinary monograph, *Legal Psychology in Australia*, in 2015, including a substantial chapter on corrections management.

Brian Norris is a professor in the Department of Criminal Justice, The Citadel, Military College of South Carolina. Dr Norris completed his BA at the University of Texas at Arlington, his MA at the University of Texas at Austin and his PhD at Johns Hopkins University in the School of Advanced International Studies. Dr Norris lived and worked in Latin America for five years and has completed 31 international research or work trips since 1997. His country experience includes Bolivia, El Salvador, Mexico, Honduras, Paraguay, Ecuador, Panama, Argentina, Cuba, Peru, India, and Zambia. *Prison Bureaucracies in the United States, Mexico, India, and Honduras* is a peer-reviewed book in production with Lexington Books, Lanham, MD (an academic imprint of Rowman & Littlefield) and is due for publication in February 2018. He is the author of scholarly publications on demographic changes in South America, on credit institutions in the US South and in South America, and on criminal justice institutions and leadership in Mexico. He is president of the World Affairs Council of Charleston and is an active promoter of area studies.

Michael Sanchez is a criminal justice professional with 20 years of domestic and international experience in many facets of the criminal justice system. Dr Sanchez served as a jailor, detention officer, police officer, investigator, patrol supervisor, investigative supervisor, training coordinator, interim chief of police, and administrator. He served four years as an international police officer for the United Nations. He served three years for the United Nations Mission in Kosovo (UNMIK) International Police, ultimately as the Director of Personnel and Administration for the UNMIK Police. He also served for one year in the United Nations Stabilization Mission in Haiti (MINUSTAH) and was the Regional Commander for the Les Cayes (SUD) Region of Haiti. Dr Sanchez was in Haiti for the January 2010 earthquake and commanded the Les Cayes Region throughout the recovery and normalisation efforts. After ending his UN mission in Haiti, Dr Sanchez entered the private sector as the training manager for a federal contractor who operates the ICE Immigration Detention Centers. After eight months, Dr. Sanchez was promoted to Assistant Project Manager (Assistant Warden) and was transferred to Texas, where he has worked for the past six years. Dr Sanchez holds a Bachelor's degree in Police Science from Ottawa University (Ottawa, KS); a Master's degree in Criminal Justice Administration from Utica College (Utica, NY); a PhD in Business Administration with a Concentration in Criminal Justice, from Northcentral University (Prescott Valley, AZ). He is a lecturer for the University of Texas Rio Grande Valley, teaching undergraduate courses in criminal justice; and an adjunct lecturer for Utica College, teaching graduate courses in Utica's Cybersecurity graduate program.

Dittita Tititampruk is a penologist and criminologist working at the Professional Level Correctional Staff Training Institute of the Department of Corrections, Thailand. Dr Dittita graduated with a PhD from the School of Criminal Justice at Texas State University, following her Masters degree in Criminal Justice Administration from Thammasat University and a BA in Business Computing from Assumption University, both in Bangkok, Thailand. Her research has ranged from the study of inmate subcultures (including inmate tattoos), inmate perceptions and attitudes, violent offenders, and criminogenic thinking.

About the Interviewees

Steven Anderson became the director of the Cherokee County Detention Center in 2015. He began his career path, though, intending to serve as an educator and religious minister. He graduated college in 2001 with a degree in religious studies and minors in English and history, and cognates in music and French. He went to work as a minister as intended. However, a turn in the economy forced him from this career, and, in 2009, he was offered a job as a duty officer for the Cherokee County Sheriff's Office; a non-sworn, non-law-enforcement position. Having excelled in this capacity, he was promoted to Captain of the Cherokee County Detention Center in 2011. Upon being promoted, he immediately sought the necessary state training through the South Carolina Criminal Justice Academy to become a certified law enforcement officer. He served in his capacity as Captain until 2015, when he was promoted to Major-Jail Director.

Adonay Davila is a criminal justice professional with over 32 years of experience in corrections and detention. Mr Davila served for 22 years in the Texas Department of Criminal Justice (TDCJ) prison system, retiring in 2003 at the rank of Senior Warden. Mr Davila served in every conceivable capacity in the TDCJ prison system, from Corrections Officer to Senior Warden. His career spanned an era of exceptional modernisation and reform within the TDCJ prison system. He frequently found himself at the leading edge of prison reform and has both an operational and strategic vision of the strengths and weaknesses of the corrections system in the United States. After his retirement from TDCJ, Mr Davila successfully transitioned his broad corrections skill set to the private corrections and detention industry. He served as a compliance auditor and inspector travelling the United States conducting inspections and audits on detention facilities around the country. As a result, Mr Davila has seen the inner workings of a very large number of facilities. He served as a new construction and startup specialist, overseeing the construction and operationalisation of ten new private corrections and detention facilities. In this capacity, Mr Davila quite literally developed a ground-up perspective on the private corrections and detention industry. He has worked for the past four years as the Project Manager (Warden) at a privately run ICE Immigration Detention Center. Mr Davila's extensive experience in both the private and public sectors of corrections and detention makes him a knowledgeable expert in comparing the pros and cons of the privatisation of corrections currently under way in the United States. Mr Davila has a broad vision of the fields of public and private corrections, having viewed both industries from so many different perspectives. He holds an Associate Degree in Law Enforcement from Texas Southmost College (Brownsville, TX), and a Bachelor's degree in Criminal Justice from West Texas State University (Canyon, TX).

Orlando Garcia Maradiaga is a colonel in the Honduran army and became Director of the National Penitentiary Institute of Honduras in May of 2015. He began his military career with the army as an enlisted man in February of 1978. He was promoted to sergeant first class, and then the army sent him to Officer Candidate School in the US to become an officer. Colonel Garcia underwent training programmes in Panama and in Fort Benning, Georgia, the latter for arms training and training in US military doctrine. He then achieved the rank of Lieutenant Colonel and was part of command staff. He commanded a company of riflemen, and then commanded, in turn, a battalion and a brigade. He became Chief of the Department of Intelligence of the Honduran army, and this trajectory sent him ultimately to his current position in the Honduran prison sector. Immediately prior to being Director of the National Penitentiary Institute, in August 2014, Colonel Garcia was named Inspector General of the Honduran National Prison system, an ombudsman-type position.

Nathee Jitsawang is a Special Adviser at the Thailand institute of Justice within the Ministry of Justice Thailand. He studied criminology and penology as an undergraduate law student at Chulalongkorn University before returning, after public service work, to Masters study, having being awarded a Royal Thai Government Scholarship to further his education with a Masters Degree in Criminology at Florida State University. Under the conditions of the scholarship, all graduates are obliged to work back in the Thai public service upon graduation, so Mr Nathee returned to work at the Department of Corrections.

Randel Latoza is Jail Superintendent of the Quezon City Jail (QCJ), Male Dormitory, Manila, in the Philippines. Superintendent Latoza has worked for more than 20 years with the Jail Bureau, during which time he has been assigned to multiple jails of varying sizes and locations. Since his appointment as Warden of the QCJ in April 2014, he has introduced numerous reforms that have improved the living conditions of the inmates and the working environment of the jail staff. In February 2017, the Quezon City Jail was awarded a designation as the 'Most Innovative Jail' in the country, and Superintendent Latoza was selected the 'Best Jail Warden' in the country.

Johan Ellis Le Grange is based within the Department of Corrections, South Africa. With a career spanning 40 years, Mr Le Grange began his career on 5 December 1977 as a 17-year-old South African Correctional Services officer (then known as the South African Prison Service). Le Grange was appointed in 1999 by the National Commissioner to lead a team to eradicate corruption and criminality that prevailed at the Johannesburg prison, and in 2014 he was appointed as Area Commissioner of the Overberg area (Western Cape province) – a position he still holds.

Martin Lulei is a doctoral graduate, researcher, social worker and project manager in the area of social work and criminal justice. He has published more than 40 articles and chapters in Slovakia and abroad (France, Czech Republic, the Netherlands, Romania, Poland, etc.) and is author of the scientific publication *Criminal Justice, Social Work and Probation* (2011). After finishing his studies in 2005, he used to work for several non-governmental organisations (NGOs) (social work, counselling) or as a university teacher (criminal justice social work, social work theory). He completed his PhD (Probation and Social Work) in 2008. Dr Lulei participated in international projects such as DOMICE (Developing offender management in corrections in Europe), GRUNTVIG, OSE (Offender supervision in Europe), ISRD 3, etc. Nowadays, he works as a project manager at the Ministry of Labour, Social Affairs and Family on national projects in the social field, and as a university teacher.

Živilė Mikėnaitė was the Director General of the Prison Department under the Ministry of Justice of the Republic of Lithuania. She oversaw 11 penitentiary establishments with a prison population of around 7,000 and provided leadership to around 3,500 staff. Her professional background shows that she was moving forward step by step, getting to know the prison system from inside, first as Head of Personnel Unit at the Prison Department, later on as the governor of Kaunas Remand Prison, witnessing the challenges it was facing and its achievements, learning from the experts in the field of corrections. Mikėnaitė was the Board member at the European Organization of Prison and Correctional Services.

Danny W. Pirtle serves as the Deputy Director of Executive and Administrative Services, where he oversees training, grants, and research initiatives. He also reports institutional data to the Juvenile Justice Information System and the Juvenile Case Management System. In 1996, he graduated from Tennessee State University and started his career in juvenile corrections as an institutional officer in Harris County, Texas. In 2001, he completed his Master of

Science in Juvenile Justice from Prairie View A&M University. He became an assessment specialist for the Juvenile Justice Charter School located in the facility and then served as a juvenile probation officer from 2002 to 2006. In 2007, he graduated from Prairie View A&M University with his PhD and embarked on a calling of teaching at Holy Family University until he was lured back to the field of juvenile corrections in 2013. In the Fall of 2016, Dr Pirtle left the juvenile justice system and became an instructor at Arizona State University at Lake Havasu, where he uses his experience as a juvenile corrections administrator to teach college students.

Satoshi Tomiyama was only the second corrections officer in Japan to be appointed to the position of Director-General of the Ministry of Justice Correction Bureau, a post traditionally held by an elite prosecutor. Studying law at Chuo University in the late 1970s, he passed the Senior Civil Service Examination as an undergraduate, leading to graduate recruitment on the Bureau's 'fast-track'. Tomiyama's 35-year career saw him rise through a diverse range of roles at penal institutions, regional headquarters and the Correction Bureau's head office in Tokyo. He also served in the Probation Bureau for two years, and as Correctional Training Institute Head Instructor for 19 months. Crucially, he was part of the special project team that investigated the Nagoya Prison incidents in late 2002, which sparked long-awaited reforms. As Special Assistant to the Director of the General Affairs Division, he was a key liaison between the Bureau and the Correctional Administration Reform Council in 2003, and assisted in the legislative drafting for the new regime enacted in 2005–2006. His senior management roles include 18 months as the Director of the Ministry of Justice Facilities Division, with responsibility for all Ministry facilities, before his appointment as Director-General in June 2016.

Chapter 1

Contextualising the Issue

Leadership in Corrections

Mark A. Nolan, Martha Henderson Hurley,
Dilip K. Das and Philip Birch

Modern correctional leaders are challenged by immediate country and system-specific dynamics and demands. Illustrated by Cavadino and Dignan (2006), for example, the political economy of countries, broadly categorised as neo-liberal, conservative corporatist, social democratic or oriental corporatist, is strongly related to the punitiveness of the penal culture and rates of imprisonment in each country. Also, few countries can ignore the evolving international norms that shape international, national, and system-based regulatory and auditing practices within their bailiwicks. Recent international developments referred to by correctional leaders in this volume include the Nelson Mandela Rules (United Nations General Assembly Resolution 70/175 of 2015) a set of human rights guidelines for correctional administrators formerly known as the United Nations Standard Minimum Rules for the Treatment of Prisoners. Noted as a rapidly-developing pressure, too, is the cooperation between national and international assessors created in those countries where UN member states have ratified the Optional Protocol to the Convention Against Torture along with the monitoring of prisoner rights by the Human Rights Committee overseeing the UN's International Covenant on Civil and Political Rights. These norms and processes are not dissimilar to the move to design and regulate official visitor regimes within regional human rights and political frameworks such as those of the European Union.

All of these developments invite norm and evidence-based evaluation of the work of correctional leaders. The reality of such monitoring in a globalised world emphasises the need for executives around the world to communicate with each other about the best way to achieve human rights compliance sensitively and effectively in their home jurisdictions, while needing to be sensitive to the peculiar history and evolution of their own correctional system. Dialogue between the holders of long-standing corporate memory within national correctional systems, who often possess highly developed unpublished ideas and theories based on decades of correctional administrative experience, is crucial in the modern context of correctional management. Responding poorly and slowly to scandals, and avoiding the chance to learn from other countries within and outside of one's home region, is no longer an adequate way to lead any particular correctional system in an era of national or international monitoring of compliance with shared standards.

The important body of insights presented in this volume speaks to the spirit of international cooperation bridging practice, theory and policy that is embodied in the work of the International Police Executive Symposium; sharing valuable perspectives among those who may not have the chance or ability to learn from other systems. This is especially the case when there is a linguistic, and/or political, and/or cultural barrier preventing easy mutual access to ideas and understanding of a correctional system and its innovation or stasis. In this series, the English speaker is treated to understanding the experience, success and challenges faced by non-English speakers in systems that feel familiar, yet can also be struck through with history, politics and pressures quite different to one's own. The tireless effort and work of bilingual or polylingual interviewers has again produced a smorgasbord of national perspectives for the English speaker, allowing them to break free from the dominant perspectives they may know best from reading and working predominately in English-language systems and correctional literatures.

In *Trends in Corrections, Volume One*, readers were introduced to the importance of understanding the perspective of correctional leaders. By viewing corrections through the lens of its international leaders, the great diversity that exists in corrections, cross-culturally, was exposed. Similarities and differences in the political, social, and economic context of the correctional system were discussed. The general conclusion drawn from the first volume was that the 12 correctional leaders interviewed shared "striking similarities" despite vast differences in the social and political climates in which they worked.

In *Trends in Corrections, Volume Two*, 12 interviews were presented from ten countries in Europe, North America and Asia. The editors of Volume Two and a co-author concluded that similar challenges, despite the country differences, exist for correctional leaders around the world. The importance for leaders to stay abreast of developments and innovations fuelled by evidence-based research and theory-driven practice was obvious. The longevity of involvement in corrections by the interviewees, even if not their intended or first-chosen career, explained the successful promotion of these leaders to executive positions within their systems in the majority of cases. There was also evidence of transfers between prison systems; career choices that demand that one is steeped in comparative correctional wisdom. Another emergent conclusion from Volume Two was that life-long learning, higher education, and interdisciplinary study shaped and benefited the correctional leaders' leadership and management work. Most interviewees endorsed the importance of international comparative and scholarly prisons research to their polycentric decision making aimed at serving many, sometimes opposing, if not competing, interests. The interviewed leaders were reformers of policy, procedure, and sometimes law, suggesting the important role correctional executives have in leaving their systems better than they found them as their main professional and occupational contribution. It was also obvious from the interviews in Volume 2 that it is often correctional philosophy that is at the forefront of leaders' thinking as they juggle the demands for community protection, secure incarceration, and rehabilitative needs within their correctional systems, whatever the political, social and scientific trajectory their system had been on before they led and shaped it.

In this current volume, Volume Three, the ten interviews presented provide unique first-hand experiential accounts of correctional practices in eight countries. Each chapter contains transcripts and summaries of in-depth, semi-structured interviews based on a standard interview protocol that was used as the basis for all interviewing also reported in Volumes One and Two. As for the earlier volumes, the selection of interviewees was based on the willingness and availability once identified through practice and research networks of the interviewers and/or the editors. Correctional officials were chosen due to their innovative leadership and their experience of holding major administrative responsibilities for a department or agency related to the field of corrections. The interviews were conducted by practitioners or scholars with intimate knowledge of correctional practice and who are familiar with the correctional system in the country from which the interviewee hails. The interview is designed to solicit and explore the views, experiences, reflections and thought processes of the interviewed correctional leader. Particular emphasis is placed on exploring how correctional leaders throughout the world think about and evaluate trends and developments. This series affords correctional leaders an unprecedented opportunity to express their views on current practices and the future of corrections in their country.

In Chapter 2, Živilė Mikėnaitė, Director-General of the Prison Department of Lithuania, relates her experience to Ilona Laurinaitytė (Čėsnienė), commenting on the challenges of prioristing supported re-entry of prisoners into the community in reaction to a new probation law that is barely five years old and a wave of additional and even more specific criminal offences being added to the prosecutors' toolkits. The Director General also discusses the need for record enhancements, interoperability between government departments, and a need to be adopting evidence-based practices that are rigorous according to international standards.

In Chapter 3, Pavol Kopinec's interview of Martin Lulei, Project Manager, Ministry of Labour, Social Affairs and Family, Slovak Republic, a data-rich picture is painted of the successes and challenges of this system. The interview reveals that, in a slightly overcrowded prison system with a moderate rate of incarceration within the neighbouring region, a focus on recidivism prevention and interagency cooperation remains key. Lulei laments that the Slovak Republic may still languish behind the international norms in terms of risk assessment tool use, evidence-based offender management and throughcare architecture.

In Chapter 4, moving from Europe to North America, David Hurley exposes the dynamics surrounding both the pathway in and pathway out of executive work within a correctional system for Danny W. Pirtle, former Deputy Director of Executive and Administrative Services of the Dallas County Juvenile Justice Department. This interview reveals the angst-ridden and stark choices some professionals face as they consider where best they can make a contribution to the refinement of criminal justice institutions and systems with their given and developing skill sets. Further trends discussed in this chapter include how the incarceration of juveniles may be decreasing in Texas and targeted rehabilitation programs may be on the rise, all at the same time that the rate of incarceration of minority youth remains alarmingly stable.

In Chapter 5, Michael Sanchez mines the long and deep experience of fellow retired Texan Adonay Davila, Senior Warden, Texas Department of Criminal Justice, who served within corrections for more than two decades. One focus of expert commentary here is about the successes and challenges of private prisons in comparison with public prisons; Davila having worked extensively in both systems. At the system level, Davila states the importance of governments demanding fine-grained contracting with private correctional providers if standards and norms of public prisons are to be achievable within privately run facilities. The final chapter to focus on North America is offered by Fred Lux in Chapter 6. Within this chapter, Major Anderson, a Director of the Cherokee County Detention Centre in South Carolina, is interviewed. Offering a unique perspective, this corrections facility is a pretrial jail and, as a consequence, provides insightful nuances for leadership within this context. A significant 'take home message' in this chapter is both the importance and application of restorative principles when dealing with offending behaviour, reminding the reader that corrections play a broader role than punishment in society. Corrections have an important role to play in rehabilitation and in supporting offenders in making amends for wrongs. Lux's chapter and his interview with Major Anderson is an excellent reminder of these principles and has implications for leaders in corrections around the world.

From North America, we travel south to Honduras in Chapter 7 to provide a perspective from a long-standing military officer recently thrust into correctional management following an intriguing policy decision taken by the Honduran government. Interviewing Coronel Orlando Garcia Maradiaga, Director, National Penitentiary Institute of Honduras in Spanish, interviewer Brian Norris reveals the cultural flux that is palpable in a system now being run by a military officer. The chapter educates the reader in the opinions that the military executive now has on many international correctional trends. In addition, the reader will learn plenty of Spanish and feel as if they were sitting across from this professional with an intriguing and, again, unexpected, career trajectory and hearing him describe his greatest challenges.

Chapter 8 is the first of three chapters from Asian correctional systems and signifies a notable willingness by the Japanese Correction Bureau to reveal in Japanese to a bilingual researcher and certified legal translator, Carol Lawson, the innovations now occurring in Japanese corrections. Director-General Satoshi Tomiyama explains in detail how many challenges facing Japanese correctional executives are being managed. For example, despite incarceration and violence rates being comparatively low in Japan, aging of the prison population is a clear challenge. Also, this experienced correctional officer elevated to executive rank reflects on an historical prisoner treatment scandal that has clearly motivated the Japanese authorities to act and reform their system. At this exciting time, the Director-General explains that the Japanese system will work best if professionalism, trust, education and sound leadership qualities are used to shape prisons culture in Japan.

In Chapter 9, Raymund Narag, himself once an incarcerated inmate (wrongfully), reports the interview with Randel Latoza, Superintendent of the Male Dormitory of the Quezon City Jail in the Philippines. The Philippines adult correctional system is facing severe stress due to massive increases in prisoner numbers between 2016 and 2017 and the perspective related in this chapter comes from the experience of the superintendent of the second most crowded prison in all of the Philippines. Latoza laments that, historically, Philippine prison staff were trained as if they needed only to be police and security officers. The introduction of Welfare Divisions (including therapeutic communities and structured rehabilitation programmes) within prisons in the Philippines is driving cultural change there and expanding the professional identity and expectations placed upon correctional staff for the better.

In Chapter 10, Dittita Tititampruk reports her interview with former Director-General of the Department of Corrections in Thailand, law graduate Nathee Jitsawang, who is optimistic that reform to Thai prisons will go hand-in-hand with proposed reforms to drug crime sentencing in Thailand. This correctional leader highlights the clear role that international monitoring of the Thai correctional system has had for decades on improving the compliance of Thai prisons with internationally accepted norms and practices. The range of reform programs and policy initiatives trialled in Thailand, including elite athlete development work, is discussed in detail in this interview.

In Chapter 11, Anni-Mari Hesselink provides the sole chapter in this volume that focuses on corrections in South Africa. This insightful and detailed chapter provides an important context with regard to the delivery of corrections in South Africa, from both a historical and contemporary perspective. The interviewee, Johan Ellis Le Grange, who has had a 40-year career in South Africa corrections, provides the reader with a deep background in corrections practice, offering evidence of practice development and enhancement in relation to offender management. This penultimate chapter in this volume reveals a complex prison system with some monumental historical moments, including both the incarceration and release of Nelson Mandela, as well as the end of apartheid. In among such social, political economical and structural change, South Africa Corrections has been able to address corruption, mismanagement and maladministration, to name but few, and emerge as an organisation that can become a global leader in corrections policy and practice.

In drawing this volume to a conclusion, the final chapter, Chapter 12, Philip Birch, along with colleagues Mark Nolan, Martha Henderson Hurley and Dilip K. Das, reflect on the key themes that have emerged from the ten interviews. Based on the interview themes, evidence-based corrections, transnational relations and correctional philosophy as examples, consideration is given to leadership theory. As a consequence, this final chapter recognises that there has been much practice development that has occurred across many countries over many years in relation to corrections, yet, there is still a journey to travel. Nevertheless, perhaps the path left to travel is as simple as the exchange of knowledge, ideas, policies and practices between correction colleagues around the world.

Section 1

Europe

Chapter 2

Živilė Mikėnaitė, Director General of the Prison Department of Lithuania

Interviewer: Ilona Laurinaityté (Česnienė)

Contents

Overview	9
Introduction	12
Career	12
Changes Experienced	13
Personal Correctional Philosophy	14
Problems and Successes Experienced	15
Theory and Practice	17
Evidence-Based Corrections	18
Transnational Relations	19
Role of Corrections	20
General Assessments	21
Conclusion	21
Glossary	21

Overview

The current mission of the Prison Department under the Ministry of Justice of the Republic of Lithuania is to ensure operation of a system that is based on just and progressive serving of awarded sentences and execution of punishment following humanistic principles. Two main strategic goals have been developed in order to carry out this mission: (1) to ensure the execution of arrests, sentences, and probation, as well as substance abuse prevention in places of confinement; (2) to create sentence serving conditions that encourage inmates' good behaviour during the term of imprisonment and discourage reoffending following release. Based on the Prison Department's structure, three main directions of activities may be distinguished. First, organisation of work with arrestees and convicted prisoners: protection and supervision of arrestees and convicted offenders, social rehabilitation of convicted prisoners, and investigation of complaints lodged by arrestees and convicted persons. Second, economic and financial operations: planning of allocations needed by the penitentiary system, distribution and accounting of funds, supplying of materials/equipment to places of confinement and correctional inspectorates, organisation of occupational activities for those convicted, etc. Third, administration of the penitentiary system's operation: creation and updating of legal authority, investigation of complaints and representation in court, personnel management, creation and control of an information system, and collection and systematisation of data. Today, the Department has 11 subordinate imprisonment institutions that house inmates who are awaiting trial and those serving their sentences and five district probation authorities executing sentences without imprisonment and supervising persons released conditionally from places of their confinement before the end of their sentence term. The Training Centre in Vilnius for new employees of subordinate institutions is also under the purview of the Prison Department. Imprisonment institutions operate branches of "Mūsų amatai" (Our Trades) state-owned enterprise. They employ inmates to preserve and develop their work skills and prepare them for employment following their release. In late 2015, there were 3,486 workers employed by the Prison Department and institutions under it. Women represented approximately 40% of the system's workforce; the majority (60%) of workers were in the age group of 30–50 years old.

As of 31 December 2015, confinement institutions housed 7,355 inmates (a decrease of 14.8% compared to the same period, 2014). Convicted women accounted for 3.7%, and minors for 1.2% of the total number of inmates. There are 120 people sentenced to lifeimprisonment in Lithuania.

On the one hand, the rate of offences more than doubled over the past 20 years, that is, from 1,003 offences per 100,000 residents in 1990 to 2,391 offences in 2010. However, the rate stabilised in 2000, remaining lower in comparison with many countries in Western or Central Europe (Dobryninas & Sakalauskas, 2011). On the other hand, according to official statistics of imprisoned people, the rate in 2015 was 254 convicts per 100,000 residents (International Centre for Prison Studies, 2016); this is more than double compared to many European countries. Significantly, real imprisonment (arrest and confinement) accounts for almost 40% of all sentences, and the frequency of awarding such sentences has increased over the past ten years (Sakalauskas & Jarutienė, 2015).

In the past several years, 6–7% of the national budget was allocated annually for the protection of public order and protection of communities in Lithuania (6% of the national budget, or €0.6 bn in 2016). Over the past decade, various offence prevention programmes have been developed and implemented on a national scale, with the purpose of facilitating changes in offending behaviour: for example, reduction of the scale of domestic violence, supply and consumption of psychoactive substances, corruption, and increasing youth employment rate, etc.

Lithuanian statehood emerged more than 1,000 years ago, but an independent state of Lithuania was restored on 16 February 1918, following the signing of the Act of Reinstating Independence of Lithuania by the Council of Lithuania. At the end of the same year, the Ministry of Justice of the Lithuanian Republic was created. Supervision/monitoring of places of confinement was one of the areas of its operation. In February of 1919, the Prison Department under the Ministry of Justice was created.

During the implementation of the Penal Statute of 1903, the following punishments were established: hard labour prison, common prison, arrest, and fine. It must be noted that Lithuania, strictly speaking, did not have any hard labour prisons. All convicts served their terms in the same prisons; only their custodial control was different. The newly emerging state of Lithuania inherited 24 prisons and other imprisonment institutions from Tsarist Russia and the occupation administration of Kaiser Germany. However, buildings specially designed to house prisoners existed only in Vilnius, Kaunas, Šiauliai and Panevėžys. Unfortunately, even these prisons failed to meet the requirements for the imprisonment and general penal policy followed by many European states at that time. Therefore, during the first years of the period between the World Wars, Lithuania put a lot of effort into adapting and modifying the existing buildings intended for the housing of prisoners.

During the years of Soviet occupation (1940–1941, 1944–1990), the Lithuanian penitentiary system was incorporated into the common penitentiary system of the Soviet Union that was overseen by the Ministry of Internal Affairs. In that period, all information about the execution of punishments in Lithuania was classified and never made public. Institutions of confinement had code names; major statistical data were available only to officers for internal use. From 1940 till 1961, the Criminal Code of the Russian Soviet Federal Socialist Republic (SFSR) was in force in the territory of Lithuania. Significantly, for four years, from 1941 till 1944, when the Lithuanian territory was occupied by Nazi Germany and became part of the eastern lands of the Reich (so-called Ostland, which consisted of Lithuania, Latvia, Estonia and a greater part of Belarus), German law was in force. In 1961, the Lithuanian Soviet Socialist Republic (SSR) Supreme Council, based on the Russian SFSR Criminal Code, adopted the Lithuanian SSR Criminal Code, which, together with its amendments and supplements, stayed in force till 2003. One of the peculiar features of that period is that the law of the time prescribed work for all convicts, so they were simply made to sustain themselves, costing nothing to the state. Their earnings were sufficient not only to sustain them throughout their term of imprisonment but also to cover part of production and administration costs, and the remaining portion of earnings was remitted to the State budget.

Following the restoration of independence to Lithuania in 1990, the Administration of Correctional Affairs, which managed the system of implementation of criminal punishments in the Soviet period, was reorganised as the Department of Correctional Affairs. Throughout the Soviet period, and for the first decade of Lithuanian independence till 2000, the Department functioned under the Ministry of Internal Affairs. In execution of the legal system reform on 1 September 2000, control over the penitentiary system was turned over to the Ministry of Justice. The Department of Correctional Affairs was given back the name it held during the period between the World Wars and of Lithuanian independence – the Prison Department under the Ministry of Justice of the Republic of Lithuania. Lithuania gained access to the European Council in 1993 and the European Union (EU) in 2004. Many positive changes were introduced into the existing legislation, including the ones made in the area of human rights implementation.

In 1991–2002, some punishments existing in the old Criminal Code were repealed: for example, exile, deportation, public reprimand, etc. In addition, a moratorium on the execution of a death penalty was declared in 1996; two years passed, and it was entirely abolished.

New important legislation (the Criminal Code, Criminal Procedure Code and Penitentiary Code) came into force on 1 May 2003. These codes from 2003, which are still in place today, introduced a more progressive and flexible system of punishments, stricter control over the conditions of pre-trial detention and imprisonment after conviction, and enhanced prisoners' rights (Dobryninas & Sakalauskas, 2011). Despite the positive effects of these changes, it must be noted that the Soviet system still has an undoubtedly strong effect on Lithuanian penal policy, including its tradition and culture; people's attitudes to offending behaviour and punishments change slowly. People are inclined to demand stricter punishments and isolation of offenders. Open discussions show that the new Criminal Code, in people's opinion, is too soft. Accordingly, by 2008, the new Criminal Code has undergone modifications as many as 14 times, the Criminal Procedure Code 15 times, and the Penitentiary Code five times (Newman, 2010).

Introduction

The key participant in this interview is Živilė Mikėnaitė, the Director General of the Prison Department under the Ministry of Justice of the Republic of Lithuania. A warm expression in her eyes, a friendly smile and an unassuming attitude was present during the length of our interview. She listened attentively to every question, consulting the latest statistical data and analytical reviews in order to provide answers to some of them.

Career

Having started her professional career as a mathematics and IT teacher at a secondary school, Mikėnaitė was soon employed as a junior inspector in the juvenile department of the Main Police Commissariat of the city of Šiauliai. Later, she worked as a senior inspector in the municipal police force and a commissar inspector in the public police force. While working in the police force, she completed her law studies at Vilnius University and was awarded a Master's degree in law. After her studies Mikėnaitė was employed by the Prison Department. There, she held the post of personnel unit head for eight years. In 2006, she received an award for exemplary service at the Prison Department. She was also involved in academic work at Mykolas Romeris University, giving lectures and participating in various projects. Later, Mikėnaitė was the successful competitor for the post of the head of the Kaunas Interrogation Facility, becoming the first female in Lithuania in charge of a confinement institution. In 2015, having spent four years in this post, she was chosen, following a competitive selection process, for the post of head of the Prison Department. The selection committee noted her exceptional qualifications, professional experience and her years of service as statutory officer.

Mikėnaitė told me that working in the correctional system was never her childhood dream; it just happened. In her opinion, her career moves were a natural progression of her activities. However, she acknowledges that many people looked surprised when they learnt about her appointment to the position. Indeed, she is the first female in Lithuania heading not only the Prison Department, but also a statutory authority. The Director enjoys new challenges, and she finds it interesting, yet her duties demand a lot of effort every day. She is an optimist focused on the future, and she does not regret the past because that does not make much sense.

My interviewee states that occasionally she hears people describing her as "an iron lady"; her true nature is, however, a bit different. Three years ago, in Paris during a lecture on Human Resources (HR), the following idea presented to the audience captured her attention:

> You could decide not to be an iron person and be sympathetic toward your subordinates, but remember that later you or your family, which lost out on time with you, may not receive sympathy. Lenience towards others puts a heavier load on your own back.

Bearing this in mind, she holds her employees accountable to help them get used to completing their work in a timely manner.

Changes Experienced

Development of the current Lithuanian correctional system was greatly influenced by legal and political, as well as by social and economic, factors. After reinstatement of independence, an urgent need to reform the Lithuanian penal policy emerged just as in other areas of government. Comparative analysis of penal justice in 1991–2002, carried out during Lithuania's EU accession period, showed the following: Lithuania was among the EU member-state leaders for the number of imprisoned people per 100,000 residents; the frequency of awarding a punishment of confinement was one of the greatest in Lithuania (Sakalauskas, 2012). However, both research findings and world practice indicate that an offender's isolation *per se* does not necessarily achieve any correction of the offender's behaviour; sometimes it even complicates his/her reintegration into society following release. It became evident that, in our country, chances offered for a convicted person's resocialisation through alternative punishments, that is, punishments not related to imprisonment (e.g., restriction of freedom, public works, conditional release, etc.) were under-utilised. Taking into consideration recommendations of the European Council Committee of Ministers in the area of penal policy, in 2002 a new Lithuanian Republic (LR) Penitentiary Code was adopted with the purpose of reducing the number of people sentenced to serve a term of imprisonment. The new Code established the principles of individualisation in punishment execution, participation of society in the process of convicted people's correction, and just and progressive serving of sentences.

It must be noted that the Law on Probation came into force in Lithuania in 2012. Taking into consideration the existing situation, it defined the aim of probation – ensuring efficacious resocialisation of people on probation and reducing the rate of recidivism. This had the purpose of creating a qualitatively new probation structure orientated towards assistance, not just control of the convicted, that implements evidence-based resocialisation forms and reacts to the various needs of sentenced people with more flexibility, etc. On the other hand, the emergence of new legislation was an important event that resulted in stricter criminalisation of certain behaviours. It affected the dynamics of a number of convictions. For example, the 2012 Law on Protection Against Domestic Violence and Criminal Code amendments influenced significant growth in the number of domestic violence pre-trial investigations. Accordingly, more people who had committed such offences found themselves under supervision provided by the probation system; this, in turn, demanded establishing efficacious methods of work.

Personal Correctional Philosophy

Penal policy neither is, nor may be, self-focused because a state, through the adoption and application of criminal laws, must pursue goals that are useful to individuals, society and the state, reflect purposefulness of penal policy, and allow evaluation of its efficaciousness. In the most general sense, penal policy must secure protection of order and conditions essential to the normal existence, functioning and evolution of individuals, society and the state against the most dangerous behaviour – criminal acts (Švedas, 2006). Numerous factors determine penal policy, both in Lithuania and abroad.

The most important of them include the status, dynamics and structure of criminality; political, legal and moral attitudes of parliament members; constitutional norms and principles; international law; court performance; criminal law and criminology as a field of study; and the mass media.

It is important to understand that offenders' integration is of interest to society because it offers better chances of securing public safety. What is more, social integration is also connected to more frequent compensation for damage, which is hardly possible if offenders are simply isolated. Accordingly, modern probation neither is, nor ever can be, merely a system for formal control and registration of events involving people on probation; it must encourage, motivate, and seek to change the behaviour of people put on probation by helping them choose a pro-social direction. Indeed, it is important not only to record formal statistical data, but also to evaluate the quality of procedures and measures, the efficiency of adopted decisions, and their effect on the lives of people on probation from a long-term perspective.

It must be noted that the modern system of probation was created in Lithuania in 2012 in the wake of the newly adopted Law on Probation; thus, we can evaluate only the first steps made towards implementation of this system. Probation authorities in five districts of Lithuania are responsible for the preparation of social research conclusions concerning accused persons, including the ones who seek conditional release: offending behaviour risk evaluation in planning supervision of people on probation; implementation of behaviour correction programmes; provision of social assistance, behaviour control and intensive supervision of people put on probation. Modernisation of the Lithuanian penitentiary system encourages serving a sentence within a community, facilitating a reduction in recidivism. However, some problems are already apparent: for example the indicators of performance evaluation of the penitentiary system do not demonstrate to what degree envisaged goals are achievable because longitudinal research that could allow evaluation of the recidivism rate, especially the rate observed upon completion of the probation term, is lacking.

Problems and Successes Experienced

The global economic crisis of 2008 significantly affected the situation in Lithuania and in many other European countries: our state resorted to the policy of strict economy of public expenses, reducing significantly its social obligations, assumed before the crisis, to various groups of society. The impact of this crisis influenced correctional system operation; for example, salaries shrank, the number of employees was reduced, and funds for the confinement modernisation programme were cut. While many positive changes can be currently observed, the situation remains complex. For example, every year the state must pay huge sums of money to convicts in compensation for unsuitable conditions of confinement; this confirms a widely held belief: once a person is sentenced in the West, it is better for them to serve their term there. What is more, the turnover of officers employed in the corrective system remains high. Causes are the huge responsibility, low salaries, complex working conditions, and insufficient benefits.

In the Director's opinion, major problems encountered by the Lithuanian correctional system are lack of systemic management, inefficacious performance processes, obsolete infrastructure at institutions under the Department, and lack of motivated human resources. Administration of Prison Department (PD) pays special attention to the solution of these problems. Thus, over the past few years, several working groups have been created and are tasked with providing detailed analysis of problem situations and suggesting solutions. However, often, unfavourable views are expressed by society and some PD employees on the subject of convicts or the penitentiary system in general, which holds back implementation of desired changes. For example, several halfway houses were opened this year in various Lithuanian towns. The intention was to offer favourable conditions to convicts motivated to live outside prison and integrate into society, thus reducing the number of prisoners in places of confinement. Understandably, a drop in the reoffending rate is also expected. It seems that society ought to be interested in the implementation of such a goal; however, opinions about this project differed, and often it encountered the hostility of local people. Obviously, chances of successful integration will be smaller without any assistance on the part of any society to which convicts wish to return.

Moreover, in order to reduce harmful effects produced by prison subcultures and to improve the quality of work carried out with convicts, much attention was paid to the professional training of officers. For example, dynamic protection was introduced at Lithuanian correctional institutions. This system of protection is successfully used in Norway. This type of protection is focused on obtaining an in-depth knowledge of the inmate and correcting his/her behaviour by using unique methods specific to the particular individual. The individualised convict correction model is also applicable to people suffering from substance or alcohol dependence. Used at special rehabilitation centres, it helps them to get rid of problems related to the abuse of psychoactive substances and, often, with transgression.

Mikėnaitė is satisfied with the success of some social projects organised by the PD. She singled out the project "Žalioji oazė" (Green Oasis) launched in 2015. This project is unique for Europe. Inmates involved in it began growing flowers and vegetables at all imprisonment institutions in Lithuania. Results achieved in one year were amazing: over a relatively short period, many institutions managed to turn their wastelands into blooming gardens without any significant investment. Obviously, the creation of beauty does not require huge funds; the only required thing is will. One institution is even considering opening a sculpture park this year.

When talking about challenges in management efficiency, Mikėnaitė stressed the insufficient number of leaders who have adopted the new mentality. There is a need for a new type of leader who can take into account the needs of today's society and can use their specific abilities and skills to create strong teams, adequately motivate employees, foster employee involvement in the work performed by institutions, formulate tasks clearly, adapt innovations, implement changes, etc. In the near future, the Director would like to see the PD become one of the most desirable employers in Lithuania, alongside some business organisations.

Theory and Practice

To Mikėnaitės' mind, cooperation between researchers and practitioners is vital. The PD has signed long-term cooperation agreements with several Lithuanian universities in the areas of research, participation in international and national projects, practical training for students, improvement of professional qualifications of employees, etc. On the other hand, the PD, as a social partner, contributes to the development of study programmes in higher education by providing suggestions for the training of future professionals. One of the main suggestions of the employers concerning the training of the specialists in higher education is to consider the demands of the labour market and trends and relating the theory with the practice accordingly. PD is one of several social partners participating in the implementation of some study programmes (for example, Law, Psychology, etc.). The social partners are actively involved in study programme development processes: they are involved, together with academic colleagues, in the consideration of both the content of the programme and the competencies to be acquired by graduates, in addition to being directly involved in the organisation and supervision of internship practice.

Additionally social partners are engaged in professional innovation discussions and projects. This way, disconnectedness between science and practice is reduced, and new ideas are developed that may be implemented in practice and investigated scientifically. Evidently, such partnerships must be developed further, by inviting researchers to help when the PD conducts its research. Since the system changes perpetually, the necessity of enquiry into various fields of knowledge is obvious.

One instance of successful cooperation is adaptation and utilisation of the most well-known and advanced instruments in the world for the risk evaluation of criminal behaviour in the Lithuanian correctional system. Application of these instruments enables scientifically based risk evaluation, which is vital for efficacious planning of a convicted person's punishment and management of the risk of offending behaviour in the future. It must be noted that due attention is given to the examination of the reliability of risk evaluation instruments, to their validity in research, and to the improvement of the professional skills of instrumental administrators.

Evidence-based Corrections

In 2007–2012, adaptation of several instruments that were used successfully for the risk assessment of offending behaviour in Western Europe and North America was requested by the PD and carried out in Lithuania. Instruments adapted to meet Lithuanian needs included The Historical, Clinical and Risk Management Scales-20 (HCR-20), PCL:SV, OASys, SARA, etc.[1] Findings of this research were presented in national and foreign publications and at conferences (Žukauskienė, Laurinavičius & Singh, 2014). Accordingly, several behaviour correctional programmes were also adapted for use with convicts with different criminogenic needs: for example, the 'One-to-One' (OTO) individual cognitive behaviour correctional programme; the 'Behaviour–Conversation–Change' programme focused on reduction of consumption of psychotropic substances and criminal behaviour problems; the 'EQUIP' treatment program for young people with antisocial behaviour problems, the Sex Offender Therapy Programme for Lithuanian Corrections SeNAT (Boer, 2009), etc. Approved in 2012 in Lithuania, these risk assessment instruments, coupled with behaviour correctional programmes, created more opportunities to individualise the implementation of punishments in concrete cases, contributing to more progressive development of the Lithuanian penitentiary system.

Significantly, involvement of convicts under the supervision of probation authorities in behaviour correctional programmes has been one of the most successful areas of performance of these authorities since 2012, when the Law on Probation came into force. In 2012, only 1,920 people participated in the programmes. However in 2014, the number of participants totalled 2,936. The quantity is growing steadily. Approximately 70% of convicts complete behaviour correction programmes.

Efficacious application of the OTO individual cognitive behaviour correctional programme (intended to work with convicts' motivation for the prevention of offending behaviour and violence or for the reduction of psychoactive substance abuse) should be mentioned separately. Findings of research carried out in Lithuania in 2016 show changes in attitudes and behaviour of the OTO participants upon programme completion in comparison with their attitudes and behaviour before starting the programme (Česnienė & Klimukienė, 2016). These results correspond with the data provided by other researchers (Besev & Gajecki, 2009; Priestley, 2008). They indicate that following OTO programme completion, problems voiced by participants were changed, and problem solving skills and social skills were improved. Understandably, in addition to some pleasing results, some problem areas exist; these problems must be addressed in the near future.

For example, it is vitally important to secure adequate distribution of time and human resources when prioritising the implementation of correctional programmes that are effective for the prevention of offending behaviour. This goal could be achieved by redistributing the functions of probation officers or using specific incentive measures to encourage officers carrying out correctional programmes, or defining various (not only quantitative) criteria of the performance evaluation results that are easy to understand and are communicated not only to administration, but to staff officers as well. It is equally important to provide professional supervision of, and consultation with, staff implementing programmes. Besides taking a broader view of the situation, there is a need for the perpetual accumulation of data evaluating the implementation of various programmes, evaluation of the efficaciousness of these programmes, and, most importantly, the creation of a database suitable for research purposes.

Transnational Relations

The PD is a member of the European Organisation of Prison and Correctional Services (EuroPris), uniting the prison authorities of approximately 20 countries. In 2015, Mikėnaitė was elected member of the Council of this organisation. It must be noted that the main goal of EuroPris is to facilitate cooperation among European prison authorities and to ensure public safety. Correspondingly, EuroPris unites professionals employed in prison systems, seeks to ensure imprisonment conditions that are ethical and based on human rights protection principles, facilitates sharing of information relevant to penitentiary systems and best practices, and seeks to influence European penitentiary policy and related legislation.

The PD actively develops international cooperation with prison authorities in Latvia, Estonia, Poland, Norway, and the Czech Republic. These countries invite each other's representatives for educational tours, seminars, conferences, sports competitions and other events, seeking to create direct ties among the leaders, officers and employees of penitentiary systems of these countries. They share information and materials on penitentiary issues, research materials and findings, and projects financed by EU funds and partner in project implementation. International cooperation is pursued not only for developing their own organisations by gaining experience from foreign partners, but also by sharing best practices. The PD Training Centre's cooperation with foreign partners must be mentioned separately. The Prison and Probation Administration of Sweden was among the first institutions cooperating with the Training Centre. It helped to develop training strategies and primary training models, supplying the Training Centre with some technical training aids. Representatives of the Training Centre had a chance to get acquainted with the features of the penitentiary systems of Canada, Germany, Finland, France, Italy, Australia, and Estonia, as well as with the best practices of personnel training in these countries, participating in the professional development events in Sweden, Germany, Poland, and Austria.

The PD emphasises that over the past few years, cooperation between Lithuania and Norway has increased significantly. Confronted with the growing number of people confined to prison, Norway, hosting, by the way, quite a few imprisoned Lithuanians, decided to solve this problem in more than one way. One of the ways is direct financial and human assistance offered to other countries, including Lithuania. It is due to the 2009–2014 Norwegian financial mechanism funds that several important projects have been launched over the past few years. The purpose of these projects is to create more humane conditions for convicts and offer them a chance to reform. For example, in 2016, the Child and Mother Home was created at a correctional institution for women in Panevėžys, the only establishment of the kind in Lithuania. This was done in order to accommodate convicted women with small children outside the prison, securing normal psychosocial development for their offspring. Women wishing for admittance to this home are selected by specific criteria. Their psychological condition and motivation for work, child-rearing, and change are assessed by psychologists and other specialists. In this way not only is the overpopulation problem at the Child and Mother Unit solved, but the measure is also intended for the improvement of inmates' chances of resocialisation and integration into society after their release. Moreover, following the "Correction including punishments without imprisonment" programme funded by the Norwegian financial mechanism, the Rehabilitation Centre for convicts suffering from substance abuse was opened at one correctional institution. In addition, a school was created at a correctional institution for minors.

Role of Corrections

Mikėnaitė states that society plays a very important role in the penitentiary system. However, society, due to its general lack of understanding of the issue, is still unaware of it. Society is more inclined to condemn than to extend a helping hand. People think that it is necessary to isolate an offender from society by putting them in prison. Evidently, this measure is not sufficient. Yes, they are offenders, yet they are still humans who need help. Volunteer work is gaining momentum and a number of nice instances demonstrating community involvement can be observed. In late 2014, there were 280 volunteers, but in 2015 their number totalled 314. Currently, the PD cooperates with 22 non-governmental organisations and 33 religious communities. Assistance given by non-governmental organisations and religious communities is focused on the satisfaction of prisoners' spiritual needs, solution of substance abuse related problems, sensible organisation of meaningful leisure activities, and facilitation of the process of social integration.

General Assessments

Penal policy and public opinion have a significant influence on the correctional system. Penal policy determines the number of convicts and prisoners at confinement places, and public opinion determines the process of convicted people's adaptation and resocialisation. In order to achieve best results, that is, a reduced rate of repeated offence, systematic work in every direction is needed.

On the one hand, it is important to increase the efficaciousness of work with the convicted person (application of correctional programmes, evaluation of criminal risk, meeting individual needs, etc.). On the other hand, it is necessary to create safe working conditions for officers employed at confinement institutions, and to provide confinement institutions with necessary equipment (convoy cars, disposable narcotic substance detection tests, wireless stations, etc.). It must be noted that in order to reduce the rate of convoying people from one place of confinement to another, video conference equipment was introduced in 2015 in Lithuania, giving the opportunity to hold distance court sessions. In the same year, a cynology (canine) operations strategy was developed which resulted in the opening of a cynology unit at one institution.[2] Electronic supervision/monitoring is more prevalent in probation, and plans are being made for the intensified use of this measure in future.

Conclusion

To summarise, Mikėnaitė stated that her priority areas were the integration of best practices and new methods into work with convicted people, openness to the interaction of various national and international organisations representing different sectors, strategic planning of employee professional development that takes into consideration their personal needs and the goals of the institution. She also noted that further research, as well as collaboration between researchers and practitioners, would foster more efficacious development of the Lithuanian correctional system.[3]

Glossary

EuroPris: The European Organisation of Prison and Correctional Services.
HCR-20: The Historical, Clinical and Risk Management Scales-20.
OASys: The Offender Assessment System.
PCL:SV: Hare Psychopathy Checklist: Screening Version.
PD: The Prison Department under the Ministry of Justice of the Republic of Lithuania.
SARA: The Spousal Assault Risk Assessment.

Notes

1 A number of offender assessment tools have been introduced into practice in Lithuania recently: The Offender Assessment System (OASys, Home Office, 2002), The Psychopathy Checklist: Screening Version (PCL:SV, Hart, Cox & Hare, 1995), The Historical, Clinical, Risk Management-20 (HCR-20, Webster, Douglas, Eaves & Hart, 2007), the Spousal Assault Risk Assessment (SARA, Kropp, Hart, Webster & Eaves, 1999), the Brief Spousal Assault Form for the Evaluation of Risk (B-SAFER, Kropp, Hart & Belfrage, 2005), and the Sexual Violence Risk-20 (SVR-20, Boer, Hart, Kropp & Webster, 1997).
2 A dog training unit established to improve and enhance safety and security.
3 The interview was conducted in summer 2016.

Chapter 3

Martin Lulei, Project Manager, Ministry of Labour, Social Affairs and Family, Slovak Republic

Interviewer: Pavol Kopinec

Contents

Overview	23
Introduction	24
Career	24
Changes Experienced	25
Personal Correctional Philosophy	28
Problems and Successes Experienced	32
Theory and Practice	33
Evidence-Based Corrections	35
Transnational Relations	36
General Assessments	36
Glossary	37

Overview

The Slovak Republic (also known as Slovakia) is in the geographic centre of Europe. It has a population of 5.5 million. The Slovak Republic was established on 1 January 1993 following the division of Czechoslovakia into two countries – the Slovak Republic, with Bratislava as its capital, and the Czech Republic. The Slovak Republic is a member of the European Union, NATO and the Eurozone. It has 18 correctional institutions capable of holding 9,500 inmates: five institutions hold only pre-trial detainees, nine hold sentenced prisoners, and four house a combination of sentenced prisoners and pre-trial detainees. All correctional institutions are operated by the state (Mačkinová, Mačkin, & Mačkinová, 2017).

The correction system is administered by the Slovak General Directorate of the Prison and Court Guard Corps under the Ministry of the Interior of the Slovak Republic. The prison system is divided into three security levels, referred to as 'the external differentiation' of prisons. Prisoners serve their sentences in differentiated groups 'A', 'B', 'C', or in specialised units.

Those sentenced to life-long imprisonment are categorised as 'D1' and 'D2'. Internal differentiation of prisons by the Ministry of Justice Decree no. 368/2008 Coll. of Law places prisoners into sections and groups at the same security level to increase the effectiveness of the treatment of prisoners. Prisoners placed in sections or groups stay together and usually also work together to assist in meeting targets for treatment (Act no. 93/2008 Coll. of Law).

The purpose of prison is defined as being to maintain the health and dignity of prisoners and, for the duration of the sentence, to develop their sense of responsibility and equip them with skills that will help them to reintegrate into society, to live and to respect the law after leaving prison (European Prison Rules). 'External differentiation' refers to the degree of imposed penalties and surveillance, governed by the principle that the higher the degree of surveillance, the greater the scope of restrictions, which are regulated differently with regard to rights and forms of treatment (Act no. 93/2008 Coll. of law). The categorisation of the individual is based on the conclusions and recommendations of psychological evaluation, the prisoner's behaviour during previous sentences, understanding of the emotional and social problems of the prisoner and the prisoner's attitudes to following a rehabilitation programme. The categorisation of a prisoner does not change if he/she is relocated between institutions of the same security level (Decree no. 368/2008). Nowadays, Slovak prisons feature modern technologies. All prisons have a working organisation's standards and security, including a good level of prison healthcare, thoughtful and functional psycho-diagnostic activities concerning the classification of convicts and the choice of internal differentiation. Applied are individual–educational methods and means (Mačkinová et al., 2017).

Introduction

The interviewee communicated with Dr Lulei via email and phone, with a transcript of questions in Slovak and English. Following his swift reply, and in order to receive further details, further questions were sent and the responses incorporated in the text.

Career

Q: What motivated you to enter the field of corrections?
A: During my university studies, I focused on the problem of probation and mediation in criminal matters. From 2004, I worked as a social worker in Victim Support Slovakia, an NGO working with victims of crime. In 2005, I won a national Slovak round for students and professionals involved in social work with the theme of

'Probation and mediation along the lines of social work'. Social work with victims of crime and social counselling in another NGO, as well as work with delinquent youths, led me to the practical, theoretical and research bases within these target groups.

Q: Did the way your career developed surprise you?

A: Not really. During my university studies I focused on working with the victims of crime and offenders and eventually with delinquent youth.

Q: Did your work prove as interesting or rewarding as you thought it would?

A: I think that the results of my work influenced the course of science and practice in this field (though not as much as I thought it would). I have published a number of articles, chapters in research monographs, also an independent scientific monograph in 2011 (*Social Work in Criminal Justice and Probation*).

Q: Do you have any regrets about an opportunity you pursued or chose not to pursue during the course of your career?

A: No.

Changes Experienced

Q: What do you see as the most important changes that have occurred in the field of corrections over the course of your career?

A: I consider the most significant change as the establishment of probation and mediation offices (initially through the pilot projects after 2000, followed by legislation in 2003). There were also significant changes in the criminal law standards (in the Criminal Law and in the Code of Criminal Procedure), which came into force on January 2006. Also very important were legislative changes related to the provision of the 'new' alternative sanctions (punishment through obligated work, home imprisonment, etc.), as well as new projects and resocialisation programmes introduced for offenders serving a prison sentence, particularly with a focus on education (graduation course, retraining courses, computer literacy, etc.).

Q: What changes in external conditions (support from communities, legal and legislative powers, relations with minority communities, resource provision, political influence, etc.) have had a significant impact on current correctional practices and policy?

A: The current prison practice is greatly influenced by the membership of the Slovak Republic in the EU. My personal view is that, in many cases, these practices are at the minimum level of EU requirements, with no effective strategies for long-term development. Probation and mediation services have existed for a decade, but have undergone minimal changes within this period. On the positive side, there is a wide range of project activities in relation to the prevention of crime implemented at the national level through a variety of organisations. These include the transfer of the project 'Night Ravens' into selected Slovak municipalities, the implementation of CCTV systems in Slovak villages, and others. Political influence has had a significant impact on the current correctional practice, particularly in the ruling political party's view of crime and criminal justice. For example, the rule 'three strikes and you're out' during the governance of the right-wing parties.

Q: Overall, has the quality of prisons, jails, and community supervision in your country/community improved or declined over the past ten years?

A: To answer this question would require an independent professional evaluation. In short, we can say that, according to statistics, Slovakia ranks 13th out of the 56 European countries, including Kosovo (Table 3.1). Approximately 30–45% of offenders of varied types of

Table 3.1 Number of detained people per 100,000 residents in selected European countries (International Centre for Prison Studies, 2012; Lulei, 2013)

Ordinal no.	State	No. of prisoners (to that date)	Repletion of prisons in % (to that date)	No. of detained people per 100,000 residents (to that date)
1	Georgia	23,653 (30.4. 2012)	100.1 (30.4. 2012)	524 (April 2012)
2	Russian Federation	738,400 (1.5. 2012)	91 (31.12. 2009)	516 (May 2012)
3	Belarus	41,525 (31.12. 2009)	96.8 (31.12. 2009)	438 (December 2009)
5	Ukraine	153,508 (1.5. 2012)	96.7 (1.9. 2010)	338 (May 2012)
11	Czech Republic	23,734 (27.4. 2012)	114.7 (31.3. 2012)	225 (April 2012)
12	Poland	84,799 (30.4. 2012)	98.6 (30.4. 2012*)	222 (April 2012)
13	Slovakia	10,086 (30.5. 2012)	102.7 (30.5. 2012)	203 (May 2012)
16	Hungary	17,210 (31.12. 2011)	136.5 (31.12. 2011)	173 (December 2011)
36	Austria	8,694 (3.6. 2011)	98 (3.6. 2011)	104 (June 2010)

*The figure does not include inmates currently awaiting implementation of a sentence (to that date)

crime are repeat offenders and unemployed people. Predominant in these figures are first-time offenders, who represented almost 80% of all in the past decade. According to a decade's worth of statistical data of reoffenders, Slovakia had in 2000 48,771 offenders, including 8,814 repeat offenders (18.07%) and in 2010 it was 53,310 offenders, including 11,007 repeat offenders (20.64%). The Annual Report of the Prison Service of the Slovak Republic for 2011 indicates that a gradually increasing trend in the number of prisoners was reflected mainly in the population of the institutes, which, at the end of 2011, was 98.1% of the total accommodation capacity (10,725 beds). In 2011, there were 55 registered suicide attempts (accused and convicted), five of which were successful. The upward movement of the number of accused and convicted is presented in Figure 3.1.

From my point of view, the quality of prisons and community supervision should be reflected by the rate of repeat criminal offenders, the proportion of crimes committed by repeat offenders, the total crime, and by the percentage of first-time offenders in respect of penalty as well as by percentage of youth committing the crime and, of course, by an index of crime. In Slovakia, we have implemented programmes, but they are few in number and reports of their effectiveness from evidence-based practise are completely absent. On the other hand, there are a number of projects, particularly in relation to the prevention of crime, which are implemented by the NGOs with varying quality. I have no information as to whether quality management of correction services exists. In terms of education, there are separate concepts of education for prison staff and independent institutions which

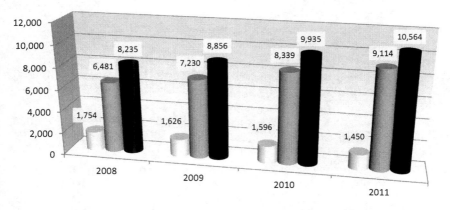

Figure 3.1 Development of the number of accused and sentenced (annual statistical report, Ministry of Justice, 2011)

provide this type of training in this field, and that is very positive. If we talk about integration or services, we can speak only about the local levels but not nationally. Cooperation and coordination mechanisms are missing within the nationwide system. Also lacking is an institution focused predominantly on researching effective measures in the professional prison practice, as is evident in the Czech Republic and their Institute for Criminology and Social Prevention.

Q: In general, is it more or less difficult to be a correctional officer (or supervisor, warden, regional management) now than in the past?

A: I think now it is more difficult. The current position of the prison director includes effective management of human resources, projects, operations, security, etc.

Personal Correctional Philosophy

Q: What should be the main job, functions and roles of prisons? What should be left to other people or organisations?

A: The primary role of prisons is the protection of society and socialisation of criminals. The priority of correctional policy should be the principle of the 'ultima ratio' (the use of a measured penalty when there are no other options). Their mission should be orientated to reduce the use of imprisonment, reduce the risk of recidivism and protection of the wider society. The whole system of criminal policy should be cross-linked and should create a synergetic effect, which, unfortunately, is not the case in the Slovak Republic. Prisons should combine with other organisations active in the field of crime, including the thirrd sector, and with state organisations included in the system. Correctional institutions are 'only' a part of the crime policy system (Figure 3.2).

Q: Which organisational arrangements work and which do not?

A: From my perspective, networking and synergy between government and non-government organisations is not working in the light of the above-mentioned approach. An effective strategy, not currently in place, for a prisoner's release would be to scientifically and practically declare their 'readiness' to respect society's norms. Offender management is missing in the Slovak Republic and has a negative effect. What is working are the activities provided inside of the prison system (projects, education and trainings of employees, etc.).

Q: What policies does your country have in regard to relations with the community, political groups, and other criminal justice organisations? Do these policies work well? What hampers cooperation with other agencies and groups?

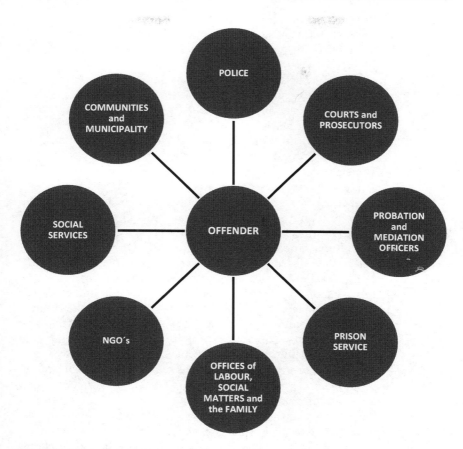

Figure 3.2 Synergy in penal policy (Lulei, 2011)

A: In relation to the community, we can talk about the crime prevention programmes which are supported by the Government Council for Crime Prevention. In Slovakia, the work of community programmes in general is undervalued. Community sentences should be used more, for example as alternatives. Groups such as probation and mediation officers, in my view representing a potentially highly effective group in the criminal policy system, but changes that would lead to their increased effectiveness are not realised and sometimes are not even politically recognised.

Q: How should corrections institutions be run? What programmes should be provided, and how would you prefer sentencing laws to be modified so as to have prisons and jails include the individuals most deserving of incarceration? What are the best correctional strategies to ensure the safety and security of the inmates, staff and community? What services should prisons and jails provide that are currently not offered? What services are provided that you believe should be cut?

A: The management of correctional institutions should be professional in accordance with procedural management and management of quality. The correctional leader should be a manager and professional expert. Emphasis should be placed on transparency of costs to the public from each correctional institution regarding cost, efficiency, the proportion of relapses, the numbers of successful social reintegration programmes and their evaluation, etc.)

There should be a special accreditation council of scientific and practical experts, who would be a part of the accreditation process of the resocialisation programmes. The enforcement of sentences by the criminal justice policy should follow the principle of 'ultima ratio', as already mentioned. Only serious offenders should be placed in prison in order to protect society. These should be facilities providing a specialised regime for offenders. In other cases, imprisonment should be used minimally or not at all, and replaced by other forms as appropriate – alternative sentences, community supervision, supervision of probation and mediation officers, specialised programmes linking the penitentiary post-penitentiary areas _ evidence-based practice, etc).

The best correctional strategy is ensuring minimal use of imprisonment (serious offenders posing a threat to society), with a system set up to implement proven resocialisation programmes inside and outside the prison, and an overall system of crime policy (synergy effect and offender management).

Q: How should supervision post-prison or post-jail (or in lieu of prison or jail) be dealt with? Is the procedure used in your country working, or do you see an increased recidivism rate due to issues experienced by those supervised in the community? How would you resolve this problem, or why is this process working in your country?

A: A natural part of the practice of probation intervention is a general intervention process: contact = risk–intervention–evaluation. Unprofessional implementation increases the risk of recurrence. The question of current probation practices in Slovakia is primarily a risk assessment system of recurrence and the individual needs of the offender and subsequent application of effective interventions. This is a continuing interlinked process and probation should be within the paradigm of researched best practice. The absence of any part of this process disrupts the system's functionality. Slovakia has seen cases in the media where offenders have relapsed seriously after release, committing murders, for example. Public attitudes towards probation are hard to measure, because most don't understand probation. Research conducted in 2008 (200 participants from 13 cities and 32 villages in Slovakia) reflected a lack of information in public about probation. Questioned 'Have you ever heard of probation?', 84.50% of respondents answered 'no' (Lulei, 2010). Probation services working in close cooperation with police, prison services and social services should ensure professional supervision. First of all, there should be an assessment of the level of risk of relapse – a risk assessment tool. Based on this, there should be continuing work with criminals, such as an adjustment programme or other interventions, etc.). See Figure 3.3.

Unfortunately, this system does not work in Slovakia. The result is the recurrence of crime, generally as a result of an incorrect policy of penalties.

Q: Do you feel that your country uses appropriate intermediate sanctions when needed, or is there a lack of such sanctions? Are intermediate sanctions such as treatment programmes, intensive supervision, or electronic monitoring utilised, and do they reduce recidivism while keeping those in the community safe? If not, what do you feel is the problem?

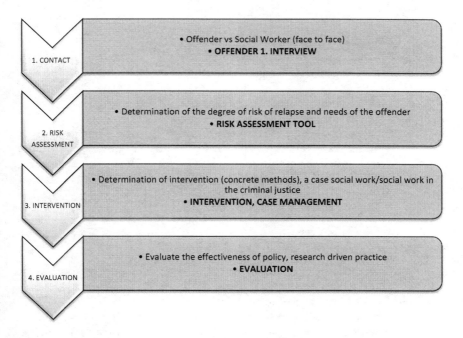

Figure 3.3 Contact = risk management–intervention–evaluation

Table 3.2 Probation summary (Cehlar, 2012)

Year	Number of allocated probations			Summary of probation per year	Number of probation and mediation officers in Slovakia
	Number of unfinished probations from the last year	New allocated probations	Number of compulsory work (alternative sanction)		
2007	5,919	6,636	302	12,555	116
2010	9,239	4,297	1,175	13,536	77
2011	11,337	7,737	2,278	19,074	63

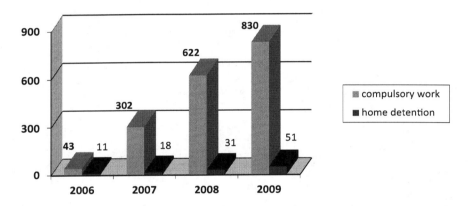

Figure 3.4 Number of chosen alternative sanctions (2006–2009) in Slovakia

A: These penalties are used only to a small extent, although increasing from year to year). The problem, for example, is that although house arrest exists, electronic monitoring is still absent. The problem is also the small number of probation and mediation officers, their working conditions and insufficient financial reward (see Table 3.2; Figure 3.4).

Problems and Successes Experienced

Q: In your experience, which policies or programmes have worked well, and which have not?
A: Employment, within this target group, reduces recurrence by almost 50%. I consider as appropriate a combination of programmes, which include increasing employability. A lot of such programmes have

been realised in many different prisons in Slovakia within the past 15 years. I also consider effective cooperation between prisons services, non-governmental organisations and academic actors.

Q: What would you consider to be the greatest problem facing the correctional system at this time?

A: Insufficient synergy and absence of offender management, absence of risk assessment tools, the small number of probation and mediation workers and an absence of programmes emphasising evidence-based practice.

Q: What problems in corrections do you find are the most difficult to deal with? What would be easy to change, internal problems (culture of the organisation, managerial deficiencies, allegations of corruption or gender related problems) or externally generated problems (resources, community support, parole or probation procedures, or lack thereof)?

A: It would be easy to change the system set up for release procedures, risk assessment evaluation, as well as the creation of effective programmes described above. What is not so easy to change is the organisation cultures in the prisons and their approach to scientific developments and the latest scientific knowledge.

Q: What is the most successful programme you have worked with in corrections? What is the most successful policy in regards to the positive improvements that have been made to prisons, jails, or community supervision?

A: As a very successful project, I would pick out the project 'option', which, unfortunately, does not apply to prisons, but to social work with delinquent youth in specialised educational institutions.

Theory and Practice

Q: What is the relationship between theory and practice right now? Does it exist? Does it work? What holds collaboration or interactions back?

A: Currently absent is the transfer of the latest scientific knowledge into practice (risk assessment tools, evidence-based practice, and so on).The reason for this is the lack of research institutions and the closed intra-organisational structure of the prison service, which has little contact with external sources. We cannot consider conferences and workshops effective without the subsequent transfer of their knowledge into concrete practice.

If we are talking about the relationship between theory and practice in relation to social work in criminal justice, I would specify four components:

- Science and research (theoretical concepts, paradigm, research findings);
- Education (theoretical framework, methods, techniques, approaches, research methodology);
- Practice (application in practice and its resources evaluation); and,
- Evaluation (assessment and change of starting points in relationship to effectiveness).

Analysis of these components would require an independent workshop, but I will try to outline how it could be. The theoretical answer is shown in Figure 3.5. Taking resocialisation of the offender as an area of interest of social work, then it is determined by the answers to the following questions:

- What are the theoretical concepts, paradigms and research in the field of social work related to resocialisation of an offender (for example, paradigm on evidence-based practice)?
- What theoretical knowledge, specific methods, techniques, approaches, methodology in the field of social reintegration of the offender is offered within social work education and through which specific subjects (e.g., forensic social work, methods such as, for example, self-help group, motivational interview, etc)?
- What, from the field of social work, is applied in practice (what methods, techniques, approaches and research methodology) (e.g., system of offender assessment) that does not exist in the current Slovak conditions)?
- How are the individual methods and techniques reviewed in relation to research and science (e.g., are changes reflected in social work in relationship to methods, which is possible based on current trends in science considered to be ineffective)?

Q: What kind of research, in what form, and on which questions would you find most useful for practice? If not very useful, what could or should creators of theory do to make their ideas more useful to you?

A: Research focused on decreasing the degree of risk of recurrence, effective resocialisation programmes, SWOT analysis of the current prison system, prepared by the external auditors, and research on protective and risk factors on committing of criminal offence.

Q: Where do you find theory-based information? Where do you look: journals, professional magazines, books, publications, reports?

A: Internships abroad, conferences, international organisations, CEP, ESC, scientific journals, international projects.

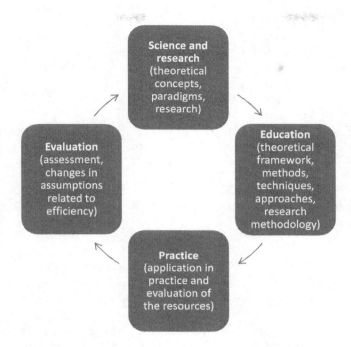

Figure 3.5 Theory and practice of social work as a system

Q: Does the department of corrections you work for conduct research on its own? On what types of issues or questions?
A: The University department participates in various international projects in the context of the correctional services (DOMICE, OSE ISRD, and so on), as well as leading students theses to address specific topics targeting different areas in the context of criminal policy.

Evidence-Based Corrections

Q: What evidence-based practices are used now in prisons, jails, for intermediate sanctions, or in community supervision? Do you agree with the use of these practices? Do you feel that using more evidence-based practices would benefit the correctional system?
A: Application of this approach is crucial. Unfortunately, I do not have any knowledge that this approach will be applied in the Slovak Republic, but it would be very useful.
Q: Do you read information on evidence-based practices? Where do you get this information? If you do not have this information, would you be interested in having access to these practices? What programmes have been proved to work best in your country?
A: Only from abroad: for example, from the Czech Republic.

Transnational Relations

Q: Have those interactions been beneficial or harmful? What kind of external international influences are beneficial and which ones less so?
A: Expertise from other foreign prison institutions is very useful. We often attend various meetings, but their effect on specific practices in prisons in Slovakia is minimal. The implementation of international projects and membership in international organisations is also very useful.
Q: How have international relationships with other countries or other political influences had an impact on correctional policy or practice in your country?
A: I do not know of any effective measures for correction practice in Slovakia, based on positive experiences abroad. The exception is a recurring transition of knowledge from the Czech Republic.

General Assessments

Q: What do you think of the relationship between sentencing laws and public opinion and whether it affects the functioning of prisons, jails and community supervision?
A: Public opinion tends towards harsh and uncompromising punishment of criminals; on the other hand, public opinion is positive towards the social reintegration of youth offenders. The public wants to punish criminals, and also needs protection against crime.
Q: How do you view the release procedures in your country and do they contribute to, or inhibit, recidivism?
A: The answer to this question is related to the setting of release procedures and to the risk management approach to decreasing the risk of recurrence. Given that, in Slovakia, there is no functioning system of declaration of effectiveness, from my perspective it contributes to relapses and Slovakia does not even have a risk assessment tool in place.
Q: What rehabilitative programmes could be offered, either in or out of prison or jail, that could decrease recidivism?
A: Only those that have been proved by research and where evidence of their effectiveness exists. There should be multi-factorial programmes which are not only based on target groups. It means not just an individual programme for offenders of domestic violence and another individual programme for addicts and so on . . . because the social situation is, in many cases, a combination of these socio-pathological phenomena.
Q: How are intermediate sanctions (such as house arrest, ankle bracelets, rehabilitative programmes in the community, or intensive

supervision, among others) in your country used, and how are they working or failing to work?

A: The use of alternative sanctions, such as community services and house arrest is increasing. They are used in complicated forms due to the lack of effective setting of probation and mediation services. Electronic monitoring is absent and, in many cases, the application of alternative penalties are associated with the individual 'confidence' placed on these forms of punishment by the justice organs – the courts and prosecutors.

Q: Which intermediate sanctions would you increase or create, and why?

A: I would support the increased application of alternative sanctions. It is unreasonable and inefficient to send a first-time offender to prison for a year. The negative effects of imprisonment on the offender's personality are scientifically declared. These types of sanctions should be enhanced and their implementation should be under the auspices of probation and mediation services of NGOs and state institutions: for example, those providing social services.

Q: How could changing the balance between intermediate sanctions affect prison and jail environments? Would that be an improvement?

A: Surely this would mean an improvement through a decrease in prison populations – but only if it were implemented systematically and controlled effectively by the management.

Q: What are the developments you see as most likely to happen in the next few years, and which developments would you prefer to see happening?

A: I think prison populations will increase, and also crime will increase globally. There will be a move towards private prisons contracted for public services and more pressure will be created on the use and utilisation of alternative measures and sanctions. Youth crime will increase, too, and especially an increase in property crime.

Q: What is most needed now to improve prisons, jails, community supervision, and the overall punishment process in your country?

A: Systematic changes in penal policy, most of which I have mentioned in the answers to the previous questions.

Glossary

Ministry of Justice Decree 368/2008 Coll. of Law: Decree issuing the Custodial Order.

Act No. 93/2008 Coll. of Law: Act amending and supplementing Act No. 475/2005 Coll. on the implementation of imprisonment and amending and supplementing certain acts.

Victim Support Slovakia: Independent Slovak civil association and counselling centre for victims of crime.

Probation and mediation services: Centralised Slovak services taking into account local specifics. Their aim is to strengthen the rights of victims damaged by crime, to help actively resocialise the offender and to return him/her into society after the crime was committed, and to educate the whole society.

The Council of the Slovak Government for Crime Prevention: An advisory, initiative, coordination and expert body of the government for the area of prevention of crime and other antisocial activities.

CEP: Confederation of European Probation.

ESC: European Society of Criminology.

DOMICE: Developing Offender Management in Corrections in Europe.

OSE: Offender Supervision in Europe.

ISRD: International Self-Report Delinquency study.

Section II

North America

Chapter 4

Danny W. Pirtle, Deputy Director of Executive and Administrative Services (former), Dallas County Juvenile Justice Department

Interviewer: David C. Hurley

Contents

Overview	41
Introduction	42
Career	43
Changes Experienced	44
Personal Correctional Philosophy	49
Problems and Successes Experienced	51
Theory and Practice	52
Evidence-Based Corrections	53
Transnational Relations	56
Role of Corrections	57
General Assessments	57
Conclusion	58
Glossary	59

Overview

The United States is distinctive in how it dispenses justice in a decentralised manner. For example, there are approximately 18,000 different law enforcement agencies within the United States, significantly more than any other country (Peak, 2014). The same is true in adult and juvenile corrections. Most juvenile correctional programmes are administered at the county level, based on state regulations. There is no comprehensive national juvenile justice system *per se*, but instead there is a disjointed conglomerate model that can appear to outsiders as a holistic system. This, however, is an illusion. Each of the 50 states is responsible for overseeing more than 3,000 counties where the bulk of juvenile justice is administered (National Association of Counties).

The Dallas County Juvenile Justice Department is one of these local juvenile agencies. It is the second largest in Texas, behind Houston or Harris County, and has over 900 employees. In the Texas system, a juvenile 'is a person who was at least 10 years old but not yet 17 at the time he or she committed an act defined as delinquent conduct or conduct in need of supervision' (www.tjjd.texas.gov). When a juvenile engages in delinquent conduct, a referral to juvenile court can be made and adjudication occurs. In 2015, the Dallas County Juvenile Department made over 5,983 referrals. Possible adjudication options are probation, treatment, diversion, detention, or placement in a residential facility. All of the processes take place in the Henry Wade Detention Center. Hence, the organisation is housed in one building with the juvenile courts on the third floor, administrative offices on the second floor and the actual Henry Way Detention Center on the first floor. In a sense it is unique, in that it is not only a detention centre but also provides post-adjudication placement. Thus, the Henry Wade Detention Center houses two types of youth: (1) those who were arrested the night before and detained, and, (2) those who have gone through the court process, were found delinquent and need some type of residential placement. The agency is structured with a Director of Juvenile Services, Assistant Director and four Deputy Directors: Executive and Administrative Services, Education Services, Field Services, and a Legal Adviser.

Introduction

Danny Pirtle was selected for this interview because of his unique perspective as both practitioner and scholar. He is a rare find, an individual who started working in juvenile corrections after college, who went on to achieve a PhD and work as a university professor, and then went back to working as an administrator in the juvenile justice system when the opportunity arose. Hence, he has a grasp of juvenile justice issues from inside the system as an entry level worker, as an administrator, and, later, outside the system as a researcher and scholar.

I conducted the interview over a series of sessions. The first session with Dr Pirtle was held at the Dallas County Juvenile Justice Department, where he provided a tour of the facilities housing the juvenile programmes, lock-up, and administrative offices. Later, an additional telephone interview was conducted in order to complete the interview. Danny was very candid concerning his experience. He freely shared how both the institutional philosophy and his outlook toward juvenile justice has changed over time. He was very open on his thoughts about what worked and what did not.

Six months after the initial interview, Dr Pirtle left his position to teach at the Lake Havasu branch of Arizona State University as a senior lecturer. This campus targets first generation college students who may have had trouble gaining admission into other universities.

Career

Q: Could you please discuss your career, including any surprises, rewards and disappointments?

A: After graduating from Tennessee State University, I moved to Houston and I knew I wanted to work with juveniles. I started out as a JSO (Juvenile Supervision Officer) in Harris County in 1997. This is an entry level position, even for those with college degrees, which is true even today, 20 years later. I did that for about a year, then I started working with the academic component, which is part of the juvenile justice system that is responsible for the education of juveniles in custody. I worked there for about three years. I became an Intake Probation Officer in 2002 and I was responsible for determining whether the kids would be locked up or released. I did that for about five years. While working in the system, I decided to complete my education by first getting a Master of Science degree in Juvenile Justice in 2001, and then by completing my PhD in Juvenile Justice in 2007. After that, I started working in academia, teaching, researching and writing on juvenile minority issues, including youth violence, gangs and risk assessment. Then, in 2013, Dr Smith, whom I went to school with, contacted me and told me she had an executive position available as the Deputy of Education in the Dallas County Juvenile Department. I knew that I wanted to finish my career in the field and at the time I was 38 years old. I knew that this was a once in a lifetime opportunity, so I got off my career path. I was up for tenure and promotion at my university at that time. I left in the middle of the tenure process because I was so excited about this opportunity. I now have been here for three years. Currently, I serve as the Deputy Director of Executive and Administrative Services.

Surprises along the way – in hindsight, when I taught I used to tell my students who wanted to intern that internships primarily are a great way to be introduced to the field. I was taught that the biggest takeaway from internships was that it was a great opportunity for you to see how good the field is. But I didn't realise internships were also a great way for you to figure out that 'I don't want to do this', that is, this career is not for you.

Where I am now is that I don't want to do this [work for the Juvenile Justice Department]. This is probably a lot different than my colleagues [who work here] but working at this level has exposed some things that I am not proud of. Although I think we do a great job with kids, we are challenged. There are a lot of unwritten and unspoken rules and politics that dominate in a department of this size. I'm sort of a born rebel, if you will, hence I couldn't see myself staying in this field, particularly at this level, and being able to maintain any real sense of satisfaction.[1]

Changes Experienced

Q: What are the most important changes that have occurred over the course of your career?

A: A great deal of change has happened since I started in juvenile corrections. I think the best place to start is by discussing the programmes we currently have that would not have been available to youth when I first started. So, in detention, we have a START programme, which is the Short Term Adolescent Residential Treatment programme. The START programme is about 90 days and focuses on youth acting responsibly through counselling and peer support while in detention. Typically, the kid in START is a first or second offence low-level offender with supervision issues at home. Maybe he was on probation but was unsuccessful for not going to school. Maybe he was taking drugs or engaging in different technical violations. So, it was determined that maybe a little slap on the wrist by putting him in placement would ideally shake him up and get him on the right track. These are low risk offenders. It is not for kids that commit serious felony offences. Even if it is their first offence, we would tend to stay away from START for a kid that had an aggravated robbery [aggravated robbery suggests high risk]. We try to be very conscious of making sure that we have similar kids [in START] because,, as the literature shows when you mix low risk offenders with high risk offenders, it doesn't lower the risk of the high risk but instead raises the risk of the low risk offenders.

Then we have the Residential Drug Treatment Programme, or RDT, also located in the detention centre. RDT is just that, a residential drug treatment programme. Generally, it is about a 90–120-day programme. Kids in RDT are not major drug abusers; they are experimenting or have had supportive outpatient [treatment] in the past for marijuana, or maybe even cocaine. But it was determined that they needed placement to deal with their drug issues. They could be pretty much considered recreational users. While the youth are detained, they receive weekly individual counselling and group sessions focusing on life skills and accountability. Upon completion of the residential portion of the programme, the youth are transitioned to an aftercare day treatment programme coupled with home supervision.

If we have kids who have major drug concerns along with behavioural issues and pretty major psychological issues, such as oppositional defiant disorder and low IQs, we tend to place those kids in our contract placements. We presently have contracts with over 30 agencies and those are going to be used for more extreme cases. There was a study completed last year titled *Closer to Home* (Fabelo, Arrigona, Thompson, Clemens and Marchbanks, 2015). Basically, what was concluded in the *Closer to Home* report is that kids tend to do better the closer they are to home. And, as simple as that may sound, it is not always feasible. We have several placements here in Dallas County but all the [risk] factors that the [risk] instrument shows need to be taken care of we may not necessarily be able to address in our local placements. So, we may have to send a kid to Glenn Mills in Pennsylvania (www.glenmillsschool.org/about/). We may have to send a female to a placement in Arizona because they can deal with her very specific need.

So, that's pretty much detention; surprising to a lot of people, the detention numbers have been decreasing. [When] I say surprisingly, I'm talking over a ten-year time period. In the late 1990s up to the mid-2000s, really across the country, especially in large urban departments, you had detention centres that were literally bursting at the seams. For example, at that time, in the late 1990s or early 2000s, I worked in the Harris County. We were authorised by TJJD, the Texas Youth Authority, to house 180 to 185 youths, but there were times we had 260–270. We had kids sleep in bunks or sleep in offices because we were so overcrowded.

A major change occurred when the Annie E. Casey Foundation came in and set the tone for decreasing juvenile detention populations. This started [as] a trend in lowering numbers of youth incarcerated. Annie E. Casey started implementing a lot of federal mandates over the past ten years or so. We are under Annie E. Casey, so we utilise certain risk assessment tools and, of course, there is money attached if we abide by their edict. Their edict is to only detain those youth who need to be removed from the community because they are dangerous to others or themselves. So, there are situations where a kid might score high on the risk assessment and you may still decide to release the youth with some services. The goal the Chief Juvenile Probation Officer for Dallas County has given us is for no more than 100 youth in detention.

There are some concerns over how realistic that is, especially in Dallas County, as large as we are and as often as delinquency occurs. Decreasing detention numbers pleased some, especially the federal government and organisations like Annie E. Casey. It hasn't really boded well with a lot of [the] line staff. A perfect example is when you are a probation officer and you have 25 kids on your caseload and you have five kids on your caseload who are having pretty significant [problems] with their adjustment to probation. They are violating their probation by not attending school, by committing curfew violations, by failing drug tests, by not participating in their programme. There was a time you could simply return a kid [like this] to court and without second guessing the judge would say [order] detention and possibly placement. Now if you talk to the average probation officer you hear the exact opposite, to their chagrin and their anger. They feel their hands are tied. They feel the kids on probation know that even if they go out and commit another offence there's still the possibility they will not go to detention. There is a possibility my [the kid's] sanction level will not really increase. So, if I'm on probation, let's say for an assault, and I get probation for 12 months, when I'm six months in and have three or four technical violations and I pick up another charge, [then] I may just get extended probation. I may get extended services. I may not ever come back to detention. So there are quite a few probation officers that [believe] we are doing the youth a disservice; but we are also doing the community a disservice because we are not really sticking it to them [the juvenile probationer]. It really just depends on what end of the pendulum you are on. If you're a hard-nosed, get tough person, then this is not the era for hard-nosed, get tough. If you are more rehabilitative by giving second and third chances, this is your era. We are far removed from the 'lock-them up' mentality of the late 1990s and early 2000s.

Beyond the foundation we had some significant events occur, especially if you're talking about the population that is most likely to be detained. This [the population most likely detained] is people of colour and poor people. So we started looking at those variables. They are really hard to ignore. Why are young blacks and browns [African Americans and Hispanics] so disproportionally impacted by the system? The areas where these minorities live are so over policed that quite often they [minority and poor youth] are accused of violating local ordinances and end up in our detention centre. So even today, when I look at the actual census, like clockwork the majority of the youth that are in our detention center are young men of colour.

Q: Do you think that has to do with the start of the 1980 drug offences and the criminalisation of drugs?

A: Let me give you an overview of the detained population. While you do have your drug offences, ironically, that would not even be close to the majority of youth that are detained. We [decide] to detain based on risk assessment. A lot of the decisions we make are not based on feelings and emotions, like it was ten years ago. A kid is arrested. He comes in and we are responsible for completing a risk assessment instrument. So, basically, that risk assessment instrument is a validated instrument that is used to determine future criminal involvement. So, depending on the score, whether it be low, medium, or high, that helps guide our decision to release or not. A kid could come in on probation for a misdemeanour offence and you come in with a new referral for, let's say, a felony, but the risk assessment instrument could still indicate you [the felony offender] are a low-risk offender. So how does that look to a kid who knows, 'Wow, I'm already on probation for possession of marijuana and assault and I just picked up a robbery which is a felony offence and they are still going to let me go home.' So it can really send a mixed message to the youth if he is already on probation and under court sanction.

Q: So when we talk about a change in programmes, have the facilities or the overall organisation changed a lot over the past ten years?

A: Good question. One of the things that has happened since I have been here is that we are constantly developing programmes, improving programmes based on the needs that we see are evident.

We are very good at making data-driven decisions. Our Chief has done an excellent job in keeping her hand on the pulse of what going on in our county as far as our youth are concerned. One of the things that she has implemented is Diversion Courts. You talk about a deincarceration model. One of the biggest [things] we can do as a department is to try our very best to divert as many youth from the formal system as possible. We know the research shows that just having a basic introduction into the system can have a long-term impact, especially if you are looking at age of first offence, socio-economic status, and academic status. The more of those variables that are present [the greater the chance they] can cause a youth to go further and further into the system. So, one of our diversion programmes, again we have some pretty unique diversion programmes, at the surface level they seem to be doing exactly what we want. So, one of our novel approaches is the Diversion Courts, the diversionary male court: the sole purpose of this Diversion Court is to divert black and brown youth [African American and Hispanic]. So a kid receives a referral from a law enforcement agency. Our staff reviews the case. We examine the youth's background and make a recommendation to the District Attorney to allow that particular youth to go through the diversion programme.

Q: Would you say that the organisation is better than it was than ten years ago?

A: I would say that we have better programmes. [We are] not trying to be politically correct. Now we have a lot more options in terms of how to address any need a youth may have than we did ten years ago. You can attribute that to time and us getting better at researching. Again, I think one of the things that probation departments have that they likely didn't have as often ten years ago is access to the data and the ability to really evaluate that data. You won't find that many departments now who develop programmes in a silo and not based on some hard data that show there is a need.

In the field for kids living in the community, we have about one probation officer and the standard caseload is between 22 and 25 youths. This is extremely low compared to ten years ago, where officers had upwards of 45–50 kids to supervise. Depending on the institution, if it is a secure facility, the ratio is going to be a little different than if it is a non-secure facility. All of those numbers are based on our oversight agency, Texas Juvenile Justice Department (TJJD).

Q: How would you say staff are trained compared to ten years ago?

A: Training is one of my areas. Training has evolved tremendously because so have the training standards. Child Informed Care is something that you would not have seen ten years ago. It is very specific training that addresses how to deal with children who have had some type of very traumatic experience.[2] PREA training, required under the Federal Prison Rape Elimination Act (Public Law 108–79), which has impacted both the juvenile and the adult system, involves training you would not have received ten years ago. For example, back then, you would not have had training on how to address a child who anatomically is a male but identifies as a female. We have received that training now and we offer that training monthly to our new staff.

There are still some problems that training won't overcome. One of the things I share with new employees in the field is that, unfortunately, in the fields of juvenile probation, corrections and law enforcement, you are likely to run into a supervisor who is a supervisor just because it was his or her turn. He or she is not any more intelligent than you are, is not any better read than you are, and may not have even as many credentials as you have, but we are a field that still places limited value on academic attainment. That is just one component. You have other people who are promoted simply because they know this person who happens to be a very powerful political figure. So their relationship with this particular person has afforded not only certain positions, but it afforded them a different rulebook. I know my Chief and assistant would probably set me on fire right now [if they heard me saying this].

Personal Correctional Philosophy

Q: What do you think should be the role of juvenile correction in society?
A: When we talk about the purpose of juvenile detention at the county level, the ultimate responsibility is to keep society safe. So we need to know that we are holding those who represent harm to themselves or others. That requires a lot of guesswork – even the best risk assessment instruments are not foolproof. I think that we continue to detain and house individuals who pose very little or no risk of reoffending or harming others and that is a major concern that I have. I believe prison correctional supervisors have a responsibility to be aware of their duty to keep society safe, to rehabilitate, and to provide options to those individuals returning to the community. The entry-level position bears the brunt of the responsibility, especially in working with juveniles, but often they don't realise how impactful their involvement is to the entire process. I think many of them [entry-level workers] come in looking at this as an entry-level job; they treat it as an entry-level job, so a lot of them, unfortunately, blow off their responsibility in the overall process.

At the other end of the spectrum, when you look at it from an administration perspective, I think many of us insulate ourselves from dealing directly with those individuals who work at the lower levels. We primarily deal with disciplinary issues when we do have interaction with them. Part of my responsibility is to train and to have meaningful training. When I looked across some of the training that I was responsible for and considered the curriculum that we were providing, I had a very difficult time thinking that any of the training [provided by the agency] was really meaningful. My responsibility at the mid-level is to find meaningful training and to find those individuals that are prepared to teach training. A lot of trainers are simply there because they were the only ones that signed up or because they were the only ones that were interested; but that doesn't mean they are capable of teaching.

We have a sort of regimen that we put all of our staff through. One of the things that I became aware of is our turnover rate. We are the second largest department in the county but we were the highest in terms of the percentage of staff loss. The greatest number in dismissals were from detention staff and so one of the things that I wanted to know and began to collect data on was why they are being terminated and which policies and procedures were being violated. We know we have had a large number of staff [members] who were terminated because of improper restraints. So you would think that we could use that data and go into our training regimen and focus on restraint techniques. Those are the types of things that are not only evidenced-based but that are also common sense that we simply didn't do. So, as our turnover rate increased, we didn't look at those areas to answer questions about why and whether there was something we could do on the front end to prevent this [the rate of turnover] from increasing.

So, as a philosophy, one should not be afraid to challenge the status quo: this is how we do our training; these are the topics we are going to cover; and these are the topics we are going to continue to cover even if we found it doesn't benefit our staff along the way. This was a major problem. We would have a staffing and firing at least once a week, so you would think having that information or access to that information you [would] want do some things differently. The organisational leader did not see value in tracking that type of information to help rectify and prevent [the problem].

If I was in charge, I think the first thing you have to do is to hire the right people. Then you have to rely on those individuals you hire to do their jobs and have confidence in their abilities to do their jobs. With that being said, I would have a *laissez-faire* type of leader. We are going to come together and those policies and issues that need to be implemented we are going to simply do. I'm going to look for achievement and involvement from those individuals that I have hired. They are going to have as much ownership in this process as I do.

Q: What programmes should be provided?
A: The bigger the facility, there has to be a major detainee education component because the reality is 95% of the youth are going to return to the community. So there has to be an education component when they [juveniles] are in and there has to be an educational or vocational component when they get out. They have to have something that they can latch on to and develop a skill set where they can make some meaningful contributions not only to their households or themselves, but to society. That is where we drop the ball. After being in the field for 20 years, from experience and research we already know the kids that we are going to be involved with. We already know the types of adults we are going to be involved with in our system. We as a society need to find a way to prevent them [juveniles] from continuing to be involved in our system.

Q: What correctional strategies are needed to insure the youth, staff and community?
A: I'm still in favor of prevention programmes. In my experience, it is important for educational institutions to be strong within the communities. The school to prison pipeline is real. Until we can say, regardless of your zip code, that you are still going to have equal access to a satisfactory education, there will be problems. Good schools can prepare our youth for avoiding the system. Schools still remain one of the top three referral agencies to juvenile departments across the country.
Q: What services do you think should be offered that are not currently offered?
A: Education. When you look at Texas, for example, you would be hard pressed to find academic programmes in state jails and prison. Part of it is due to the backlash that individuals in the community have about providing a free education to someone who has violated the law. While I understand that disconnect and the feelings people may have about prisoners receiving a college education, or even a high school diploma, when they pay $25,000 for their son or daughter to have that same opportunity, what has to be realised is that these individuals are returning to the community underprepared to live a functioning, normal adult life and part of that is due to their lack of education and/or vocational preparation. So they can't contribute anything to society.

Problems and Successes Experienced

Q: In your experience, what programmes have worked well and which have not?
A: I'm a big fan of Diversion Courts; I would definitely say the Diversion Courts have been the most successful. While I can't speak directly to the efficacy of the diversion programme developed and implemented in Dallas County, I do support the research on the success of diverting youths from the formal system. I haven't been as happy with the results of shock treatments like scared straight and juvenile boot camps. Although they came in with a bang, made everyone feel good about unruly youth that needed discipline, they were sort of a colossal failure. Luckily, in most jurisdictions, while they [shock programmes and boot camps] are not all gone, [jurisdictions] have sort of repurposed their boot camps. While other cuts [to programmes] are possible, I really like electronic monitoring (EM). I like [that] it is used especially for those low- to medium-risk kids who are sitting in detention. Some of the youth are sitting in detention because they don't have a family member willing to

take them into their home. Others are sitting there because they don't have the technology to install the device nor can their family afford it. What EM does is allow us to decrease the population in our detention centre and even in our adult correctional facilities. We are simply locking up too many people who are not going to present any harm or any major harm to those in society.

Theory and Practice

Q: What do you think the relationship is between theory and practice?
A: I think that is one of those areas where some of my colleagues may not have any experience. My experience is that I don't have the staff to do this [conduct research]. Our department is the second largest in Dallas County, but my research team consisted of me, my deputy, a research manager, and a couple of assistants. For a department of this size and level of responsibility, you would think there would be more resources available for my particular unit. We were constantly short of manpower because we were responsible for all things data-related for our department. It was simply impossible for us, with our manpower, to do evaluations. We would be bogged down in simple day-to-day requests. If the Chief had to present anything to do with department statistics, she would call my researcher manager. He would have to drop everything he was doing and crunch this data then explain them [the data] to her so she could explain it. Only then could he go back to doing what he was supposed to be doing.

At the organisational level there is not much of a relationship between theory and practice due to the lack of manpower and a lack of interest. There continues to be an academic/practitioner schism. There are those individuals who do all the research but have never set foot inside of an institution, compared to those practitioners who have worked every day for the last 15–20 years and are very reluctant to embrace information from those people who have never actually done [the work]. I think that one of the things that could continue to be beneficial is when you have practitioners who have academic experience and when you have academics who have practical experience. It is rare for someone in a juvenile probation department to have a terminal degree and be familiar with research methodology, theories and best practices. I really think that departments should invest more in developing relationships with academics and to bringing in various areas of expertise, perhaps in the role of consultants. I think the relationships have not occurred because of the fear of being wrong or simply admitting when you don't know something. Maybe you have some workers who have an ego too big to accept recommendations from someone [an academic] who may have a better way of handling an issue or analysing it. Once you have achieved the highest level [in the organisation] it is hard to admit that you don't know something. You very rarely hear someone at the highest level say 'I don't know.'

For example, one of the biggest arguments we continue to have in juvenile justice departments is over-representation [of minorities]. We have a ton of research and data regarding this phenomenon and why it occurs and how to prevent it; but again, how many departments actually use that? Why is it that we continue to have juvenile departments that are 70–80% populated by minority youth when all of this research is out there? There has to be a concerted effort by those individuals who can make decisions to review the research and to replicate the research in their own individual juvenile justice departments so they can, in fact, do something that has been recommended by a number of agencies.

The Dallas County Juvenile Department provides information to the juvenile board regarding quarterly reports that we are required to present. Those quarterly reports really only provide demographic information [rather] than actual research. For example, they want to know specifically how many kids are in this type of programme, during this quarter how many of those kids completed the programme successfully, how many youths ran from a particular programme, how many kid were discharged successfully and unsuccessfully. Real basic, generic, and generalised information is what we would provide on a quarterly basis. Much of what we were asked to produce was descriptive statistics. There were really no formalised evaluations with inferential statistical analyses that were accepted. Now, the one thing I was able to do with the help of academics from University of Houston was to get across a proposal for an evaluation of the Diversion Courts. So there is an evaluation being started in August and they will have a year to complete the evaluation and submit it to the board.

Evidence-Based Corrections

Q: Describe evidence based/best practices in your institution.
A: Research is also a part of my division. So much of what we do [in terms of best practice] is not dictated by our knowledge or experience or capability, but dictated by the power brokers. The decisions that are being made in our department, and I can speak from experience, are made by people not on my floor. They are in other

buildings and have positions much higher than me or my director. The department, and in Dallas County in general, there are two or three people that make the majority of decisions about what happens: one of them is a commissioner, another, of course, is a county judge, and even the juvenile board has a major impact on the things that we do and don't do.

One of those things, for example, in my last position, is that I was over quality assurance, research, and training. As an academic, we know there are certain things that [should happen] especially when you talk about implementing new programmes or policies. We know that best practice is to evaluate those programmes and policies to see if they have been implemented correctly and also to determine if they are effective. That simply didn't happen to the extent that it really needs to. We have a risk assessment instrument, for example, that was totally developed by someone in the juvenile department. That's the crazy thing, we [the department] have access to validated juvenile risk assessment instruments that could easily be adopted but the powers that be, if you will, sort of tied our hands and made use the risk assessment instrument that was developed in Dallas County by a worker. When I began to ask questions about: (1) who created this instrument, and (2) when was it validated, the answers I got were ridiculous. The instrument was created sometime in 2007 or 2008 was one answer I got. I'm thinking that's seven or eight years ago and we still don't know the origin of this instrument. So why are we using it? Why are we basing our detention and release on a document that is seven or eight years old that we don't even know the origin of. That is just one of many examples.

Q: How were evidence based changes or best practices implemented?
A: One of the things our Director really touted as her major accomplishment was these Diversion Courts. With these courts, there is a lot of research to support their advocacy. So, our department was really at the forefront of this really in Texas in developing and implementing these diversionary programmes, Diversion Courts in particular. So, in Texas, we have the first of their kind Diversion Courts, where the court was specifically designed for black and brown youth [African American and Hispanic]. The purpose of the court was to adjudge those certain black and brown youthful violators in a more informal setting and hopefully setting them up to have their case expunged and keep them from moving deeper into the system. Again, because we know that formal contact with the criminal justice system, especially for minority youth, does not generally end well. So the Diversion Court has been around for four or five years and I, as well as others, began to question

its effectiveness. We want to evaluate and get some results on this court so we can determine how effective it has been in doing what we say the purpose of the court was. But we had to jump through a million hoops to get that evaluation process started and in fact it almost felt that we were being stonewalled for collecting the data and [getting] a neutral party to evaluate it. Those were some of the tough questions that I was asking as my position as the head of research. Why aren't we doing more of this, it is not like we don't have the ability or capability. Why is there no interest in getting this done? Why are we continuing to create new programmes when we haven't even evaluated the ones we have?

Q: Was it just a problem of evaluation, or implementation as well?

A: I don't doubt that they were implemented well; I think the research that went into the development of the courts was thoroughly researched. There was definitely a need, there was research to support the need and we followed very strict guidelines in setting up these courts. I think where we failed in many of our programmes that were implemented across the department was the evaluation. We in fact had five different Diversion Court programmes. There was only one of those courts that has been evaluated and that was the ESTEEM Court, and that was only a process evaluation and that was conducted by a graduate student from UT-Dallas in 2010 or 2011. Other than that, there have been no formal evaluations of any of our diversion programmes. Without a formal outcome evaluation, how can you explain, with all of these diversion programmes, what these are capable of doing or what they will do if you have no outcome measures or outcome evaluation and most of these programmes are going on their fourth or fifth year. Tracking the success and failures and analysing that information, that has not been done.

The new programmes that were developed were evidence-based programmes. That is one thing I can say we did a good job of. I can remember a time when I started in Juvenile Probation 15 or 20 years ago I remember being part of those feel-good programmes. Those were programmes that we implemented because they sounded good or they were copy-cats from other programmes but we really had no clear indication on (1) how to implement them properly, and (2) if they were going to even help the youth. I remember, when I was in education, we used to get a lot of feedback from individuals who knew we had funding available. They wanted to bring in certain types of programmes for our youth; when I would challenge them on the evidence behind the programme they were attempting to sell me by asking for outcome data, they would look at me as if I had three heads.

Evidenced-based programmes more likely than not were introduced by the Chief or the assistant. Normally, we would have manager meetings once month. For example, the initial idea might start with someone from detention who starts seeing certain trends or begins to question certain things. They might bring it up in the large meeting. The leadership in the room, if we felt it was something that needed to be addressed, then would send an informational query about the issues to the Chief and she would take it from there. For example, the initial idea of the diversion male court started from a probation officer who was concerned about first-hand experiences he dealt with so he took that idea to the Chief and she took it from there.

Staff knowledge on evidence-based practices really varied. It often depended on organisational position. I can say from my experience most of the supervisors were well versed in best practices and the research behind best practices. Especially in meetings and discussing issues, they were pretty articulate and well-spoken about best practices in their particular area.

Transnational Relations

Q: Has your organisation been affected by any transnational issues?

A: The Letot Center is a result of the transnational concern with human smuggling. Letot was born and built on the idea that human trafficking was not only a regional issue, but a national and transnational issue. This is the one programme that I have a lot of high hopes for. Currently, there is not a lot of research on this particular type of programme so I'll be interested in seeing what happens over the next few years. Letot Center was opened with the sole purpose of addressing human trafficking. It is an all-female facility, designed to address human trafficking. The DFW area is the second largest area in the US known for human smuggling for sexual purposes. This was a population that was very often overlooked in our previous efforts. We simply placed them on probation or put them in facilities that didn't address why they were becoming involved with the system in the first place. [The programme is designed for] these young ladies, who are 10–16 years old. The average age is 14–15 years old and they have been involved in some form of human trafficking. These young ladies have not been formally introduced into the system because they only engaged in minor deviant acts. These are girls who have serious runaway issues, sometimes with an adult male friend, are often truant, and have been arrested for prostitution. They may have a possession of marijuana charge and might have some delinquency issues from fighting with their parents or guardians. Our system was not dealing with, or didn't have the resources to deal with, them because we didn't have a programme designed to do so. Let's take, for example, a young lady that fits this description when she came in to the court; more likely than not she was just going to get probation and returned home. While she would be provided services within the community, the reality is, if she is a habitual runaway, she is not going to participate in those programmes to begin with. We would have to institutionalise her in order to help save her from herself in that regard.

Role of Corrections

Q: How does the public view corrections in your community?
A: For the most part, until there is a noteworthy media event, people are satisfied with the job that is being done. When people don't hear anything about corrections, it is okay. The average person in the community I don't believe really has any concerns about juvenile issues unless those issues directly impact them in their particular neighborhood or they have a personal involvement because of a child or a family member. Generally, people don't get concerned until they have some type [of] impact or connection. This always changes when there is a media event. If you have a teenager who was accused of a murder or serious crime, then individuals that remained silent before all of sudden have an opinion on what should happen. Other than that, unless it has something to do with them, most individuals are not going to get involved.

General Assessments

Q: Are you basically satisfied or dissatisfied with the developments in the role of corrections?
A: I'm generally satisfied with the developments in the field of corrections. I'm satisfied with the research aspect of it; I'm not satisfied with the implementation. Again, I have concerns about overrepresentation and it is an issue that we have dealt with for a number of years and we still have not adequately addressed it. We have all this information and we have all this research, we have best practices, but how is it that we continue to arrest and detain such large percentages of minority populations? I always tell my kids in detention it is hell being poor and now it is not just

cultural minorities, it is individuals who identify as being from a lower socio-economic background. Why is it different that we have two totally different outcomes for youth that have very similar or same charges and backgrounds, but one has means and one doesn't, and yet there are two totally different outcomes? It seems to happen in our system at both the adult and juvenile level.

I still have full support in probation; the problem we were having 10–15 years ago were these huge caseloads that the average probation officer had. Now that is not nearly as much of a problem; however, the problem is the inability of the probation officer to prepare the youth for what is expected. Those probation officers receive the training but they don't necessarily implement what should be implemented in order to prepare those youth.

Again, I would not trade this experience. It is the one thing I have under my repertoire, when I do go back to academia full-time, that I have to share. It is one thing to teach a Criminal Justice Administration course from the text or PowerPoint, but I am able to share some real-life situations to really help the students understand the topics that we discuss. I think this experience would help me in my teaching.

Q: Why did you switch and leave juvenile corrections and go back to an academic position?
A: I got sort of tired of the BS [bullshit] in the field and not feeling that I was making any impact. I missed the direct contact with students.

Conclusion

Dr Pirtle was very forthcoming in his appraisal of the juvenile justice field and the Dallas County Juvenile Justice Department. He acknowledges both the positive and negative developments and issues in the field. The positive is that best practices are being introduced into juvenile corrections and that multiple programmes are available to youth based on their individual need. Fewer youths are being detained and the recidivism rate of those released has decreased. Probation officers' caseloads are more reasonable compared to when he started. The county is trying new diversion programmes aimed at specific populations, that is, African Americans, Hispanics, and those at risk of becoming a victim of human trafficking.

The negative is that minority youth still are greatly over-represented in juvenile and adult corrections. Dr Pirtle expressed an underlying frustration with the political nature of the field that relationships and longevity were often more important than merit and knowledge in determining the organisation's position and the ability to make decisions. Moreover, he was disturbed that even when the data were available or obtainable to evaluate programmes or improve training, they were not used or collected.

Glossary

Adjudication: a court ruling that a youth was found delinquent or in conduct in need of supervision; because they are not of legal age, juveniles can be adjudicated for behaviour such as truancy that they could not be convicted of as an adult (see www.tjjd.texas.gov/about/overview.aspx).

Annie E. Casey: a foundation that advocates and funds alternatives to locking up juvenile offenders. This foundation frequently works in partnership with state and local agencies and provides them with additional funding providing the partnership agencies agree to follow certain policies and procedures (see www.aecf.org/).

Closer to Home: an internal report and study of success factors in juvenile corrections. The major finding is that detained youths perform better and have lower recidivism rates the closer to home their supervision takes place.

Conduct in need of supervision: status offences prohibited due to the individual still being categorised as a minor. These acts, if committed by an adult, would at most result in a fine and in most cases would not be considered a law violation at all: that is, they are only offences due to the offender's age (see www.tjjd.texas.gov/about/overview.aspx).

Delinquent conduct: acts that, if committed by an adult, could result in some form of incarceration (see www.tjjd.texas.gov/about/overview.aspx).

ESTEEM programme: Experiencing Success Through Empowerment, Encouragement and Mentoring is a diversion programme designed for girls whose behaviours and risk factors put them in jeopardy of becoming a victim of human trafficking (see www.dallascounty.org/department/juvenile/esteem.php).

Juvenile: defined by the State of Texas as someone who is at least ten years old but has not reached their 17th birthday before perpetrating an offence, considered delinquent or in need of supervision (see www.tjjd.texas.gov/about/overview.aspx).

Juvenile Board: defined by the State of Texas as: 'county juvenile justice departments are maintained under the leadership and direction of a juvenile board. In Dallas County, the juvenile board is comprised of district judges, elected county officials, and a representative from the Youth Services Advisory Board. The Juvenile Board ensures that the juvenile department efficiently and effectively meets the needs of Dallas County citizens" (see www.dallascounty.org/department/juvenile/juvenile_board.php).

Letot Center: a multi-use facility that houses a crises intervention programme and serves as a runaway shelter. It is also where the ESTEEM programme operates.

Prison Rape Elimination Act (PREA): a federal law (PUBLIC LAW 108-79—SEPT. 4, 2003) designed to target, reduce and eradicate the prevalence of sexual abuse among imprisoned population. This act seeks to hold correctional administrator responsible if they fail take steps to eliminate or decrease such conduct (see www.tjjd.texas.gov/programs/prea.aspx for more details).

Texas Juvenile Justice Department (TJJD): the state agency in charge of juvenile correction. It sets the standards and provides oversight to all of juvenile justice efforts in Texas.

Notes

1 Dr Pirtle, in fact, left his position in the Fall of 2016 to return to teaching as an instructor at Arizona State University at Lake Havasu.
2 According to Ko et al. (2008), young children who have experienced trauma such as violence and neglect are vastly over-represented in the child welfare system and often end up in the juvenile justice system. Unless this trauma is both recognised and addressed, successful treatment of juvenile offenders becomes increasingly unlikely.

Chapter 5

Adonay Davila, Senior Warden (retired), Texas Department of Criminal Justice

Interviewer: Michael Sanchez

Contents

Overview	61
Introduction	62
Career	62
Changes Experienced	68
Personal Correctional Philosophy	70
Problems and Successes Experienced	71
Theory and Practice	74
General Assessments	76
Transnational Relations	80
Glossary	82

Overview

The Texas Department of Criminal Justice (TDCJ) is the prison system for the State of Texas. The Texas prison system was formed in 1848 with the construction of a single prison in Huntsville. A second prison in Hodge was opened in 1883 (Texas State Prison Board, 2017). In 1983, the Texas prison system was housing 36,769 prisoners with fewer than 20 prisons (Lucko, 2010). By 2015, TDCJ was housing 148,146 prisoners in 122 prison units statewide (TDCJ, 2016). Within a 32-year period, the number of Texas prison facilities increased by more than 500% and prison population increased by more than 400%. The TDCJ's operating budget for fiscal year 2015 was $3,175,589,052 (TDCJ, 2016).

In order to save money and ease overcrowding, Texas began to use private contractors to house Texas State inmates. In 1989, the Texas prison system included four privately owned and operated prison facilities. The private facilities were relatively small, all being 500-bed facilities (Lucko, 2010). By 2015, the footprint of private prisons in Texas had increased to 16 privately owned facilities with a combined capacity of 12,908 beds

(TDCJ, 2016). In 26 years, TDCJ's reliance of private contract prisons increased by 400% and the number of privately managed prison bed space increased by more than 600%.

The use of private correctional and detention facilities has expanded exponentially in the United States over the past 20 years. While more cost effective than government run facilities, the private prison industry is controversial. In order to gain context and perspective into the controversial nature of the private prison industry, the author interviewed a corrections professional who has extensive experience with the Texas State prison system, the private prison industry, and as a compliance auditor.

Introduction

Texas Department of Criminal Justice (TDCJ) retired Senior Warden Adonay (Andy) Davila was selected for interview. Mr Davila retired from TDCJ in 2003 after 23 years' service. He then embarked on a very successful career in private sector contract corrections and detention services. He has been in the private sector for 14 years[1] and is currently the Project Manager (Warden) for a private contractor that operates immigration detention centres for the United States Immigration and Customs Enforcement (ICE) service. Mr Davila manages an immigration detention centre and supervises over 530 employees who deliver security, detention, transportation, and food services to the 1,200 federal detainees.

Mr Davila also worked as an auditor for the Nakamoto Group. He travelled the United States conducting compliance audits on various jails and detention centres. Mr Davila's broad base of experience in both the public and private sectors of corrections and detention make him an ideal candidate to discuss, compare, and contrast public sector corrections with private sector efforts. His experience as an auditor is compelling, as Mr Davila has a deep understanding of how things should be according to standards, and how those same things really exist in operations. The interview was very conversational and took place in Mr Davila's office.

The interviewer's main goal in interviewing Mr Davila was to access his considerable knowledge of both the public and private sectors of corrections and detention. The subject of the privatisation of corrections and detention in the US has always been a contentious one. Mr Davila has the background to bridge the understanding gap between the public and private sectors and bring some perspective to the strengths and weaknesses of both the public and private sectors in the field of corrections and detention.

Career

Q: Mr. Davila, could you please provide me with a synopsis of your public and private careers in corrections?

A: I actually did not intend to pursue a career in corrections, I sort of fell into it. My initial career goal was to join the Texas Department of Public Safety (DPS). I wanted to be a State Trooper, but I had some problems with getting into DPS. I had too many speeding tickets as a youth and had to wait before I could be approved for hire by DPS. I decided that I needed a job until I could get into DPS, which could take several years. I saw an advertisement for Correctional Officers at TDCJ and decided to pursue this as a job to hold me over until my application with DPS was approved.

I started out as a correctional officer at the Clemens unit down in Brazoria County, Texas. At that time, in 1981, the Clemens unit was an 850-bed facility. We had up to 1,600 inmates in that place, sometimes with as many as three inmates to a single cell. Clemens was a minimum–medium security prison and was my first experience dealing with the significant prison violence that occurred in the early 1980s. There was considerable gang activity, violence, stabbings and killings. I made sergeant and lieutenant while working at Clemens. The Clemens unit was one of the first facilities in TDCJ that had a trusty camp. I was actually placed in charge of opening the new trusty camp, which had 200 beds. A trusty camp was a minimum-security subunit specifically for non-violent and good behaviour inmates, who worked there. I stayed at Clemens until 1987.

In 1987, I took a lateral transfer to the TDCJ hospital in Galveston, Texas, as a lieutenant. This was a prison hospital facility with 200 beds. I took the hospital posting because I wanted to try something different. I was in Galveston for two years. This was a very interesting post because I got to experience that unique aspect of the prison system. I found myself dealing with inmates from all over the state. I came to understand all of the different reasons why these inmates were in the hospital. Many inmates died at the Galveston hospital unit, so I found myself having to deal with the inmates' families, which was a very different experience.

From Galveston, I went to Amarillo, Texas to open up a 3,000-bed prison there, confusingly named Clements (after Governor Bill Clements). The Clements unit was interesting because this facility had a psychiatric unit. A programme came out in 1990 called the Program for Aggressive Mentally Ill Offenders (PAMIO). TDCJ picked up all the worst offenders who were classified with mental illness, many of whom were on segregation status, and sent them to the Clements PAMIO unit. The PAMIO unit was a 750-bed subunit with all kinds of mentally ill violent offenders. This place just rocked and rolled 24 hours per day. These inmates were burning things, throwing stuff, cutting themselves, hanging themselves . . . we were constantly fighting with them trying to maintain control of the unit. Of course, the facility itself was classified as a minimum–maximum security, as we had all three levels of security there. I was there as a lieutenant for about two years. It was a very interesting environment to work in. I enjoy studying human behaviour and this unit had all kinds of behaviours.

In 1992, I was promoted to captain and moved to the Roach unit in Childress, Texas. Childress was a 1,800-bed facility that had a boot camp subunit. The boot camp was mainly used for shock probation, which lasted for 90–120 days. The environment in this subunit was just like a military boot camp. I was in Childress for about two years.

I then transferred to the Darrington unit in the Houston area. Darrington was an older 1,800-bed facility, which housed minimum–maximum security inmates. This facility had a tyre recapping shop staffed by inmates as a part of the facility. I was at Darrington when we had three inmates escape. I was there for about a year and then was promoted to major and moved to the Briscoe unit in Dilly, Texas. I was in Dilly for about four and a half years as a major. The Briscoe unit was also a 1,800-bed facility. We had two big riots while I was there. From Briscoe I promoted to the rank of Assistant Warden and transferred to the Preston Smith unit in La Mesa, Texas. At the Smith unit, I was assigned to open up a high security subunit that was about 800 beds for high security inmates. The unit was brand new, so I had to start it from the ground up. Learning how to start up a unit from scratch would be a huge benefit to me later on in my career. Once again, they brought me the worst inmates from around the state. Once I got that unit up and running, I was sent to the Middleton unit in Abilene, Texas. The Middleton unit was very different in that it was an intake facility. This facility would receive sentenced inmates from the county jails all over the north Texas area. These inmates would be processed in to the TDCJ system. We would do an intake procedure with each inmate. We would do the inmates' medical exams, sociological exams, classification interviews, and determine what job skills each inmate had. Inmates who completed intake would be housed at Middleton until the TDCJ Bureau of Classification in Huntsville, Texas determined to which facility in the system they should go. I occasionally received requests from wardens around Texas who were looking for inmates with particular skills, such as a barber or farrier. I would maintain a list of inmates with particular skills and would try to get inmates with particular skills where they could do the most good.

After Middleton, I went to the Central unit, previously known as the Imperial State Prison Farm and the Central State Prison Farm, in Sugarland, Texas. This facility was a minimum–medium security prison, with a 200-bed trusty camp. The Central unit was also a logistical distribution centre for the entire TDCJ prison system. The Central unit was one of the oldest prisons in Texas, having been opened in 1878. It was part of the old Imperial Sugar factory complex, which used inmates, leased from the state prison system, for labour in the late 19th and early 20th centuries. When I was there, I helped to get this facility recognised as a historical landmark by the Texas Historical Society. I made Senior Warden at the Central unit.

All totalled, I did 23 years at TDCJ. I worked other facilities on a short-term or temporary basis to assist these facilities. I moved around quite a bit during my career. I enjoyed working in so many places. Each facility was different and represented a different environment and different challenges to be overcome.

Q: After you retired from TDCJ, you embarked on a career in the private sector. Can you give me a synopsis of your private sector career post TDCJ?

A: After I left TDCJ, I really had no plans to stay in the correctional field. A good friend of mine recruited me to go work in the private sector. I was going through a divorce at the time, and was not really tied down, so I decided to give the private sector a try. I went to work for Emerald Correctional Management, who hired me as a warden in Haskell, Texas. Haskell was a 580-bed hybrid facility that was part private detention facility and part county jail. Although inmates and detainees could be county, state, or federal prisoners, the contractor operated the entire facility. When I went to Haskell, Emerald was taking over the contract from MTC. I oversaw the handover of the contract, employees, and operations. This was my first exposure to the federal side of detention, through ICE and the US Marshals. My experience in transitioning to the private sector was very interesting to me because working the private sector showed me how institutionalised I was. I had to adapt to the different use of force protocols that applied to detainees as opposed to inmates. In TDCJ, everyone locked up was a convicted felon, so use of force was more definitive. When there would be a disturbance in a dormitory at Haskell, my first instinct was to throw tear gas into the unit. This is not an acceptable level of force in a detention environment. I also found myself using prison jargon with detainees. They would look at me in confusion as if I was talking crazy. It also took me a long time to learn to say detainee instead of inmate. There was an intergovernmental service agreement (IGSA) contract with the county that allowed us to operate this homogenous facility and house a variety of detainees. I worked in Haskell for about one year.

I was then asked to go down to Cotulla, Texas to operate a small jail contract that handled approximately 50 detainees for the US Marshals. While I was at Cotulla, I was also supervising the construction of a new jail in Encinal, Texas, which was about 30 miles south of Cotulla. The Encinal facility was a 550-bed facility under construction by Emerald for the detention of US Marshals' prisoners. I was at Encinal until the facility was built and fully operational. I was responsible for all of the hiring, policy writing, inspections, and certifications required to get this facility operational. Once I got Encinal up and running, I was asked to go to Sierra Blanca, Texas, to open up a new facility there. The Sierra Blanca facility was also an IGSA facility, in cooperation with the county, which handled county prisoners, Marshals' detainees, and ICE detainees. As with Encinal, I was responsible for creating and implementing policies, procedures, and accomplishing the required certifications for the facility to become operational. I was in Sierra Blanca for approximately a year and a half, again, until the facility was up and running.

After Encinal, I went to work for Civigenics, which was bought out by Community Education Centers. I went to Lufkin, Texas and ran a 100-bed facility. The facility was an old county jail that was bought and converted to house detainees from Fort Bend County and ICE. I was there as an assistant warden and was specifically tasked to rewrite all of the facility policies and procedures. After I finished with updating all of the policies and procedures in Lufkin, they moved me over to Livingston, Texas. Livingston was a 600-bed facility that was an IGSA facility, which housed a mixture of county prisoners, US Marshals, ICE, and Federal Bureau of Prisoners (BOP) inmates. I was in Livingston for approximately six months, to oversee the construction of an addition to this facility. I then moved to San Luis, Arizona to oversee the construction of another 600-bed IGSA facility there. I moved to the Yuma area and, as with the other new construction project I had been working on, got this facility up and running. I stayed in San Luis for approximately two years. I then went to oversee the construction of a facility in Coastal Bend, Texas. Again, I was responsible for implementing policies and procedures. I brought the facility to a level where it would pass the requisite inspections for operation.

About this time, I was recruited by Nakamoto to be a compliance reviewer at the Willacy Detention Center, which was an ICE service-processing centre in Raymondville, Texas. Willacy was an ICE contract detention facility that housed only immigration detainees. Rather than work for the primary operational contractor, I worked for Nakamoto as an independent compliance reviewer. My job was to ensure that the facility complied with American Correctional Association (ACA) and the ICE Performance Based National Detention Standards (PBNDS) standards. I was at Willacy for approximately 6–8 months when Natkamoto put me on the road doing PBNDS inspections at facilities all over America. I did this for approximately one year. I went all over the country inspecting public and private detention centres, ensuring that they were compliant with PBNDS standards. During my tenure with Nakamoto, I inspected well over 30 facilities.

When Nakamoto's contract with ICE ended, I was recruited to work as the Project Manager (Warden) for the Port Isabel Detention Center (PIDC), where I am still employed. I oversee all operations of a 1,200 bed ICE Service Processing Center. We currently have approximately 570 contract staff performing detention, security, transportation, administration, training, quality control, and food service operations. My career in the private sector mirrored my career in TDCJ in that I moved around quite a bit. I really enjoyed this aspect of my career. I got to see so much, learn new things, see and experience different places. I learned to be an effective troubleshooter. Having conducted the start up of multiple facilities, I came to develop a deep understanding of the operations of these facilities.

Q: You said that you wanted to get into corrections because it was a job to keep you busy until you could get into DPS. At what time did you realise that corrections was your career?

A: In my third year with TDCJ, I was promoted to sergeant. About the same time, I received a call from DPS to become a state trooper. This was when I really had to make a decision as to which path I wanted to take. I discovered that I really did enjoy working at TDCJ, although going in I did not expect that I would enjoy the job as much as I did. What I really enjoyed most was the environment I was in at TDCJ. I found the job to be very interesting because it was helping me to understand human behaviour. I had a real interest at the time in psychology and sociology, so being around convicted felons, and even employees, and the behaviours I saw in that environment was so interesting that I decided to stick it out. I also dealt with inmates from many different backgrounds and different cultures, which was also very interesting.

Q: Did anything in your career surprise you?

A: I think what surprised me the most was how well I was able to handle violence. Growing up, you would see your share of indirect violence.

You see people on TV getting shot and stabbed, or you might see fights here and there. But when I started as a correctional officer, the level of violence in prison was shocking. Inmates were stabbing each other and killing each other right in front of you. I was very surprised to discover how well I would handle that level of violence.

Q: Do you mean handling violence psychologically or professionally?

A: Both... Throughout my career, I was involved in a lot of violent incidents. I have seen riots, homicides, beat downs, and other such violence. It was interesting to observe the way my fellow correctional officers would react to these violent incidents. Many of them would be traumatised by what they had seen or experienced. There were also correctional officers who would simply run the other way. I was able to deal with the psychological implications of witnessing so much violence, as well as react appropriately in the moment. Trying to understand such aspects of human behaviour, on the part of both inmates and correctional officers, and trying to figure out why they reacted in certain ways, kept me interested.

As I moved up the ranks in the TDCJ system, I realised that I was able to make more of a difference with both inmates and correctional staff. Both would come to me for advice or guidance. I learned how to assess the behaviours of the inmates. If you became a student of human psychology, you could always tell which inmates were sincere about trying to change from those who are just trying to play a game on you. Throughout my career, I feel that there were some positive impacts that I was able to make with both inmates and correctional officers, and I felt good about that.

Q: Which position in the TDCJ career ladder did you find to be the most challenging?

A: Major... the Major was essentially the Chief of Security in a prison, and was ultimately responsible for all operations and policy writing. The Major had a lot of duties delegated to him by the Warden. The thing about being a major is that you are responsible for everything that happens below you. Anything that happens in the facility is your direct responsibility. You are really depended on to run the facility for the Warden, so there is a significant level of responsibility for this position.

Changes Experienced

Q: What significant changes did you see in corrections during your career?

A: The most obvious change was the big change after the ruling in the landmark *Ruiz* v. *Estelle* case. That case lasted 20 years, but it was the impetus for the first real prison reform regarding conditions such as overcrowding, access to health care, and punitive security policies. I saw a radical change in TDCJ start in the early 1980s, largely as a result of *Ruiz* v. *Estelle*. When I started as a correctional officer in TDCJ, we had building tender and turnkeys. These were inmates who actually helped run the facility. In the 1980s, you did not have the prison staffing levels that are in place now. Staffing of corrections officers has increased considerably. When I first started in TDCJ, I was at Clemens with 1,600 inmates, working on the evening shift. At the time, we had 13 correctional officers running the entire prison. Six officers were staffing the pickets [guard towers]. That left seven correctional officers to supervise 1,600 inmates [a ratio of more than 228:1], so the inmates had to help run the facility. In those days, inmates actually helped with discipline and, for the most part, the inmates were pretty much running the prison. When TDCJ killed the building tender programme in 1982, I was one of the first officers at the Clemens unit to take the keys away from an inmate. A notice went out to all facilities and the Major told me to take the keys away from the building tender and lock him up. This was the start of a trend of significant improvements in the living conditions and quality of life of inmates; you could definitely see changes for the better.

When I first started in TDCJ, prisons were dirty and nasty. There were no regulations for sanitation, healthy conditions, etc. After *Ruiz* v. *Estelle*, systems were put in place to improve all aspects of the quality of life of inmates in the system. I believe that these changes were for the better.

The post *Ruiz* v. *Estelle* changes also included putting more systems in place as far as classification and due process, which also had a beneficial effect. There were more programmes implemented for inmate rehabilitation, such as educational and vocational training, arts and crafts to develop the inmates and keep them busy. These were all very positive changes. When I was a sergeant, I was one of the first gang intelligence officers in TDCJ. In 1984, TDCJ locked down the system to identify all of the gang members. Each facility appointed a couple of sergeants to develop procedures for classifying and identifying gang members. When I was a lieutenant at the Clemens unit in Amarillo, TDCJ came up with a perimeter security programme. I was involved in developing what was called the perimeter security team, made up of several lieutenants, who developed perimeter security policies for the entire TDCJ system. Our job was to conduct quarterly training, improve efficiency, prevent escapes, etc. My main focus throughout my career was security. If my facility did not have any escapes or killings, I felt that I was being successful in my job.

Personal Correctional Philosophy

Q: Do you see the primary goal of the prison system to rehabilitate offenders? Or is the simple incapacitation of offenders the most important goal?

A: It would have to be rehabilitation. With a few exceptions, at some point in time they are going to come out of prison. When an inmate leaves prison he is going to do one of two things. He is either going to go to work, or he is going to go back to crime. If he goes back to crime, that is going to cost the taxpayers money in a lot of different ways. That offender is going to have to go back through the entire criminal justice system. If we can invest a little to develop that offender, to give him job skills or education, then the odds that an ex-inmate will take the legitimate path in life are much more likely. As I said earlier, I think vocational programmes were among the most successful because they gave inmates an immediately marketable skill when they get released.

When it comes to recidivism, separating non-violent offenders is very important. In my experience, before Texas instituted the State Jail felony charge and State Jail facilities, you had inmates who were sentenced to two to three years for a simple non-violent crime thrown in a cellblock with murderers and rapists. These non-violent offenders, who might have been convicted of theft or drug charges, would come out of prison harder and more violent than when they entered the system. This is why Texas created the State Jail programme in 1993. People who are non-violent minor felons, who commit drug crimes, felony theft, or felony DWI offences, are sent to State Jail. State Jails are completely separate from regular institutions and are minimum security. Having a completely separate system keeps these non-violent offenders away from the hardcore violent offenders. Again, the problem with integrating non-violent offenders with the general prison population is the effect of peer pressure. The correctional environment in a regular prison encourages, and, at times, forces, new inmates to conform to the prison subculture. New inmates want to survive in prison and they desperately want to fit in with the subculture and become a part of it, if for no other reason than for their personal safety.

Q: What are your opinions on parole?

A: I think parole is overburdened with too many parolees. I do not think that there is an effective system to keep these ex-offenders from going back. Back when I was in, we had one institutional parole officer that was in charge of 1,000 inmates. His job was to filter out the inmates and move them through the parole process. However, in the state of Texas, parole officers have huge caseloads. Parole officers are so overworked that they cannot be proactive about checking on their parolees. They have to rely on the parolee to come in for short interviews and maybe drug tests, but they do not have time to be more proactive. There has to be a better system. A lot of the problems with the parole system actually have to do with legislation. When legislators make decisions on parole or crime, each decision has a profound impact on prison overcrowding. There were some legislative years where prison overcrowding caused legislation that gave more good time so inmates could get out earlier, alleviating overcrowding. What would ultimately happen is that we would have inmates going out the door early, and coming right back because they did not have enough time in the system to rehabilitate.

There was one legislative year where the legislature was trying to get tough on crime. It was determined that an inmate had to do at least half of his time before becoming eligible for parole. Prior to this legislation, inmates were eligible for parole after serving one fourth of their sentence. The result of that decision was that prisons became overcrowded again. When you let inmates out before they are ready to re-enter society, the offender only recidivates and comes back to prison. Such policies might relieve overcrowding in the short term, but in the long run, overcrowding was only exacerbated.

Problems and Successes Experienced

Q: Do you feel that rehabilitation programmes worked?
A: In the early 1980s, TDCJ had a very high recidivism rate, well over 50%.
The only advantage back then for inmates was that education was free. Inmates could get an Associates or a Bachelor's Degree at no cost. Some inmates took advantage of these programmes. However, the system did not have the broad base of programmes that are in place now that would guide an inmate from day one and guide them through a rehabilitation process until the time the inmate re-enters society.

The prison culture could steer inmates away from rehabilitation through peer pressure. Once a newly arrived inmate was processed and put into general population, he had to find his own way inside the prison. A lot of inmates grouped up based on where they came from. If the inmate was fortunate enough to find a group that was clean, meaning that the group was not violent, gang affiliated, or into drugs, then that new inmate had a chance.

If the newly arrived inmate ran into a group that was full of gang members and thugs, then the inmate would get caught up in that violent culture. Once a new inmate becomes a part of a group, he would have no choice but to conform to the culture of the group. Back then, either an inmate got involved in his group's activities, or he got stomped on.

Q: Were there some rehabilitation programmes that were a waste of time?
A: Some programmes were ultimately a waste. This frequently happened because the state did not allow that programme to mature and grow. After a certain number of years, the state would cut the funding before the programme had a chance to develop. There were times when legislation and funding issues would cause programmes to be cut out. The programmes never had the time to evolve to full effectiveness. This made it very difficult for rehabilitation programmes to mature, and for inmates to try and rehabilitate themselves.

One of the best types of programmes that we had was vocational programmes. They still have some vocational programmes, but not as many as they used to. Vocational programmes address an inmate's immediate need when he is released, which is finding a job. Many inmates are released with a resolve to live a straight life; however, if they cannot find a decent job, they slide back quickly into their old behavioural patterns. An inmate who is released with the skill set to get a decent job has a real chance to re-enter society successfully. TDCJ used to have many vocationally orientated programmes such as welding, auto body and mechanic programmes. When inmates would complete these vocational programmes, they would receive certifications through partnerships with local colleges and vocational training centres. A lot of inmates took pride in completing a programme because they got something for it that could actually help them in a meaningful way on the outside. Once an inmate completed a programme, he was certified in that skill set. Once certified, the inmate might be transferred to another facility that could then use that skill. For example, the TDCJ prison in Huntsville has a bus barn where they would repair all of the school buses every year. An inmate who completed a diesel mechanic or auto body vocational programme might be sent to Huntsville to put those skills to work. This allows them to hone their skills and make the inmates even more employable when they get out. This type of vocational programme was a rehabilitation programme that, in my opinion, really was really beneficial to the inmates in TDCJ.

Q: Were there a lot of inmates who genuinely wanted to change?
A: In my experience, it was very few. Only a small percentage of inmates were really genuine about changing. The way you can tell who is

genuine about rehabilitation is to track their progress throughout their incarceration. You might have an inmate who is in your facility for two or three years. During that time, you can see the programmes they get involved in, such as educational programmes, vocational programmes, Alcoholics Anonymous, etc. You can see if the inmate holds a steady job inside the facility. You can also look at their institutional behaviour, to see if they have had discipline problems. Through these methods, you can see how they interact with programmes, staff and other inmates. This gives you a clear view of how dedicated an inmate is to self-improvement, rehabilitation, and successful re-entry after release. Of course, there are inmates who participate in programmes just to keep busy, but it is relatively easy to detect the ones who are genuine about self-improvement. Of course, some people just do not care and are marking time until they can return to the street. There were people who would say, 'Hey ... give me another chance ...', or '... let me have a job over here and I'll do a real good job for you ...' but over time, you figure out at some point there was something in it for them ... you just had to learn how to recognise it.

Q: Do you think programs, rehabilitation, and safety decline in the private sector because of the bottom line?

A: Unless the contract spells out precisely what must be provided, private companies will not take the initiative to develop programmes that will cost them money. If you are housing temporary detainees such as Border Patrol, ICE, US Marshals, then extensive rehabilitation programmes are not needed. However, if you are housing in state or out of state convicted inmates, then there is a need for rehabilitation programmes. There might be parole or court ordered programmes, such as Alcoholics Anonymous, that the inmate is mandated to complete. These programmes should be included in the contract. There is inflexibility in the private sector in that a programme or a need that is not included in the contract will not be implemented. I would like to see the private sector take the initiative to invest in programmes that will benefit the inmate or detainee. In the long run, if you keep them busy ... they stay out of trouble.

Q: How effective was upper management in the TDCJ system?

A: When I started in TDCJ, prison management was very similar to what we would call micromanagement today. The Warden was the ultimate authority and frequently maintained an autocratic my-way-or-the-highway mentality. There was also a definitive good old boy system in place. Wardens managed through fear, rather than good leadership practices. This type of system worked only because we had so much to do that there was no time to think '... my job is in jeopardy'. Nowadays, an employee who feels he or she was treated unfairly can file grievances and EEO complaints. Back when I started, if the Warden said, 'This is how we are going to do it...', you followed. Wardens were very autonomous and frequently dictatorial. The prison was his prison and he would run it any way he saw fit. As I moved up the organisational ladder in the 1990s, I started to see significant changes in leadership and management training and methods throughout the TDCJ system. TDCJ had a very difficult time transitioning from the old dictatorial style of facility management to a more business-like model. The organisation was really stuck in the 1990s, when I was developing as a leader. They were trying many different systems of leadership and training, but had a hard time sticking to one method. Every year we would go to a different training, so you never had time to fully commit to a particular system before they moved on to try another system. They were trying everything to see what would work, but never really gave any one method enough time to take hold.

When I was promoted to Major in 1993, and I went to Majors' training, there was still a division of the old school autocratic managers and the new breed, who were searching for leadership and managerial development. Each group would actually sit on opposite sides of the classroom. At that time, the ratio of dinosaurs to new breed was about 50:50. As I got closer to retirement, the ratios slowly started to change. This changeover started to pick up speed in the late 1990s. The dinosaurs were leaving and the new breed was coming to prominence. Now, there might be 1% of the old school leaders left.

Theory and Practice

Q: In the TDCJ system, particularly in management, did you perceive any gaps between theory and application?

A: TDCJ was always looking for ways to separate non-violent inmates with programmes that really did not work. For example, they had a Youth Offender Program (YOP) that would separate youthful offenders from the general population. The idea was that youthful offenders could be dealt with more effectively away from the adult population. However, the youthful offenders were still housed in an adult correctional environment. When the programme came out, they emptied out a cellblock in the Clemens unit and housed YOP prisoners there. The problem was the cellblock was adjacent to three other cellblocks that housed adult inmates. Because of the proximity, the YOP offenders were still exposed to the adult prisoners. The adults and YOPs would yell back and forth to each other. When you put 13-, 14-, or 15-year-olds in an adult setting, exposed to that type of environment, it has a negative effect on them. They are going to buy in to the prison subculture that an adult correctional environment creates and try to compete to be badder than the next inmate. There were a lot of fights and staff assaults in YOP because the youths were trying to impress the inmates in the adjacent cellblocks. Instead of housing these youthful offenders in an adult setting, if they had been housed in a juvenile environment in a separate facility, I think the programme would be more effective. The youthful offenders would be surrounded by inmates in their own age group, and in an environment designed to meet the needs of a juvenile offender.

Many times, people with theoretically based programme ideas would sell the idea to the TDCJ administrative hierarchy; however, they did not fully utilise the expertise of field experts, who are knowledgeable in operations and making things work. What happens is that the theorists sell the idea to the higher-ups without really knowing where to put the programme or how to implement it effectively. We would get theoreticians who would come in and say, 'We think this programme might work . . .' The problem was that the programme might work if the theoreticians would allow the experts in daily operations help with the conceptualisation of the programme. This is the only way to effectively take a theoretical idea and make it operationally feasible. Nevertheless, the site-level managers were rarely asked to help figure out how to make the programme work.

Some of these programmes were very good programmes, but they were put in the wrong place, or the implementation of the programme was not thoroughly thought out. Take the TDCJ Gang Renunciation and Disassociation (GRAD) programme, for example. The GRAD programme was for gang members who wanted to renounce their gang memberships and move away from the gang-orientated lifestyle. This programme was effective; however, when an inmate completed this programme and had renounced his gang, rather than send that inmate to a facility that would be more conducive to non-gang affiliated inmates, these GRAD programme inmates were put back into general population, which is full-on gangs. Once again, peer pressure would draw the inmate back into the gang culture. So the programme was ultimately self-defeating. A little more clarity and realistic vision in implementing this programme would have made it much more successful.

General Assessments

Q: You have worked in corrections extensively in both the public and the private sector. In your experience, are the private sector efforts in detention and corrections effective?

A: The public has a split mind when it comes to detention and corrections. Take Sheriff Joe Arpaio from Arizona: everyone seems to hate him, but he also keeps getting re-elected. The public's general perception of corrections in America is the same way. Texas has that hard line mentality of '. . . lock 'em up and throw away the key . . .', and then the public turns around and complains that the inmates are being treated too harshly, or that they are made to work too hard. The public certainly has a right to voice their opinion. Corrections does cost the taxpayer a considerable amount of money. Even though TDCJ has more staff and more prisons today, the job is more difficult in some ways. When I started with TDCJ, there were 13 prisons in Texas. Now there are over 116, eight of which are for females.

The problem in TDCJ now is that staff turnover is very high. High turnover rates causes the mean level of experience for correctional staff in the prison system keeps going down. When I was moving up the ranks, most people in positions of captain, major, assistant warden and warden had over 15–20 years of experience before they moved up to those positions. Now there are officers with 2–3 years making captain and people with five years of experience making warden.

Part of the excessive turnover problem in TDCJ is budgetary. At approximately $3 bn per year, TDCJ has the biggest budget in the State of Texas. One year, when I was in TDCJ, we were tasked with finding $200–300 mn dollars to cut from the budget. TDCJ got all the wardens together to brainstorm on where we can find areas to cut. The more you cut the budget, the harder it becomes effectively run a prison. So you start cutting programmes, then you have no choice but to start cutting employee benefits and raises. Employees become disgruntled and morale suffers because they are distracted by all of the political budgetary machinations.

One of my biggest issues running an IGSA facility was the county. The County Commissioners and County Judge saw the facility as 'My' prison. They had a sense of entitlement that caused them to try to tell me how to run the facility, without any of the liability if their idea went wrong. This interfered significantly with the effective operation of the facility.

Private sector corrections and detention can be effective, and they are to an extent. There is always that ongoing debate about the efficacy of the corrections and detention private sector. Knowing what I know from being inside of both systems, the difference in the private sector is that it is a business . . . it is all about making money. So, your task as a warden in the private sector, on the surface, is to show the client that he can be provided with all the services and security they need. You have to do whatever it takes to meet this expectation. However, without making it seem that you are compromising this expectation, you also have to generate a profit.

Working in the private sector, a lot of people feel that they have lost the personal integrity and satisfaction of being a public servant who is doing something for the people. Because private corrections and detention has turned into such a big business, it has sort of overshadowed the feeling of providing a meaningful public service. There are so many companies out there providing private prison services that the industry is becoming like Wal-Mart. A lot of retired wardens get into the private sector without fully realising what is involved in operating a private facility.

In the debate about the differences between public and private corrections and detention, the place where the private sector really fails is in oversight. When the federal government, state, or county bring in a correctional or detention contractor, they lose control of the facility and of what the company is doing. TDCJ actually has a contracts division that oversees any state contracted services. This division has people who actually go to the contracted sites and conduct audits, inspections, and contract compliance. If a contractor is not meeting their obligations, they will get cut loose. A lot of governmental entities do not do this. When I was in Arizona, the State of Arizona did not do this. They were contracting out inmates with minimal oversight.

Another area where a state will lose control is when they contract to house prisoners out of state. There were inmates in Phoenix, AZ that were from Hawaii. They opened up a private correctional facility in Michigan to house inmates that were from California. Because of the distances involved, the states lose even more oversight potential and are unable to ensure that the inmates' needs are being met. Having more oversight would keep the private contractors in check and force them to provide all of the services at the agreed upon standards.

The strength of private sector corrections and detention is that, to an extent, there is going to be a saving of taxpayers' money. Where the state really saves by privatising is in not having to pay state employee benefits. They no longer have to pay retirement and other benefits for employees, which can be substantial amounts of money. Privatisation allows for the relief of overcrowding by being able to supervise more inmates for less money.

Another problem with the private sector is staffing. When you turn over corrections and detention to the private sector, there is a problem in the quality of staff. Unless you are able to hire people with experience (which is not always the case), it takes considerable time, money, and training to develop someone into an effective correctional officer. One problem that bears directly on staffing circles back to the fact that private corrections and detention is a business. Most private companies do not pay very well. Essentially, you get what you pay for. If a company is only paying $8–9 per hour for a correctional officer, they are not going to get the quality of employee that a state prison, with state retirement and benefits, will be able to attract.

Another problem in the private sector is that the client, usually a governmental agency, can have unrealistic expectations of the duties of the contractor. Sometimes these expectations can become overbearing. For example, a private company may have a contract to house federal detainees. Then the client says, 'Hey, I need your guys to work a cellblock in another facility'. Then they ask your personnel to make a transportation run to the far side of the state and back. They start asking for more, without paying for it. This is normal in the public sector, but when dealing with private contractors, the client frequently does not understand that any services they request of the contractor that are above and beyond what the contract specifies costs the contractor money.

Based on my personal experience, the private sector is able to provide a better service. The private sector can go outside of the entrenched bureaucratic boundaries of the public sector to accomplish their mission. When I was in the public sector, we were very constrained by budgetary allocations and bureaucratic inflexibility. In the public sector, if a facility needs a particular piece of equipment, and there is no budgetary allocation for that piece of equipment, the facility must simply do without. In the private sector, the contractor has much more flexibility in their ability to move money or line items around to get that critical piece of equipment. This agility is a very positive aspect of the private sector corrections and detention.

Q: What are the strengths of the public sector?
A: The public sector has more formalised training. There is more room for staff advancement and development. The public sector offers more staff development programmes, training, promotions, retirement, etc. There is a critical perceptual difference where people in public sector corrections and detention feel that they have a

career where people in the private sector feel that they have a job. If there were more opportunities for professional growth in the private sector, this might change. In order to have the public sector's level of opportunity, one must work for a private company that is large enough to have sufficient opportunities. I worked for a small company that had a few detention centres. Even though there is some room for professional growth, the opportunities are not as broad as with larger companies, such as CCA or GEO. These large companies have multiple divisions, districts, regional and corporate management positions. There are more avenues for advancement. The mentality in the private sector is still stuck in that 'This is just a job' mentality. It seems that people working for private corrections and detention are working to pay the bills, not building a career *per se*.

Q: Having worked in both the public and private sectors, do you think this slow march toward privatisation of what has historically been a public function is a good thing?

A: Privatisation of prisons and detention is starting to become a quick fix for problems that states are having, such as overcrowding. The problem is that the move toward privatisation is often not well thought out. A state that has problems with overcrowding in their prisons is looking for a way out. A good example is what happened in Mississippi. They were experiencing significant problems within their correctional system throughout the state. There was a lot of violence and corruption in the prison system. The solution was to put their prisoners into private facilities. That is when GEO came in and took over state facilities. The problem was that this solution did not work. GEO was utilising either the same staff, or at least the same correctional mentality, so there was no real change. Mississippi started cancelling contracts because the whole programme was not working. If privatisation is planned out well, and has definitive goals, it can work effectively. Contracts need to outline oversight, compliance and requirements so that the contractor can be fully prepared to meet those requirements. In the absence of this level of attention to detail in planning, private corrections becomes simply warehousing of inmates, without any programmes to benefit the inmate. That is when you have problems, violence, and unrest. Inmates know there should be programmes, and many of them want programmes to help them.

A perfect example of this lack of careful consideration occurred when I was in Arizona. The State of California wanted to house inmates in our facility. What they wanted was to put all of their problematic violent inmates in our facility. My response to California's representatives was that the design of my facility was not conducive to the type of inmates California wanted to send to us. This facility utilised 100% dormitory style housing, which is totally inappropriate for violent and problematic inmates. However, this facility was constructed with a lot of multi-purpose rooms. I proposed that this facility would be ideal for inmates who are preparing to parole out within a year. They can be housed together. They would all have a unified purpose, which would be preparing for their parole. The multi-purpose rooms could be used as classrooms to provide GED classes, Alcoholics Anonymous, Narcotics Anonymous, or to facilitate and deliver whatever pre-parole training California requires. Once these inmates parole out, they can transported back to California. Now, if the facility design had incorporated cellblocks, then it may have been appropriate for the problem inmates. The problem is that California was not carefully planning the privatisation of the supervision of these particular inmates; they just wanted to find somewhere to put them. Privatisation would really work if the state wanting to privatise did so with careful consideration and planning. Many times, the privatisation of the supervision of inmates is more of a knee-jerk reaction to pressure from the courts, public, or legislature, rather than a careful, well thought out process. They look for a quick way out, and this is where the concept of privatisation goes wrong.

When I was in Sierra Blanca, we were housing inmates from Wyoming. The inmates started asking for programmes to keep busy or improve themselves. When they discovered that there were no such programmes, and realised that they were simply being warehoused, their morale went down. This is a recipe for inmates to go bad.

Transnational Relations

Q: Do you think that the American privatisation model is something that could work in other countries?
A: When I was with Emerald, I was helping them to propose a private prison in Honduras. We put the entire package together and pitched the entire plan to the Honduran government, and they loved it. The problem was that they could not afford it. This is part of the problem in trying to bring privatisation to other countries. The private companies see an opportunity to go abroad and make some money. However, it does not work that way because many of the countries that could benefit from privatisation cannot afford it. In the US, in the private facilities I ran, the average we were charging per inmate per day was about $45–50, and that is cheap in

America. Most other countries could not afford that level of cost. So, bringing the level of privatisation expertise from America to other countries would be very difficult because the company could not function at the level of pay these countries could afford.

The privatisation model might work for an indigenous company because they would operate within the means of their own economy. One big problem they would have would be government interference. A country that is corrupt and/or autocratic will dictate policy to a private company, run up the costs, and drive that company out of business. A friend of mine worked an international mission as a correctional specialist. His job was to provide guidance to the corrections departments in other countries. A significant portion of the time, these national authorities would not listen to the guidance this correctional specialist was providing. They have their own ways of doing things that were so far from the American correctional methodology that reform seemed almost impossible. Prison wardens would take bribes from family members to let a prisoner go. There would have to be fundamental paradigm shift in the correctional and criminal justice mentality. I would like to see implementation of international correctional standards. Each country that came on board with the creation of such standards would be more likely to accept reform and move their correctional systems in a more positive direction.

The US has come a long way in this past century in correctional standards. Both the public and private sectors have gone through significant reform. We have ACA standards, ACA facility certification, which ensures that ACA standards are met, PBNDS detention standards that regulate detention. All of these standards have improved the level of our corrections programmes, whether it is public or private. When we try to bring American-level correctional standards to other countries, we have to realise that it took us 100 years to get to where we are today. A key factor is simply whether or not a struggling country can afford such broad reform. Take a country where there are 20–30 inmates in a 15 x 15 foot cell, with only a bucket on the floor as a toilet. A country at that level cannot possibly afford to bring their correctional systems up to US standards. More developed countries might be able to afford to reform their healthcare, nutritional, and rehabilitative services, but most countries probably could not. Corrections systems are a very expensive undertaking. The only way to do it is what we are doing now, which is to send specialists abroad to try and guide these countries to shift their perceptions and paradigms first. They have to want to buy into reform before it can be delivered. We have to continue the trend of education and guidance, produce international standards, and ease these countries in the right direction, but it will take time.

Q: Do you think use of private prisons would be feasible in a country with institutionalised corruption, like Mexico?

A: If we could do it in Texas . . . they can do it in Mexico. When I started in the Texas prison system in the early 1980s, it was very tough. I have been to some of the prisons in Mexico. I would compare their prisons now to where Texas prisons were in the 1970s and 1980s. Therefore, they do not have as far to come as we might think they do. However, the government has to want to change and reform, otherwise nothing will change. We were fortunate in Texas to have governors like Ann Richards and Bill Clements, who put their foot down and wanted meaningful reform. You have to have real leadership to get reform moving and to sustain it. I think a lack of committed leadership is what is really lacking in bringing other countries up to some meaningful level of correctional standards.

Glossary

American Correctional Association (ACA): Founded in 1870 as the National Prison Association, the ACA is the oldest correctional association in the world. The ACA provides research, training, support, and standards for the corrections industry. ACA accreditation of a detention facility is an important indicator of the facility's adherence to national standards.

Building Tender (Turnkey): Building Tenders were trustys who actually supervised areas of a correctional facility. Although the Building Tenders were inmates, they were actually issued keys to certain areas of a facility. This was seen as a necessary step in the pre-1980s, as there was insufficient staff to effectively operate a correctional facility. Inmates were sometimes used in the Building Tender role to augment staffing.

Bureau of Classification: The bureau within the Texas Department of Criminal Justice that classifies prison inmates during in-processing. The classification procedure reviews the inmate's criminal history, previous incarceration records, disciplinary history, and other factors to determine the custody level (low, medium, high, or maximum security) an inmate should be assigned.

Federal Bureau of Prisons (BOP): The prison system operated by the Federal Government of the United States. Offenders convicted of federal crimes are incarcerated in BOP facilities.

Immigration and Customs Enforcement: ICE is the principal law enforcement arm of the Department of Homeland Security and is the result of a 2003 merger between the Immigration and Naturalization Service, and the US Customs Service. ICE's responsibilities include criminal and civil enforcement of federal border, immigration, trade, and customs laws.

Intergovernmental Service Agreement (IGSA): An IGSA contract is a service contract between multiple governmental organisations. An IGSA can be between municipalities, counties, the federal government, or any combination.

Performance Based National Detention Standards (PBNDS): PBNDS standards are detention standards that every ICE detention facility must adhere to. Based loosely on ACA standards, but designed specifically for immigration detention, the PBNDS standards are an important tool in the efficient operation of an immigration detention centre. ICE detention centres are inspected annually in a week-long audit to ensure that the facility meets PBNDS standards.

Port Isabel Detention Center (PIDC): The Port Isabel Detention Center is the largest ICE service processing centre and is located in Los Fresnos, TX. PIDC houses up to 1,200 immigration detainees at any given time; and processes well over 100,000 Border Patrol and ICE detainees annually.

Program for Aggressive Mentally Ill Offenders (PAMIO): The PAMIO programme is a voluntary behavioural programme for mentally ill offenders at the TDCJ Clements unit, which is not a mental health facility. This specialised programme, and the violent mentally ill offenders it treats, results in a very high number of violent incidents at the Clements unit.

Ruiz v. Estelle: *Ruiz* v. *Estelle* was a landmark court case, decided by the United States District Court for the Southern District of Texas in 1979, that declared that conditions within the TDCJ prison system constituted a violation of the 8th Amendment to the US Constitution banning cruel and unusual punishment. This case sparked a prison reform movement in TDCJ that saw vast improvements in the quality of life and services available to convicts in the Texas prison system.

TDCJ Gang Renunciation and Disassociation Programme (GRAD): The TDCJ GRAD programme is an inmate programme specifically designed to assist gang affiliated inmates with breaking away from a gang-orientated life. The voluntary programme guides inmates away from gangs and ultimately assists them in renouncing gang membership. The rehabilitative concept is that renouncing gang affiliation will allow an inmate to lead a more normal and productive life upon release from prison.

TDCJ Youth Offender Programme (YOP): The TDCJ YOP programme is a programme specially designed for juveniles between the ages of 14 and 19 who are certified to stand trial as adults and convicted of violent crimes as an adult. The YOP was instituted in 1995 and rarely exceeds 250 participants.

Texas Department of Criminal Justice (TDCJ): Texas is one of the 50 states that comprise the United States of America. Each state, and the Federal Government, maintains their own prison systems. The TDCJ system consists of 112 correctional facilities containing approximately 112,000 convicted felons.

Trusty Camp: Trusty inmates (also called Trustys) are prison inmates who are vetted to be allowed to work within a correctional institution with minimal or no direct supervision. Trustys tend to be convicted on non-violent offences and generally have good institutional disciplinary records. A Trusty Camp is a subunit within a correctional facility where Trustys are housed. Placing Trustys in a very minimal setting, with minimal security, allows the institution to utilise the more secure housing areas and staff to effectively house more inmates. Trustys perform a variety of duties within a facility.

Note

1 Mr Davila had been working in the private sector for 11 years at the time of the interview.

Chapter 6

Stephen Anderson, Major for Cherokee County Sheriff's Office, and Director of Cherokee County Detention Facility Gaffney, SC, USA

Interviewer: Fred Lux

Contents

Overview	85
Introduction	86
Career	88
Personal Correctional Philosophy	89
Problems and Successes Experienced	94
Theory and Practice	98
Evidence-Based Corrections	99
Transnational Relations	99
Role of Corrections	99
General Assessments	100
Conclusion	101
Glossary	102

Overview

On 6 February 2019, Major Stephen Anderson discussed his career and his views of corrections in America. We met in his office at the Cherokee County Detention Center (CCDC) after having just completed a walk-through of the facility he manages. Over the course of several hours, Major Anderson detailed his work in the field of corrections, his views of correctional policy, and his opinions with regard to the field of corrections, including his concerns for the relationship between the field and the justice system as a whole as well as the communities it is poised to serve. Major Anderson is the Director of the CCDC, a county level pretrial jail facility, in Cherokee County, South Carolina, USA. The CCDC is located in Gaffney, South Carolina and serves the surrounding county – Cherokee County – by providing temporary detention facilities and bond and arraignment proceedings for inmates charged with criminal offences that have not been adjudicated. Despite the limited use of the facility within the parameters of the American justice system as a whole, the CCDC faces challenges that are faced by countless facilities similar in nature to the CCDC as well as those with larger inmate populations and correctional responsibilities.

Introduction

The American justice system functions in a tiered fashion by which jurisdiction for justice is divided between federal, state, and local subdivisions. Generally, the nature of the offence or judicial question at hand, coupled with geographical parameters, dictate jurisdiction. Hence, a local or county facility such as CCDC would have jurisdiction for incarceration of inmates justice-involved for matters arising with the bounds of its own county and no other. In turn, those inmates held in its facility will, as a general rule, be held only for matters under the jurisdiction of the Cherokee County Courts. As South Carolina – much like the rest of the US – is deemed to function through a retributive justice process, acts committed by an offender are viewed as offences against society as a whole. Further, South Carolina judicial jurisdictions are divided not only by geographical bounds of their jurisdiction, but also by the gravity of the offence at hand. Thus, lesser offences commonly deemed low misdemeanours fall under the purview of Cherokee County Courts. Greater offences commonly deemed felonies and high misdemeanours fall under the purview of the South Carolina State Courts. Therefore, offences falling under the jurisdiction of state courts will result in sentencing and corrections actions governed by the state correctional institutions – South Carolina Department of Corrections (SCDoC). The CCDC, then, is responsible for the incarceration and monitoring only of those inmates whose cases are to be decided in the county courts. And the courts of Cherokee County have carried out a local tradition of using lesser sanctions against offenders convicted at the county level that either do not result in post-conviction incarceration or incur no more than 90 days of incarceration.

The surrounding county that the local justice system and this facility serves, Cherokee County, is home to a little more than 57,000 residents. This rural community is centred directly between two major metropolitan areas – Greenville/Spartanburg, SC and Charlotte, NC – with a major transportation thoroughfare passing directly through its jurisdiction and connecting it to these metropolitan areas (United States Census Bureau, 2017). This positioning greatly shapes the natured of crime in that area. The CCDC itself is home to approximately 250 of those residents as inmates on an average daily basis. Of those 250, approximately 90% of the inmates are pre-adjudication. The remaining 10% comprises post-adjudication incarceration and the occasional contracted inmate from SCDOC of federal prisons (although, the latter is rare since Major Anderson became director of the facility).

Correctional Institution

The CDCC was built and opened in 1997 to house 140 male inmates and ten female inmates in a five-pod environment. By 2011, the facility was already overcrowded and housing more than 300 inmates at a time, with many of those being state and federal post-adjudication inmates held under contract with the respective judicial entity. In 2011, Major Anderson became Deputy Director of the facility and was tasked with addressing the issue of overcrowding. In doing so, he eliminated those contracts with state and federal entities, citing that the facility could not continue to house inmates above such egregious levels that violate human and constitutional rights, and that by housing inmates from other facilities, the CCDC was not providing adequate and professional services to its own community. Additionally, the design of the facility was revamped to account for the rising number of inmates. The conventional jail-cell pod-model was eliminated and the jail converted to a direct supervision environment in which three of the five pods were converted to a linear model with open bunk areas (no doors or cells). The fourth pod remained a conventional celled pod, while the fifth was converted to a maximum security or disciplinary pod.

Facility Services and Programmes

Beyond the expected services of incarcerating inmates, the CCDC provides programmes set to improve the quality of life – within the facility and throughout the community – of those who come in contact with the justice system. By way of the retributive nature of the American criminal justice system, it was conceived that incarceration as a threat and subsequent punishment was the most effective way to reduce crime and recidivism. Since the late 1970s, the system has seen an exponential increase in the use of incarceration as a means of judicial corrections, yet recidivism steadily climbed throughout the nation alongside the numbers of incarcerated individuals. Many scholars note, and Major Anderson echoes the notion, that incarceration, while sometimes a warranted and effective means of punishment, is not always the most effective means of correction (Warren, 2008).

In some instances, seemingly criminal acts are the result of mental health disorders suffered by the offender. As such, CCDC offers a referral programme by which inmates can seek subcontracted mental health evaluations and treatment from a third-party source. Similarly, offenders are often incarcerated for not being able to meet financial obligations (court fines, child support obligations, and such). Many recognise incarceration for such matters as counterintuitive (Swank, 2003). Accordingly, the CCDC offers remote monitoring programmes by which inmates can be released into the community under global positioning system (GPS) monitoring so as to be afforded the opportunity to work and fulfil their financial obligations. Also, they do house inmates sentenced to mixed sentences or weekend time to afford them the opportunity to work during the week but still be held accountable to society for their offences; thus, fulfilling that retributive model of justice so notably American. Last, the facility and its administrators recognise the need to maintain the morale of the inmates. Despite being criminal or alleged criminal offenders, they still must be afforded certain human dignities. As such, the CCDC makes us of a work release programme, allowing inmates to leave the correctional facility and perform work throughout the community while supervised by corrections personnel. While the work is limited and the inmates are still under direct supervision, it affords those who choose to participate in this programme an opportunity to leave the confines of the facility and to fulfil some semblance of a sense of purpose despite their immediate circumstances.

Career

While Major Anderson started his direction of the CCDC in 2011 with fervour and zeal that resulted in a reduction of inmate overcrowding and a redesign of the facility he was directed to manage, his career path was unconventional and not with intentions of being employed in the corrections profession. Major Anderson set out to be an educator or religious minister, having graduated from college with a degree in religious studies and minors in English and history, and cognates in music and French. Throughout college, he was employed in various capacities in the retail industry and eventually gained employment as a manager. This would prove to serve him well later, as it shaped his management and leadership theories with regard to the corrections field that would eventually become his profession.

Following college, Major Anderson became a full time religious minster for more than seven years. As the economy turned, though, the church that employed him could no longer pay him. It was then that he was offered employment with the Cherokee County Sheriff's Office. He worked predominantly in an administrative capacity for the sheriff's office from 2002 until the sheriff appointed him Captain-Deputy Director – of the jail in 2011. Up to this point in time, though, Major Anderson had never truly served in a law enforcement capacity, as he was not formally trained, and he had no experience in the field of corrections at all. But he recognised that he had been appointed to a role of management and this was a professional capacity he knew well. He immersed himself in the field of corrections, attending the state's training academy, and assigning himself to work shifts as a line-level corrections officer. As he had been promoted and set the task of correcting the overcrowding issues of the jail, he recognised that the facility needed a cultural change as well; one that was reflective of policies and procedures set to minimise recidivism and ensure the efficacy of the justice system that dictated the number of inmates housed in the facility.

Major Anderson recognised the need for change in the CCDC and that other facilities had already suffered from, and corrected, the same dilemmas that he was faced with (Lurigio, 2016). He reached out to various correctional facilities in the region and requested copies of their policies, procedures, missions and values, and design plans for their facilities. He learned the foundations of corrections through these readings, while seeking ways to improve the facility he oversaw. In 2012, he implemented a new Records Management System (RMS) that allowed easier access to police records and inmate records between the sheriff's office and the jail. This afforded him an opportunity to build a collaboration between corrections and law enforcement that he describes as greatly lacking in American justice. During this time, he also implemented the new logistical and structural changes previously discussed. And, in 2015, he was promoted to the rank of Major-Director. By 2017, he noted the disparity in rank and pay between corrections professionals and law enforcement professionals, and the subsequent ramification this has on the morale, and, in turn, professional nature of the work, of corrections officers (MacDonald, 2016). As such, he restructured the rank and pay system of the CCDC to allow for recruitment of personnel better suited to the corrections environment and profession.

Major Anderson's unconventional career development did not detract from his abilities as a successful and professional correctional facility director. Rather, his varied background developed rather progressive notions for how corrections in his local jurisdiction should be managed. His education and religious background have greatly shaped not only how he manages his personnel, but also how he manages corrections as an effective means to justice. He notes his 'Christian core values are greatly reflected in the opportunities the job has provided' and these values are what shape his correctional philosophies.

Personal Correctional Philosophy

While American justice, and subsequently corrections, operates in a federal capacity (shared authorities between the states and the national government), this is in a very limited manner. In many regards, law enforcement and corrections in this country are left to the states to manage and facilitate. Similarly, corrections at the local level – in this discussion, the county level – are left to the oversight of local authorities (United States, Department of State . . ., 2004). However, despite no nationally consolidated corrections system, there often seems to be consensus in correctional philosophy among practitioners. Over the course of the history of our nation's correctional system, we have evolved through several philosophical eras; some that persisted more than others. At its inception, the system focused on revenge; seeking the proverbial 'pound of flesh'. This gave way to a society seeking merely to eliminate the threat of the criminal's presence and remove them from society altogether. Eventually, the American people recognised the detriment of inhumane practices in corrections settings and sought to reform these ways. But they did so while adhering to the principles that offenders be punished and kept away from law-abiding society. Finally, philosophy has shifted to one concerned with rehabilitation and reintegration of the offender back into productive society (Blakely, 2008). This notion of effective rehabilitation and reintegration into society is what greatly shapes Major Anderson's personal philosophy.

In addressing his personal notions concerning the purpose of corrections, Major Anderson opened by explaining that he takes a 'common sense' approach to everything he does. Further, his approach is tempered by the desire to ensure that those in the custody of his facility 'feel as if they were treated fairly and with dignity.' He seeks to ensure that every action taken within the CCDC gives 'no reason for any inmate to ever leave citing any form of mistreatment.' He strives to balance the role of corrections and the overall justice process with basic human rights first and constitutional rights second. Further, in treating people with dignity and respect, he feels that he can better serve them to the system's overall end – preventing crime by preventing their recidivism.

Major Anderson cited a cultural mindset throughout the United States and the justice system that tends to view offenders as 'scum or bad people who must be dealt with.' He contends, though, that it is this mentality that lends to the retributive justice that has predicated much of corrections philosophy and resulted in the high rates of recidivism (Warren, 2008). He holds that corrections is a misnomer in the justice system and states that those of the profession 'don't correct people; [they] teach people to make better choices.' Corrections implies an inherent fault in the person, whereas his philosophy is more in line with the notion of continuing education. Offenders are not inherently bad or possessing some fault. They merely have not fully learned their obligation to, and role in, society and need to be taught this. He returns to his educational and religious roots in this manner.

In addition to his own experience and professional background shaping his philosophy, Major Anderson cites his work environment – namely, his agency's conveying of core values – for shaping his professional philosophy. He prominently displays the core values of the Cherokee County Sheriff's Office (of which the CCDC is a subordinate entity) and turned to indicate them: Dedication, Honour, Integrity, Excellence, and Professionalism, as he explained their impact on his professional life. Major Anderson stated that he has taken them to heart and applied them to every facet of decision making in his capacity as Director of the CCDC. He holds them in high regard, as he feels that they are indicative of the effort that should be put forth in every facet of justice to ensure that the justice entities commonly referred to as public service agencies truly provide the public service obligated to their community.

Corrections in the Community

Major Anderson contends that corrections serves to prevent crime and reduce recidivism, not through punishment, but through education. That education requires the fostering of partnerships within the community (Byrne, Taxman & Young, 2002). As noted previously, he holds that the most effective means to reducing recidivism is to ensure that those who leave the CCDC do so with the skills and ability to lead productive lives within the bounds of the rule of law. This requires ensuring that the necessary partnerships are developed to dissuade negative views of those being released from corrections programmes and facilities and back into the public forum. Major Anderson indicates his perception that certain facets of society – media and entertainment, news media, and so on – tend to glamourise criminal behaviours and a criminal life. This furthers the criminal actions of the offender, as this poses a dilemma within their mind as to whether criminal acts are acceptable within orderly society. Conversely, as an offender reintegrates into society, they are faced with countless difficulties, as being viewed as a criminal precludes them from obtaining jobs. Employers within his community are hesitant to hire persons under bond or having been adjudicated for a criminal offence. Thus, their dilemma is only reinforced, in that those they hope will help them reintegrate into orderly society shun them, while the proverbial life of crime is still willing to accept them as they are.

By developing partnerships with those in the community, Major Anderson hopes to apply corrections or education to the community at large in an effort to curb these debilitating notions. He views his and his agency's responsibility as one as much to the community as it is to those incarcerated within it. To that end, he strives to change the perception of the public community so that reintegration is possible and without unnecessary biases. He spoke on collaborative efforts often being stifled by a lack of understanding of corrections' roles and obligations, coupled with the perception that 'offenders are bad people as opposed to people who have made a bad decision.' In turn, he feels that education needs to occur inside the CCDC as well as in the community.

Major Anderson stated that 'the people want justice and structure, and they will seek punishment' with regard to offenders. However, as was addressed earlier, his facility is generally not one of punishment, but one of pre-trial detainment. Further, he espouses that what many perceive as justice and punishment is not fitting with our nation's modern application of civil and constitutional rights. Major Anderson indicated that he had taken note that the administrators and staff of the CCDC often recognise the liability of confusing society's concept of justice with the reality of civil and constitutional rights. However, it is only through collaborative and educational efforts between his staff and the community that similar understandings can be held by the community at large.

In all of this, Major Anderson suggests that the perceptions that preclude reintegrating offenders back into society and those that fuel the harsh punishment tactics of society cannot be overcome without the proper information being imparted. And this information must be imparted by those who know, first-hand, the implications of faulty perceptions. This equates to an understanding that it is the responsibility of him and his staff to be involved beyond the bounds of their facility. As such, he has implemented several programmes to ensure that the public is given that opportunity to better understand the true nature of corrections in Cherokee County. Since being employed as the director of CCDC, Major Anderson has implemented three notable programmes in his effort to interject his agency and its mission into the community it serves.

Inmates in the Community. Major Anderson has instituted a programme in which inmates are allowed to make public appearances. In some instances, they appear before community organisations, in many, they appear in schools speaking before students. They speak to the need to learn and further grow as a member of society. They speak to the end of asking that others be the example of what is desired in society. They speak of the consequences of their actions and the impact their actions had on the community, their friends, their family, and their life. These opportunities, Major Anderson says, relate back to his overall correctional philosophies while serving towards reparation for all stakeholders in the community.

The American criminal justice system is a system of a retributive nature, seeking punishment of an offender for an offence against society. But a restorative based system has been argued to be more effective at rehabilitation of an offender in that offenders are afforded an opportunity to interact with the victim of their offence – be it members of society at large or the victim directly affected by their offence (Wenzel, Okimoto, Feather & Platow, 2008). In keeping with the notion of rehabilitating all stakeholders, programmes have been implemented by which incarcerated offenders are afforded the opportunity to speak publicly about their offences and the ramifications of those. These programmes afford the opportunity for the public to see the effectiveness of the corrections system. They also serve to an end of general deterrence in that the community at large hears first hand of the consequences of lawbreaking behaviours. And these programmes allow the offender an opportunity to impact the community and feel a certain growth in their life (Gilligan & Lee, 2005). These nationally implemented programmes serve the same ends through the same means as the one implemented by Major Anderson. They have proven effective on a national level and Major Anderson feels certain they have been in his community as well.

Scared Straight. Scared Straight programmes were first implemented in the US in the 1970s. These programmes served to introduce juveniles to the consequences that adult offenders face for lawbreaking actions. The programmes hoped to scare deviant juveniles into a life of societal orderliness. They often entailed talks by incarcerated offenders telling of the horrors of violence, sexual abuse, and generally being confined, in an effort to dissuade juveniles from any desire to commit any act that may result their being faced with such horrors. Many of these programmes were eventually abandoned – despite public appeal – as they were determined to be ineffective. However, similar programmes that afforded juveniles the opportunity to merely receive guidance and encouragement from inmates and corrections personnel alike in a non-confrontational manner demonstrated effectiveness in reducing juvenile offending and recidivism (Klenowski, Bell & Dodson, 2010).

Recognising the value in such programmes for both the community and his personnel, Major Anderson implemented a similar, but less formal, programme. His programme affords parents and guardians the opportunity to discuss their concerns regarding their children with Major Anderson. Collaboratively, they determine various courses of action that might best suit the juvenile. Major Anderson then speaks with the juvenile and, based upon their reaction to him, the best course of action is determined. Often the programme minimally entails the juvenile meeting with an inmate, a corrections officer and Major Anderson. It will also result in his providing his contact information to the juvenile for follow-up conversations should he or she find the need.

Adopt a School. Corrections is often the least recognised facet of the criminal justice system. They are equally forgotten by the community at large, as well as their justice colleagues in law enforcement and courts (Peak & Giacomazzi, 2019). This lack of recognition among the community is demoralising to the professionals within the field and poses challenges (as previously discussed) with effective reintegration and reducing of recidivism of offenders. To that end, Major Anderson implemented the Adopt a School programme within his agency. The programme had already been implemented locally by law enforcement and afforded officers the opportunity to speak in classrooms concerning the profession, thus garnering awareness, support, and recognition for police efforts. To similar ends, Major Anderson has afforded his officers the opportunity to take on similar roles and tasks. However, doing so presents another opportunity – fostering of collaboration between the professional corrections and law enforcement communities.

Problems and Successes Experienced

Major Anderson concedes that he has been employed in the corrections profession only for the past eight years. In that time, though, he has noted the various changes in the field prior to his promotion as well as since. Similarly, he has effected a fair number of changes within the CCDC. The mere remodelling of the CCDC was not only a change, but a solution to a problem brought on by change. Corrections systems are interdependent upon the rest of the criminal justice system, and that system is interdependent upon the society it serves. As society has evolved and changed, so must the system and so must corrections.

Probably the most impacting change noted by Major Anderson has been the insertion of the victim into the justice process. As the American criminal justice system has evolved, victims' rights have become more of a forefront issue. A push for more recognition by the system of the victim has proved to be a double-edged sword. The concept of restorative justice has helped in many regards towards rehabilitative efforts for the sake of the offender, as well as restoring the victim (Wenzel, Okimoto, Feather & Platow, 2008). Major Anderson relates, though, that it has caused somewhat of a burden for the correctional system. Prior to this shift in the nature of the system, sentencing decisions were made in a very pragmatic and detached manner, with the judge ruling merely on the facts and the law as to what punishment should be appropriate. With the interjection of the victim into the process, though, emotion has come to be acknowledged in making these rulings. While evidence would suggest that victim's statements have less impact on sentencing decisions than expected (Roberts, 2009), Major Anderson holds that he has personally seen cases where the victim's interaction has resulted in a sentence of incarceration that would have otherwise been one of a fine or community monitoring. This, in turn, results in another inmate in an already overcrowded correctional facility (as perceived by Major Anderson).

Overcrowding

This brings about the discussion recognised by many as the crux of correctional institutions around the world – overcrowded populations. CCDC is no exception to this dilemma, as noted at the onset of this chapter. As American society has sought to win the 'war on drugs' and maintain its stance of 'tough on crime', it has often sought to remove the offender from society permanently through incarceration rather than rehabilitate them through effective correctional programmes. This has equated to greater correctional facility populations than those facilities were ever intended to house (Travis, Western & Redburn, 2014). Similarly, local implications with regard to victims' input (as related by Major Anderson) has resulted in CCDC housing approximately 60% more inmates than the facility was intended for.

In an effort to reduce overcrowding and the human rights violations inherent in those conditions, the CCDC was remodelled in such a manner as to allow for the housing of more inmates. Major Anderson points out, though, that this is only a temporary solution, as populations have continued to grow and the remodel only mitigated the problem as opposed to truly solving it. He conveys that the solution to the issue of overcrowding is not one of larger correctional facilities, but a change in justice programmes. He holds that it is necessary to implement programmes that more effectively prevent crime, reduce recidivism, and provide a means to accomplish these without the use of incarceration when appropriate.

Further Needs in Community Efforts

Major Anderson spoke of a host of challenges in the implementation of efforts to foster community collaborations. However, he noted that one major hurdle to be overcome is with regard to the children of those incarcerated. To some extent, he sees them as victimised by the inherent process and scenario of parental incarceration. He has implemented several programmes through which he interjects corrections personnel as well as inmates into the school environment. He notes that many of these programmes, though, seek to raise awareness of the corrections role and impact. However, this facet of every community – that is, the school community – not only knows the impact but *feels* the impact of corrections in the community through no fault of their own. Major Anderson realised that, all too often, incarcerated persons in the CCDC leave behind children who know their parent is incarcerated. Parental incarceration fosters a disdain for the justice system, a lack of interest in school and school attendance, and any number of subsequent mental and emotional developmental issues among the children (Murray & Farrington, 2008). As such, he has seen the need to provide for these children in a manner that maintains relationships with their parents, ensures proper development, and encourages lawful behaviour on their part. While he has not yet instituted a formal programme to do so, he has begun planning for one.

Mental Health

The National Alliance on Mental Illness (NAMI) reports that persons with mental illnesses are more likely to encounter police than mental health or medical personnel. As such, approximately 15% of all men and 30% of all women booked into jails are suffering from a mental health condition (n.d.). The deinstitutionalising of America's mental health discipline has resulted in fewer mental health hospitals and fewer mental health patients being treated. Thus, there are more mental health patients in America' jails and prisons than in hospitals (Torrey, Kennard, Eslinger, Lamb & Pavle, 2010).

Major Anderson relates that mental health recognition and treatment has become a greater focus in the corrections field within the past 5–10 years. Hence, he states that it is necessary for jail facilities such as CCDC to ensure that they are providing for the mental health care that hospitals are not. He states there comes a point where you 'realise that mental health will preclude justice rehab.' You cannot seek and successfully provide for rehabilitation of an offender if you cannot identify and tend to the underlying cause of their actions. Further, punishing an offender for an act that they carried out as a result of a mental health disorder is neither effective nor fitting of justice. However, Major Anderson stated multiple times throughout the interview that corrections officers are not mental health treatment professionals. Many of his officers have no more than a high school education and the training and certificates required of their job. Yet, they are the people that the inmates suffering from mental health disorders come into contact with on a daily basis. And these officers are the ones who see the behaviours that best reflect the true condition of that inmate. His officers, though, are not properly trained to diagnose or treat those conditions. They must be able to, however, as 'nobody else in the community is.'

When asked what the correctional system can do to alleviate this growing dilemma, he pointed to his own efforts in Cherokee County. Major Anderson serves on a task force comprising professionals from the law enforcement community, correctional field, medical field, and mental health discipline. This task force serves to evaluate the mental health condition within the community and identify its impact on the justice system. To be precise, they recognise that many mental health patients are identified through justice involvement and eventual incarceration. Acknowledging that government institutions such as CCDC cannot afford the necessary health care professionals within the facility, the task force attempts to identify other sufficient resources to provide the essential care to patients who are incarcerated. The most recent resource and solution for CCDC has been the implementation of the use of Telepsych.

Telepsych, in the broad sense, is a subset of treatment options, referred to as teletreatment, that was implemented in the medical field to provide medical advice without the need to travel to a physician. Recognising the success in the medical field, similar programmes were implemented in the mental health field. Since their inception, these programmes have proved equally successful in the mental health field, bringing much needed care to an otherwise marginalised population of mental health patients – the incarcerated. Research has indicated that these programmes are effective at providing necessary treatment that results in improved living conditions and overall safety within incarceration settings (Deslich, 2013). Major Anderson has noted that the provision of these services has afforded inmates the opportunity to seek mental health treatment otherwise not available to them in an effort to grow and improve themselves – the overall goal of corrections, as Major Anderson sees it. Also, the programme affords correctional personnel a source of expertise to better provide services expected of them, as it allows those personnel to contact the same providers to discuss their observations and the best courses of action to take with inmates suspected of dealing with mental health issues.

Medical Care

Along the same thread, Major Anderson noted challenges in providing competent and ethically obligated medical care to inmates. Since 1976, American jails and prisons have been deemed obligated to provide for the healthcare of inmates in their charge. Beyond the legal obligations, though, the medical field acknowledges that there are social obligations to providing health care as well. Inmates will eventually be released back into the general population and need to be in a state of health that will not pose a medical danger to the public they reintegrate into (Paris, 2008). Similarly, Major Anderson notes the necessity of those inmates being healthy enough to hold jobs and be successful in life as they reintegrate.

Major Anderson described the scenario in which the CCDC could not afford, or justify to the public trying to afford, a full-time medical professional at the facility. As a solution to balancing the need for care and the lack of funding for a full-time medical professional, he opted to contract with a local doctor to come into the facility on a regular basis to examine and treat patients. However, just as society has a perception of the 'bad guy', Major Anderson found that medical professionals are subject to similar views. He described how the contracted doctor would provide minimal services and then leave having not truly treated the inmate. The doctor would come in and review the files of the inmate without ever seeing the inmate. They would make a few recommendations based upon notes written in the file by corrections personnel – not medical professionals – and then move on to the next file. When questioned about the level of service, or lack thereof, provided, the doctor indicated that his actions were sufficient.

Major Anderson recognises the need for competent medical care within his facility. He states that he has found that doctors in the Cherokee County area refuse to see patients from his facility because they are inmates. This leaves the CCDC forced to transport inmates to neighbouring counties to facilities that are as many as 20–30 miles away to find medical professionals willing to treat the inmates. The facility cannot afford this, so Major Anderson has resorted to the solution described above, which results in inadequate care being provided. All in all, Major Anderson says that it is necessary for 'corrections to collaborate with medical professionals to view patients as patients and not inmates; the fact that they are wearing a jail jumpsuit does not change the fact they should be afforded proper medical care.' Only by changing the perception of the person as an inmate to the person as a person – a patient – will appropriate medical services be afforded to those in the charge of correctional institutions. Likewise, until the public perception is changed in the same manner, the necessary funds will not be devoted to the endeavour of providing competent medical care in jails and prisons.

Lack of Resources

The CCDC operating budget is approximately half that of the Cherokee County Sheriff's Office and tends to remain the same from year to year, according to Major Anderson. Globally, and throughout the US, this trend holds. Corrections receives significantly less funding than any other facet of the criminal justice system (Farrell & Clark, 2004). Major Anderson spoke to the detriment that this lack of funding and resources has on the effective operation of any correctional facility and related programmes. He specifically addressed the impact on hiring competent and effective personnel. A lower budget than other justice disciplines equates to lower salaries for those employed in the corrections field. Thus, he cannot hire and retain employees of a calibre necessary to further the goals of the field. Similarly, the issues of overcrowding within the facilities cannot be addressed with monies to build larger facilities or programmes to make use of community monitoring programmes. Major Anderson indicates that in order for correctional practices to grow in effectiveness, their budgets need to grow first. He says that corrections is too much 'tied to legislation and law enforcement in a subordinate sense' rather than as equals in efforts towards a common goal. Until this status is changed, the resources in personnel, financing, and the like will never be equally provided for and services will continue to be hampered.

Theory and Practice

Major Anderson cites an abundance of academic journals, and professional sources by which he seeks out best practices for implementation within CCDC. But he cites that often these sources are theoretical. with no collaborative efforts to devise them in a practical setting. He contends that the efforts to derive theoretical best practices are done in controlled academic environments with no input from the practitioners in the field who will need to implement these practices. This disconnect leads to hesitance on the part of the practitioners to implement practices suggested by academicians because of a certain scepticism brought on by a lack of involvement that would lead to understanding if it existed, and a fear of liability that comes with the lack of understanding.

His comments and concerns are echoed and furthered throughout the field. Many in the corrections field are concerned that the suggested best practices are not, and will not be, effective because they are not developed in concert with a collaboration of relevant research in a practical environment – the real world; further, they are not developed in concert with other facets of the criminal justice system – law enforcement and courts. It is acknowledged, though, that this needs to change, as Major Anderson has contended. Evidence-based practices are necessary in developing effective practices and evaluating them for their effectiveness (Hooley, 2010).

Evidence-Based Corrections

Efforts to achieve the most effective corrections policies, procedures, and programmes will only be successful if they are implemented through appropriate means. The implementation of evidence-based practices has afforded the most *à propos* manner of ensuring success in these endeavours. Major Anderson, having noted the disconnect between theory and practice, has similarly not fully embraced evidence-based practices in the truest sense – the use of social science research to direct practice. When asked about his use of evidence-based practices, though, he indicated that he implements them in the most basic manner of the premise. He spoke of accounts of recognising problems within the CDCC, seeking out solutions, implementing those solutions, and evaluating their effectiveness. While not turning to social science for the evidence, he does apply the principles.

Transnational Relations

The CCDC is a local facility and institution serving local needs. Major Anderson reflected on that premise when asked about the influence that international research, trends, and issues had on the operation of the CCDC. He indicated that most of his operation is shaped through the rulings of the United States Supreme Court and the United States Constitution. He conceded that there are evident human rights violations in the international realm of corrections and that the US and its facilities are not immune to such transgressions. However, he holds that noting these transgressions in the international community only serves to iterate the need for American corrections – in this case, the CCDC – to focus on those rights afforded by the United States Constitution.

Role of Corrections

As the CCDC has striven to improve efforts towards reducing crime and recidivism by being active in the community, Major Anderson acknowledges that the facility still exists to serve to a purpose of justice as well. The noted efforts rest no more solely with the community then they do with the correctional facility. As such, Major Anderson has sought to integrate programmes within the facility to encourage growth and learning on the part of those incarcerated in it. He recognises that these programmes are predicated, though, on an understanding that those incarcerated in the facility – while stripped of certain rights of citizenry – must still be afforded rights of basic human dignity.

Major Anderson echoes considerations that all persons – even those incarcerated as part of a justice involvement – are deserving of basic human rights. It is only by being afforded those human rights that any further efforts to rehabilitate an incarcerated offender will be successful (United Nations, 2005). First, to this point, Major Anderson holds that 'force is not the answer.' Compelling inmates to do what is expected is far more labour intensive and far less effective than asking and convincing the inmate to do what is expected (McCamey & Carper, 1998). Further, if they comply only as a result of the use of force in the correctional facility, they will not comply with rules of order when integrated back into society. To this end, Major Anderson has adhered to a policy of open dialogue with the inmates of the CCDC. He states that talking them through their situations, their transgressions, and their growth and learning helps to reduce the necessity of the use of force. Further, he has experienced instances where inmates remember, recall, and speak of those conversations long past their time incarcerated in the facility. This has led to the implementation of policies and training programmes that educate and encourage his personnel to perform their duties according to the same philosophy.

The ultimate goal of the correctional system – as espoused by Major Anderson – is to ensure effective reintegration of offenders into society. He, once again, contends that punishment will not serve this end. Rather, programmes that educate inmates and develop skills and traits useful to society as a whole better serve this end (Davis, Bozick, Steele, Saunders & Miles, 2013). Noting this, CCDC employs programmes set to provide education and development of job skills. Inmates work through programmes while in the facility and then are afforded the benefit of placement services that assist them with seeking employment upon their release.

All of these efforts on the part of CCDC under the direction of Major Anderson serve the end of his overriding corrections philosophy. Again, he maintains that the role of corrections within the justice system is not one of correcting, but one of educating. But that education needs to extend beyond the walls of the facility and beyond the inmate themselves. It is necessary that education extend into the community through the application of the inmate's learning in a community environment, as well as education of the community in the role of corrections and the effectiveness of programmes designed to rehabilitate offenders.

General Assessments

When asked about his personal reflections on successes and faults in the field of corrections in general, Major Anderson stated, 'the field has taken steps in the right direction but is teetering between a desire for harsh punishment and restoring or educating offenders.' Efforts have been taken to improve relations and perspectives with regard to the intertwining of corrections, the larger justice system, and society as a whole. but greater efforts are still necessary. Society is constantly evolving and so must the justice system and correctional system that serves it. Efforts to build greater collaboration between correctional programmes and community resources need to grow. 'Corrections programmes need to be less babysitting', as described by Major Anderson, and more education.

Major Anderson sees a need for greater use of community-based monitoring such as global positioning system (GPS) monitors and home detention programmes that provide some semblance of restriction while still affording opportunities for offenders to work and garner education so as to better their role in society. With advancement in technology equating to lower costs for the use of GPS monitoring, the use of such methods has grown considerably in recent years (PEW Charitable Trust, 2016). Major Anderson feels that these methods would serve far more beneficially than traditional incarceration, as they are more conducive to rehabilitation as opposed to punishment. He suggests that these practices will likely be used far more often in both pre- and post-adjudication correctional facilities in years to come.

While there is little indication of this happening in the near future, Major Anderson also indicated a prediction that the American Justice system will likely see more federal influence. Given the recent climate throughout American society, and calls for more transparency and more restriction on justice practices, he foresees more standardisation across the field at the hands of federal government directives. While he states he does not advocate this, he believes that federalisation of law enforcement and corrections is likely to be inevitable at this point.

Conclusion

While Major Anderson's career in corrections came about quickly and has been short compared to some, he has embraced the field of corrections with a desire to better himself in the capacity of a competent administrator in the field as well as a desire to improve the correctional system as a whole by the example he and his facility can set. Major Anderson has embraced the notions of evidence-based practices in implementing best practices within his facility while balancing these with the necessity of ensuring justice as is deemed fitting from the American perspective. He sees justice, though, not as retributive and punitive, but as restorative. He maintains that the role of his facility and its personnel is not to isolate 'bad people' from society, but to educate offenders in 'how to make better choices' and how to be more productive members of a law-abiding society.

Meanwhile, he strives to educate the public against misconceived notions about the often-forgotten corrections system as well as the perception of offenders as 'bad people'. With the advent of new technologies, new theories on the treatment of offenders, and pushes for more community-focused justice throughout the American criminal justice system, he sees the role of American corrections as one of fostering the growth of people. And he advocates for more efforts throughout the system to implement programmes and make use of resources to that end, even if his efforts are constrained to the local community he and his facility serve.

Glossary

CCDC: The Cherokee County Detention Center is a county-level, pretrial, jail facility serving the law enforcement and judicial jurisdiction of Cherokee County, SC, USA.

GPS: Global positioning system refers to the technology by which space satellites are used to determine the location of electronic devices on the Earth's surface; these are commonly used for navigation purposes.

Section III

South America

Chapter 7

Orlando Garcia Maradiaga, Director, National Penitentiary Institute of Honduras

Interviewer: Brian Norris

Contents

Overview	105
Introduction	109
Career	109
Changes Experienced	110
Personal Correctional Philosophy	112
Problems and Successes Experienced	113
Theory and Practice	115
Evidence-Based Corrections	115
Transnational Relations	116
General Assessments	117
Conclusion	119
Glossary	121

Overview

Colonel Orlando Garcia Maradiaga took over as the Director of the National Penitentiary Institute of Honduras in May of 2015, about two and a half months before this interview took place. The presence of the military at the highest echelons of the 15,000-inmate and 1,600-employee national prison system was relatively recent, dating back only to August of 2014. The decision of Honduran President, Juan Orlando Hernandez, to replace civilian leadership with that of a temporary military leadership was influenced in no small measure by a tragic fire that killed 362 inmates in Comayagua prison in the country in 2014 (Santana & Romero, 2015, p. 25), and the resulting perception that the prison system in the country was spiralling out of control. This chapter relates the contents of the interview with Colonel Garcia conducted in his office in Tegucigalpa, the capital of Honduras, and further contains information from a tour of La Tamara prison, a 4,300-inmate male facility housing about 29% of the country's total inmate population.

An assessment of Honduras's modern prison institutions must be contextualised by knowledge of the historical evolution of some of the country's basic governing structures. In the 16th century, the land occupied by modern Honduras lacked advanced indigenous populations, such as the Aztecs of Mexico, the Quiche and Cakchiquel of Guatemala, and the Pipil of El Salvador. Spaniards arrived in the land that would become Honduras as early as the 1520s when the competing Conquistadors Pedro de Alvarado and Pedrarias Davila fought each other there. Honduras would be defined as a discrete political unit in the Kingdom of Guatemala, a political subunit that included Chiapas, Guatemala (including El Salvador), Honduras, Nicaragua and Costa Rica during Spanish Habsburg rule (c. 1520–1760). The *encomienda*, a quintessential Habsburg institution, was a grant of indigenous labour to Spaniards, and this institution laid the basis for the creation of the Spanish-speaking *ladino* class of mixed European and indigenous ethnicities that would become increasingly important in the country. In the 1760s, Bourbon rule established in Honduras an intendancy, a local office loyal to the royal crown, and, upon independence from Spain in 1821, Honduras became a member of the short-lived United Provinces, an independent nation composed of Guatemala, El Salvador, Honduras, Nicaragua and Costa Rica. In 1824, the United Provinces gave Honduras its first constitution, a liberal document influenced by the US Constitution of 1789 and one that enshrined individual rights that are the basis of due process in the modern US criminal justice system. Honduras seceded from the imploding Kingdom of Guatemala in 1838 and, thus, became a modern nation state with its current borders. *Mestizaje* (miscegenation between European and indigenous groups) in the mid-19th century was more advanced in Honduras than in neighbouring conservative and paternalistic Guatemala, which maintained relatively large indigenous populations through much of the 20th century. Tegucigalpa, the capital of Honduras, developed a silver industry in the late 19th century to complement and justify its role as an administrative centre. But, to this day, the centrally located and Pacific-orientated Tegucigalpa remains isolated from the commercially dominant Caribbean coast city of San Pero Sula, long linked to New Orleans by the banana industry that developed in Honduras in the late 19th century. From 1876 to 1933, Honduras had so-called liberal authoritarian leaders, that is, non-democratically elected leaders that nonetheless pursued policies of free trade and allowed civil liberties such as freedom of the press. From 1933 to 1948, Honduras had a military dictator, Tiburcio Carias Andino, who paralleled the military dictators of Guatemala (Jorge Ubico, 1931–1944) and El Salvador (Maximilian Hernandez Martinez, 1931–1944). From 1948 to 1963, Honduras was part of the worldwide second wave of global democratic expansion, but the country briefly slipped back into military dictatorship from 1963 to 1980. In 1969, Honduras fought neighbouring El Salvador in the Soccer War, a military conflict with a border dispute and Salvadoran immigration to Honduras as its driving causes. Since 1980, Honduras has remained democratic, and the country wrote a new constitution in 1982 (Woodward, 1999).[1]

Today, Honduras is a small Spanish-speaking country in the Central American Isthmus. Its population of 8.7 million is 98th out of 138 countries worldwide, about the size of Sweden or Israel. Its per capita GDP is about $4,700 (PPP), ranked 173 out of 230 countries, and similar to that of Pakistan or Sudan. About 97% of Hondurans are Catholic,[2] a great difference from neighbouring El Salvador and Guatemala, where up to 30% are Evangelical Protestant (Garrard-Burnett, 1998; Offutt, 2015, p. 3). In 2011, 98% of Hondurans spoke Spanish.[3] Health indicators are poor but improving in Honduras. In 2013, the infant mortality rate was 19 per 1,000 live births, about three times that of the United States, but dramatically down from Honduras's 1960 rate of 142 per 1,000.[4] Freedom House rated the Honduras 'partly free' in 2015 (Freedom House, 2015, p. 23), though lingering distrust from a 2009 constitutional crisis remains among the political class of the country. Honduras has recently gained notoriety for having extremely high per capita murder rates, estimated by the United Nations Office of Drugs and Crime in 2012 to be 90 murders per 100,000 population, highest in the world, while that of Mexico was 22 per 100,000 and that of the United States was 5 per 100,000 (UNODC, 2013, p. 126).

There are four major pillars of the modern criminal justice system in Honduras: the judicial branch (Poder Judicial), the attorney general (Ministerio Publico), the public defender's office (Defensa Publica), and police forces. As this structure suggests, there is greater autonomy and likely resources for Honduras's public defender's office compared with that of the US, where the public defender is an adjunct of the judicial branch of government. Important legal bases for the criminal justice system include the Constitution of 1982, the Judicial Civil Service Law of 1980 (Ley de la Carrera Judicial de 1980), and the Criminal Procedural Code of 1984 (Codigo Procesal Penal de 1984). Basic quantitative measures of the Honduran criminal justice system are comparable with other similarly situated countries. For instance, the World Bank estimated that Honduras had about ten judges per 100,000 population in 2006, which was comparable to Argentina's 11 per 100,000, Costa Rica's 17 per 100,000, France's ten per 100,000, and the US's ten per 100,000 (Hammergren, 2009).[5]

The history of the modern Honduran prison dates back to the 19th century. The Livingston Codes, mentioned by Tocqueville and Beaumont in *On the Penitentiary System in the United States* (1833), were penal codes developed by Edward Livingston for Louisiana in 1826. The codes were not adopted in Louisiana, but they were adopted by Honduras's influential neighbour, Guatemala, in 1836. The Livingston Codes, which called for impractical jails with separate cells for prisoners, were abolished in 1837 (Woodward, 1999, pp. 103–105), and certainly their attempted implementation would have been known to Honduran leaders. In 1870, the Yoro Yoro prison was the first prison constructed in Honduras. Under the modernising liberal dictator, Marco Aurelio Soto (1876–1883), a protégé of the influential dictator of Mexico from 1876 to 1910, Porfirio Diaz, Honduras adopted the Penal Code of 1880 and in 1889 opened the Central Penitentiary for 1,459 inmates, 1,338, or 92%, of whom were male (Santana & Romero, 2015, p. 18). The Positivist thinking of Auguste Comte and Herbert Spencer, which emphasised the pre-eminence of rational and scientific principles in guiding public policy, was influential for leaders like Soto (Woodward, 1999, pp. 155–156). Between 1870 and 1967, Honduras constructed nine of its 25 currently functioning prisons. In 1957, Honduras formally incorporated the concepts of 'security, social defense, and rehabilitation of the criminal' as the mission of the penitentiary system. Between 1974 and 1984, the executive branch of government, beginning with President Oswaldo Lopez Arellano, built ten prisons, dramatically increasing the capacity of the system. The last prison completed was the National Penitentiary at Juticalpa, Olancho in 2007 (Comision Interamericana de Derechos Humanos (CIDH), 2013, pp. 6–7; Santana & Romero, 2015, pp. 18–30). Honduras is currently constructing four new prisons.

Today in Honduras, there are about 15,000 inmates in 25 prisons. For comparison, South Carolina has about 22,000 inmates in 24 institutions, and Mexico City has about 40,000 inmates in ten institutions. In Honduras, there are about 1,600 prison employees, giving the country a staff to inmate ratio of around 1:10, which is right at the recommended United Nations threshold. La Tamara prison, visited during this research visit, also has a 1:10 staff to inmate ratio, with 460 staff and 4,300 inmates. Honduras has an incarceration rate of about 180 inmates per 100,000 population, while that of neighboring Mexico is about 240 per 100,000 and that of the US is about 500 per 100,000. Today, about 55% of the inmates in Honduran prisons are awaiting criminal sentences (*procesados*), and this is down from about 87% in 1990. The 2014 budget was estimated to be about 460 million Lempiras (about $21 m), about 10% of which was dedicated to inmate food and 80% of which was dedicated to prison employees' salaries. All prisons in Honduras are managed by the federal (i.e., national) government. Since 1982, three federal agencies have managed prisons. From the 1970s to 1998, the Ministry of Governing and Justice (Gobernacion and Justicia) managed prisons. From 1998 to 2012, the civilian Secretariat of Security (Secretaria de Seguridad) managed the institutions, and from 2012 to the present the newly created National Penitentiary Institute, under the Secretariat of Human Rights, Justice, Government, and Decentralisation (akin to an interior ministry), manages prisons. Honduras has no national penitentiary academy, and police from the country's national police force provide security in the country's prisons.

In 2012, a tragic fire in the Comayagua prison took the lives of 360 inmates and galvanised decision leaders in the country. This was not the first mass loss of life in a Honduran prison, because, in 2004, 107 inmates died in a fire at the San Pedro Sula Prison (Centro Penal San Pedro Sula). In 2014, one report estimated that up to 85% of Honduras's prison populations were in a condition of *autogobierno*, that is, self-government by inmates.[6] In 2014, President Juan Orlando Hernandez, judging that the system was in a state of emergency, appointed military leaders to run the prison system, and the second of these national penitentiary leaders was Colonel Orlando Garcia.

Introduction

This interview was conducted Spanish in the headquarters of the Honduran National Penitentiary Institute, housed in a Spanish villa-style two-storey house in the Florencia Sur neighbourhood of Tegucigalpa, the capital city. Interview notes were hand-written in a legal pad, and a tour of La Tamara prison, a complex housing 4,000 male inmates, or approximately 27% of Honduras's total inmate population, complemented the interview in the headquarters. The date of the interview was 20 July 2015 and the date of the tour of La Tamara was 23 July 2015.

Colonel Orlando Garcia Maradiaga is a tidy-looking man of about mid-fifties with mostly dark salt-and-pepper hair. He was cleanly shaven, wearing glasses and camouflage fatigues and combat boots the day of the interview. He had a blue and white Honduran flag patch on his shoulder, and the nametag "Garcia" on his breast pocket. Arriving at the office, one is greeted at the street level by armed guards in fatigues. Blue-uniformed guards are members of the Honduran national police, and green-uniformed guards are members of the Honduran army. Walking up to the second floor, one encounters about six administrators with desktop computers working in an open room with a ceiling fan lazily rotating above. Colonel Garcia's office is large, but not ostentatious. One sees a framed picture of President Juan Orlando Hernandez, or 'JOHA', as he is called, in the centre of the wall, a bookshelf with a few reports on it, and, in the corner, a cutout with a picture of a soldier with a signpost in the background pointing toward 'Victory'.

Career

Col. Garcia is a 37-year veteran of the Honduran army. He began his career with the army as an enlisted man (*tropa* or 'troop') in February of 1978. 'I did not go to the [military] academy,'[7] he said. Rather, he ascended the ranks by taking opportunities as they came. Initially, he was first sergeant, and then the army sent him to Officer Candidate School (OCS) in the US to become an officer. He underwent training programmes in Panama and in Fort Benning, Georgia, the latter for arms training and training in

US military doctrine. He then achieved the rank of Lieutenant Coronel (*Teniente Coronel*) and was part of command staff. He commanded a company of riflemen (*fusileros*), and then commanded, sequentially, a battalion and a brigade. He became Chief of the Department of Intelligence of the Honduran army, and this trajectory sent him ultimately to his current position in the Honduran prison sector.

In August 2014, Cololonel Garcia was named Inspector General of the Honduran National Prison system, an ombudsman-type position, and Colonel Francisco Galvez Granados was named by President Hernandez as the first military director of the system at the same time. On 1 May 1 2015, only two months before our interview, Colonel Garcia replaced Colonel Galvez as the National Director of the penitentiary system.

Colonel Garcia's eyes grew large, his eyebrows raised, and he slowed his speech when he said, 'It is not common that a military person be in charge of the National Penitentiary System,' a point he repeated during the interview. It was the decision of the 'President of the Republic', President Hernandez, to appoint a military director of the system. The Honduran system was in a 'state of crisis' (*etapa de crisis*), and the system "had collapsed". The idea was for the military to 'lend a hand' (*echar mano del ejercito*). Advantages accruing to the military in this situation included the 'confidence'" the public had in the military, and its 'credibility' (*confianza* and *credibilidad*). But his is a directorship that is meant only to address circumstances that have arisen at this critical moment (*coyutural*). It is "temporary" (*temporal*) command. He would serve temporarily, and 'leave [the system] better than it was before."'

Changes Experienced

The most important changes experienced deal with the changes in leadership in the penitentiary sector. Three different government entities have housed the directorship of the national prison system in the past three decades. The prison sector was housed in the Secretary of State's department of Government and Justice (*Secretaria de Estado, despacho Gobernacion y Justicia*) 'for 10–15 years.'[8] 'For about ten years' the prison sector was run by the civilian Department of Defence (the *Secretaria de Seguridad*). In 2013, the Commission for Transition was created to transfer the system to the newly created National Penitentiary Institute, which was placed under the Secretariat of Human Rights, Justice, Government and Decentralisation (effectively an interior ministry).

The prison sector had been neglected (*en olvido*) for many years and had been progressively "weakening" (*debilitando*), but President Hernandez changed this. He gave the sector a lot of attention.

The crisis in the prison sector encompassed many dimensions. First, there was overcrowding (*hacinamiento*) in prisons. For instance, La Tamara prison, by one estimation, was designed for 2,000 inmates, but has 4,300 housed in it now. Second, prisons were ungovernable. Authorities did not exercise control in the institutions. Third, there was a need to orientate the system toward rehabilitation or social reinsertion (*rehabilitacion* or *reinsercion*).

There are several changes that the prison sector is implementing to address these deficiencies. To address overpopulation, there is a dual-pronged approach. On the one hand, new prisons must be constructed. On the other, judges in criminal courts need to send fewer individuals to prison.

In terms of construction, Honduras is building four 'mega-prisons' as a stop-gap measure. These include El Porvenir (The Future), with a capacity of 2,000 inmates, La Acequia, with a capacity of 2,500 inmates, Moroceli (El Paraiso department, i.e., state), with a capacity of 1,500 inmates, Ilama (Santa Barbara department), with a capacity of 1,500. This is 'not a long-term' solution, but it must be done. Honduras prisons, Colonel Garcia said, are 80% overcrowded now. 'Some say, "Constructing [prisons] is not the solution",' he said. Yes, he concedes, but is quick to add that now there is a need to build prisons, irrespective of other policies that are pursued. He wants to reduce overcrowding from its current 80% level to 10%. The new prisons, in addition to reducing overcrowding, will be pilot institutions that will serve as models to other prisons in the system to accomplish some of the goals mentioned below.

In addition to new prison construction, a complementary strategy of reducing the number of individuals that judges sentence to prison must be pursued to address the overcrowding problem. According to Colonel Garcia, criminal court judges in Honduras must understand that the system 'has filled up' (*ha llegado la tope*). Judges must understand that 'they absolutely cannot continue to send [this quantity of defendants to prison]' (*ya no puede mas*). His ideas on how these judges might be convinced are related below in the 'Transnational Relations' section.

Reducing overcrowding is a humanitarian goal in and of itself, but it also serves the second major goal that Colonel Garcia sees as important, that of reducing the 'ungovernability' of the prisons. To regain control of the prisons, there needs to be a 'purification' (*depuracion*) of the 1,700 employees that staff the system. Some of the existing workers are 'in collusion' (*coludidos*), and do not want change. However, it is necessary that there be a 'new vision' among the ranks of prison workers, and up to 700 newly recruited workers might provide the system with a clean slate.

A new penitentiary professional academy will be completed next year, and this is a key component in improving the workforce in order to regain control of the prisons. The goal of the new academy will be in part to instil a sense of professional pride and a sense of 'identity' (*identidad*) in the workforce. This *esprit de corps* does not exist now among prison workers. 'Everything is negative [now]' (*Todo es negativo*), according to Colonel

Garcia. The result of the training at the new academy will produce a workforce that is 'clean and honest' (*limpio, honesto*). The academy will produce technically competent penitentiary workers with specialisations such as psychologists, socioeconomic [analysts], toxicologists, and polygraph technicians. The model for this penitentiary academy is taken from the Dominican Republic (discussed below).

The third necessary change in the prison sector deals with the need to strengthen the rehabilitation programmes, the subject of the next section.

Personal Correctional Philosophy

Rehabilitation (*rehabilitacion*) or social reinsertion (*reincersion social*, i.e., reintroduction to society) is a major focus of the prison system, and, in the opinion of Colonel Garcia, this must be improved. There are several pillars to rehabilitation. First, vocational training should be emphasised. Training workshops in tailoring (*sastreria*), carpentry (*carpenteria*), shoe repair (*zapateria*), agricultural production (agro-industrial), welding (*soldaduria*), and electrical work (*electricidad*) were among the vocational trainings to be offered.

A second pillar is that of spirituality (*capacitacion spiritual*). Citations from the Bible filled the walls of La Tamara prison. One read, 'Jesus Christ is the same yesterday, today, and forever' (Hebrews 13:8).[9]

A third pillar is that of education. Elementary education (*primaria*) and high school (*segundaria*) would be offered. The Honduran Ministry of Education offers educational programmes through elementary for inmates, and the Catholic Church has a programme called *Alfa sí*, a literacy programme for inmates who cannot read or write. The high school programmes are run by an entity other than the Ministry of Education. The National Autonomous University of Honduras (*Universidad Nacional Autonomo de Honduras*, UNAH) offers some bachelor's degree programmes, but there is little demand for this level of education, perhaps 8–10 inmates.

I ask, 'But don't these educational and rehabilitative programmes exist now?' 'Yes,' he conceded. 'But they do not yield fruit' (*No da frutos*).

Colonel Garcia also mentions national initiatives to institutionalise indeterminate sentencing (*sentencia indeterminada*). He speaks of a 'new vision' (*nueva vision*) from the Secretary of Government (*Secretaria de Gobernacion*, that is, the *Secretaria de Derechos Humanos, Justicia, Gobernacion, y Decentralizacion*, a.k.a., the Interior Ministry) on this aspect. The indeterminate sentencing in this context would be seen as a grace (*indulto*) or a dispensation, presumably for good behaviour. However, at the operational level, he does not deal with this ("*Yo no lo manejo*").

A cross-cutting philosophical principle for rehabilitation and possibly for restoring and maintaining order in the prisons, for Colonel Garcia, is the need to reduce or eliminate idleness among the inmates. 'Zero idleness'

(*Zero ociosidad*), he says. His eyes grow large and he raises his hand in a 'stop' gesture to emphasise the importance of this. 'The inmates should not be [just] playing card games' ([*Que*] *no jueguen a naipe*).

Problems and Successes Experienced

The greatest challenge faced is that of restoring order in the prisons. There is a need to 'restore peace in the prisons' (*recuperar paz en los centros penales*), according to Colonel Garcia. What is more, the infrastructure has collapsed.

The very organisation of the inmate population of La Tamara prison suggests a severe lack of official influence within the walls of the prison because inmates are categorised, in some instances, based on affiliation with gangs or other autonomous inmate governance structures. For instance, La Tamara has two dormitories for processed but not sentenced inmates (*procesados*), two dormitories for sentenced inmates, one diagnostic or triage dormitory for inmates entering prison for the first time, one dormitory each for the MS-13 and 18th Street gangs, one dormitory for individuals who have left gangs, one for ex-police and ex-military personnel, and one maximum security dormitory, itself subdivided into units for dangerous inmates and inmates who fear for their safety.

Another example of the lack of control by authorities is the practice of inmate ownership of businesses in prisons. This ownership includes not only workshops that produce arts and crafts, but, in the case of La Tamara prison, it extends to inmate ownership of sundries shops (*pulperia*), including the inventory in the shop.

A specific acute need is that of classification of inmates. As the system exists now, there is not a proper classification regime in place. Currently, it is possible that a murderer and a narcotics trafficker (i.e., two very different types of offenders) could be placed together in one cell. There needs to be a better 'criminological typology' (*tipologia criminal*) employed in the penitentiary system. There is a need to develop interdisciplinary teams, called technical councils (*consejos tecnicos*), composed of psychologists, social workers, physicians, and 'judges' (perhaps 'legal counsel', 'juridical'?]. One important component of this is the digitalisation of inmate information. 'Where is Juan Perez [invented name]?' asks Colonel Garcia. One needs to be able to consult an electronic database and immediately know the inmate's whereabouts.

A related set of problems deals with the lack of appropriate security technology and procedures. Security concerns in this context revolve around the issue of confiscation of illicit materials being introduced into the prisons through legitimate searches from authorities (*requisas*). Colonel Garcia feels that prison personnel need technology such as X-ray machines, metal detectors, and cell phone signal blocking equipment.

Another problem to overcome is the lack of follow-up after an inmate leaves the penitentiary system. There are no post-prison programmes. There are some not-for-profits (ONGs, or, in English, NGOs, non-governmental organisations) and some religious groups, but these are not part of the governmental system.

There have been successes, too. There has been an improvement in the quality of inmate food. In the recent past, the average economic amount dedicated to inmate food was nine Lempiras (about $0.50) per inmate per day. This has increased to 30 Lempiras per inmate per day.

The second example of success is that of the construction of new prisons. The infrastructure of the system is reportedly improving as we speak.

A third example of success is that of transparency (*transparencia*). Transparency in this context deals with incentivising employees to not be corrupt (*no corrompido*) without necessarily changing employees. Lower-level employees (*subalternos*) look to the leader as a role model (*lider es ejemplar*), and the improvement in leadership under the military has yielded fruit in terms of having a less corrupt workforce. Before, part of the administrative system was corrupt, but not now. Colonel Garcia's headquarters office handles human resources and manages money, functions that had been previously managed by other units in the penitentiary system. His people are loyal and non-corrupt. 'This is going well. This is a good system,' he said.

Lieutenant Colonel Guillermo Eduardo Sandoval Aguilar, Director (i.e., Warden) of La Tamara prison, told a similar story of his management. Before his arrival at La Tamara, there were several disparate units and specialisations, including medical personnel, psychologists, social workers, legal advisers, teachers, administrators, and security elements. He said, '[But these groups] never met each other and never worked together.' The first leadership imperative was to convey to the employees that 'we all work together. Security depends on administration [and vice versa.] There is not one unit on top of another. We are all equal.'

Regarding security measures taken, Lieutenant Colonel Sandoval talked of removing the 'inmate leaders' (*jefes de internos*, i.e., inmates who supervised other inmates, akin to tank bosses or con-bosses) and isolating them.

When asked about metrics for success, Lieutenant Col.onel Sandoval gave declining pistol confiscations as a metric that suggested improvement. In one raid in La Tamara, authorities confiscated 60 pistols. In another raid, they confiscated 22 pistols. In the latest raid, they only confiscated four pistols.

He also mentioned improvement with regard to escapes. In six months, there had not been a successful escape from La Tamara. Within an unspecified time period, there had been three escape attempts and four inmates recaptured and returned to the prison 'with new charges' (*con nuevas cargas*).

Colonel Garcia is sanguine about the trajectory the penitentiary system signalled with these successes. 'We have to reorganise,' he said. 'We have to put our house in order. We need to get more money to the inmates [*privados de libertad*, those deprived of liberty]. More benefits. More construction. More improvements," he concluded.

Theory and Practice

Colonel Garcia did not mention any direct collaboration with academics aside from the collaborations with professional researchers,[10] particularly those from the Dominican Republic mentioned below. The National Autonomous University of Honduras (UNAH) is the major university in Tegucigalpa and in the coastal and Pacific-orientated portions of the country that it influences. Perusal of titles in the bookstore of the UNAH revealed titles on advanced economics, project management, GIS and related engineering and graphical design software, a number of cultural or interpretative works, one book titled *Los aviones de la Fuerza Aerea Hundureña* (The Aeroplanes of the Honduran Air Force), and a memoir from General Romeo Vasquez Velasquez, titled *Dangerous Ambitions: The Temptations of Power*, detailing his intervention in 2009 to stop what he deemed to be an attempt by President Mel Zelaya to circumvent constitutional term limits. There was no criminal justice section visible, but more research would need to be done to ascertain whether Honduras in fact has a developed criminological literature.[11]

Evidence-Based[12] Corrections

As suggested above, because there is not a developed criminological analytical tradition in Honduras that is easily discernible, it is further unlikely that there is deep familiarity with analysts' writings in the 'what works' school of thought. The phrase 'evidence-based corrections' itself is not intelligible in translation to Honduran Spanish. An alternative approach to this topic was taken in the interview. I asked, 'What do you read that informs your decision-making?' Colonel Garcia produced three reports from his bookshelf, and it was possible to analyse the sources of these documents to determine the level of engagement with the 'what works' literature.

Of the three reports, only the full citation of MNP-CONAPREV's *IV Informe Anual a la Nacion* (2014) is reproducible here. The contents of a second report that Colonel Garcia provided were produced by a not-for-profit organisation. Its contents are summarised elsewhere in this chapter, but some markings on the report read 'confidential'. The third report that Colonel Garcia pointed to is not yet public and, moreover, contains confidential budgetary information.

Four of the six authors of the *IV Informe Anual a la Nacion* (2014) have legal training (*Abogado* is 'lawyer' in Spanish: Abogada Odalis Aleyda Najera Medina, Abogada Sandra Palacios, Abogada Soraya Morales, and Abogada

Linda Lizzie Rivera). One is a priest (Sacerdote Marco Renieri Sanchez). And another has a Master's in science (Msc. Claudia Ferrari [*sic.*]). The report summarises human rights incidents, such as the detention of Zenia Marazita and Ramon Eduardo Diaz Rodriguez. The report compiles basic data on the penitentiary system, such as the number of inmates, percentage of inmates processed (*procesados*, i.e., not yet sentenced) and the percentage convicted (*condenado*). Other tallies, such as the number of prison visits employees of MNP-CONAPREV have made to Honduran prisons, are included. The report does, importantly, estimate that 85% of the Honduran inmates are in a state of *autogobierno* (government by inmates, not by authorities), but the origins of this calculation are not made explicit. The document gives an extended list of recommendations, many of which are very general and deal with planning activities. For instance, the report recommends that the National Penitentiary Institute 'carry out in a responsible and opportune manner its annual budget . . . with adequate personnel . . . and under the guidelines of a previously adopted plan', such as the 2013–2022 plan that MNP-CONAPREV created with the European Union in 2013 (p. 43). The *IV Informe Anual* document contains, in its first pages, the past four years' budget for MNP-CONAPREV in a summary chart (p. 9).

There was no evidence in the two reports consulted of citations from evidence-based practice research.

Transnational Relations

The most important transnational or international relation by far for the national penitentiary system in Honduras is that forged between reformers in the country and prison reformers in the Dominican Republic. Collaboration with Dr Roberto Santana, a prison reformer in the Dominican Republic, was particularly useful for the Hondurans. Colonel Garcia believes that the Dominican Republic system is functioning at a much higher level than is the Honduran system. While Honduras has a recidivism rate of 48%, that of the Dominican Republic is only 2%. In the Dominican Republic, reformers not only increased prison capacity through the construction of new prisons, but they were also successful in getting criminal court judges to sentence fewer defendants to prison time. 'How did you do this?' the Hondurans asked the Dominicans. While the Dominican reformers found their criminal court judges reluctant to change their sentencing, the reformers were able to convince Supreme Court justices, who then forced lower courts to lower their use of prison for guilty verdicts. The diagnostic report for Honduras that Santana and his team produced has an eight-axis strategy for the reform of the Honduran system, and, importantly, there is a budget estimate for the implementation of the plan. Colonel Garcia emphasises time and time again the importance of the budget estimates being an integral part of the diagnostic plan: 'This is not just a plan of recommendations without a budget. There is an estimate of how much each component costs for this,' he said.

Other international collaborations mentioned included the assistance that the International Red Cross (ICRC) has given the Honduran National Penitentiary system in introducing electricity and water into some prisons where these services were lacking or deficient. The ICRC provided assistance in organising firefighting teams (*bomberos*), and, in fact, it was after the Comayagua fire that ICRC began working in Honduras with the explicit goal of improving fire safety in Honduran prisons.[13] The European Economic Community (EEC) provided legal analysis to Honduran prison managers, and Honduran officials have plans to travel to Argentina to learn from that country's security forces. This is what Colonel Garcia calls 'south-to-south' (*sur-a-sur*) cooperation. SICA, the Inter-American Integration System (*Sistema de Integracion Interamericana*) has provided technical support in rehabilitation and social reinsertion and for the creation of an electronic database of inmate information (*digitalizacion sistema*). There are a host of organisations, both international and local, that provide human rights assessments, including the the National Committee for the Prevention of Torture, Cruel, Inhuman, or Degrading Treatments (MNP-CONAPREV) mentioned above, the Center for the Prevention, Treatment and Rehabilitation of the Victims of Torture and Their Friends (CPTRT), the Organization of the American States (OAS), and the United Nations Development Programme (UNDP). The Honduran Red Cross, as distinguished from the International Red Cross, provides services for the prison system including medical services for the prevention and treatment of tuberculosis and HIV-AIDS,[14] improving the nutrition of inmates' diets, self-esteem classes (*auto-estima*), classes on a 'culture of peace' (*cultura de paz*), and consciousness raising exercises (*concientizar a las personas*).[15]

While not a 'transnational relation', other sectors of the Honduran government play an important role at times for the prison sector in the country. For instance, INFOP, the National Institute of Professional Education, provided computers and training for the La Tamara prison so that the prison could offer computer literacy classes for inmates.

General Assessments

Having only been in the job since May, Colonel Garcia seemed well informed about the complex organisation he oversaw. His information was, on the whole, accurate, and he seemed forthcoming in the interview.

Colonel Garcia was right when he asserted that the public trusted the military more than other major institutions in the country. The surveys from the Latin American Public Opinion Project (LAPOP) found that, in 2012, Protestant churches (*Iglesia Evangelica*, 63%) and the Catholic Church (63%) were the public institutions that had the most trust from a representative sample of Hondurans, followed closely by the military (*ejercito*, 48%). The national police were the least trusted (29%), and the justice system (*Sistema de Justicia*) had the trust of 37% of the respondents (Perez, 2013, p. 135). Similarly, the local advocacy group, CPTRT, found that police were more likely to be the perpetrators of torture than the military by a factor of from 3:1 to 10:1 during the period 2009 to 2014, where torture was defined as

> any action by which a public functionary or other person directed by the public functionary intentionally inflicts on a person punishments (*penas*) or severe suffering (*sufrimientos graves*), whether these actions be physical or mental, with the goal being to obtain from the person or a third party information or a confession, or to punish the person for an act already committed or suspected to have been committed, or to intimidate this person or others. (Galeano & Tabora, 2015, pp. 14, 133, 156–157)

Based on news reports, Colonel Garcia's estimates of the inmate capacity of the four new prisons under construction was accurate,[16] and so was his estimate of the number of employees working for the National Penitentiary Institute. In an interesting exchange, Colonel Garcia defended his estimation of the size of the workforce when challenged. He had said '1,700' in the interview, but one report estimated the size to be 1,354 (Santana & Romero, p. 90). When Colonel Garcia was asked in a follow-up interview, one of his employees, overhearing the conversation, made a phone call to get the exact number. The number was 1,619, much closer to Colonel Garcia's estimate than to that of the report: 'I knew it was in this range,' he said. 'I knew this because I just signed off on the payment of salaries' (*Pagué hace poco la planilla*)!

The assessment of the severity of the security situation by both Colonel Garcia and Lieutenant Colonel Sandoval seemed reasonable. My tour of La Tamara prison was originally scheduled for a morning, but had to be postponed because an 'operation' was being undertaken. I completed the tour in the afternoon. Newspaper reports from the following day clarified that 100 soldiers from the National Inter-institutional Security Force (*La Fuerza de Seguridad Interinstitucional Nacional*, Fusina) had conducted a raid in La Tamara in which 'only one pistol' was confiscated,[17] and this had occurred just at the time I was scheduled to go into the prison. Additionally, security officials in La Tamara carry weapons with live ammunition, a policy that I have not seen elsewhere in the US, Mexico, or India.

Similarly, the overcrowding mentioned by Colonel Garcia is immediately evident upon doing a tour of La Tamara. In one sleeping bay in the prison, one sees 12 occupied bunks separated by a narrow corridor in a tight space. The visual appearance of these inmate sleeping accommodations did not appear to be that of a prison so much as that of a submarine.

Some facts and figures mentioned were unverifiable, or possibly inaccurate. The 48% recidivism rate for the Honduran prison system and the 2% recidivism rate for the Dominican prison system that Colonel Garcia mentioned could not be verified. The 2% recidivism rate for the Dominican Republic, moreover, seems unlikely. The driver for the La Tamara tour seemed to think that there was cell phone blocking equipment in the prison, though Colonel Garcia had commented that this equipment did not exist or was inadequate.

On the whole, Colonel Garcia and Lieutenant Colonel Sandoval seemed knowledgeable and forthcoming.

Conclusion

The spectre of the Comayagua disaster haunts the Honduran prison system and has given reformers a special licence to make changes. Perceptions of the causes of the fire are relevant for reformers. One interpretation of the fire was that civilians had managed the prison system since 1998 and had badly mismanaged them, leaving up to 85% of inmates in a state of self-government. Fiefdoms based on gang affiliations, legal status, status as a former police or military man within the walls of the prisons made it impossible to implement uniform safety policies, such as evacuation procedures and fire extinguisher introduction and maintenance. When an inmate set a mattress on fire in the Comayagua prison, this led to the great catastrophe that cost 360 human lives. An alternative conspiracy theory repeated by a prominent human rights activist, was that authorities had intentionally set the fire to reduce the inmate population. There is not one shred of evidence that this second theory is true, but, whatever the cause, the Comayagua fire of 2012 forced authorities to seriously focus on improving the prison system.[18]

Given the context, the reforms that are being made seem reasonable and salutary. Many of the reforms, such as the construction of the four new prisons and the creation of a national penitentiary worker academy, were not the brainchildren of the military, but are, nonetheless, initiatives that will probably benefit from the management effectiveness of the military leadership in the short run. Other changes, such as the implementation of fire safety regimes and procedures, employee vetting (*depuracion*), centralised cash control, and removal and concentration of some inmate leaders are likely policies of military authorship, and on the whole benefit the system.

The great future challenge the Honduran prison system faces is to make the transition from the current stewardship of the military to a civilian-led arrangement that avoids the pitfalls of previous civilian leadership in the sector. This is a complex question that only the Hondurans can answer, but, on some level, it seems that there must be an institutional synthesis that balances, on the one hand, a civilian leadership, including an emphasis on human rights and rehabilitation programmes, with, on the other hand, a robust and functional security system.[19]

The most important reforms are being made by Honduran government officials, whether military or civilian, from within government. There are a number of external groups with an interest in some facet of the prison sector, and government officials make opportunistic use of resources and expertise that these groups sometimes provide. But these modest contributions by external groups should be put into context. For instance, one major international philanthropic group (i.e., NGO) has four full-time employees dedicated to prison reform in the country, while the Honduran prison system itself has 1,600 employees.

Scholars who write in the tradition of evidence-based practice have an opportunity in the coming decades to influence the development of rehabilitation programmes in Honduras. This is so because there is a desire for, and commitment to, rehabilitation (*reinseercion social*) among several influential groups managing the prison system. Furthermore, the fluid and reform-orientated nature of the Honduran system as it exists today seems to favour the insinuation of novel research and practices.

However, evidence-based practice scholars should be sober in their assessment of the relative priorities of Honduran prison managers. The system is experiencing nothing less than a total reconfiguration today, and basic issues such as the structure of senior leadership, new prison construction, the creation of a civil service system and professional career track for penitentiary workers, and basic safety issues take priority over nuanced approaches to configuring rehabilitation programmes. The evidence-based practice literature has developed in mature prison systems that are seeking to refine approaches to rehabilitation, and some of its conclusions about 'what works' would surely have to be adapted to the local conditions.

Four recommendations seem reasonable based on the Honduras case. First, translations of select evidence-based practice publications to Spanish would be a necessary condition for influence in Honduras. Spanish is the only effective language in the country. There is a small bilingual English-speaking policy group involved in prison policy in Honduras, but its impact is very limited, and any broadly effective policy information would have to be accessible to various Spanish-language-only groups involved in prison policy in the country.

Second, evidence-based practice scholars should identify areas of the literature most of interest to the Hondurans. For instance, leaders complained about both the lack of post-incarceration programmes for inmates and the lack of a link between existing private post-incarceration programmes and the formal prison system.

Third, evidence-based practice scholars should look for strategic partners operating in Honduras. The American Corrections Association (ACA), which has been very influential in Mexico (Norris, 2015), was not found to be present at all in Honduras. In contrast, the International Red Cross, the United Nations Development Program, and the Organization of American States, all groups with headquarters in Washington, DC, were present and influential in the prison sector in Honduras. Any long-term initiative to influence the intellectual landscape of the prison sector in the country must also incorporate the National Autonomous University of Honduras (UNAH). UNAH plays a key and dominant role in the formation of the country's elite, at least in the central and Pacific regions of the country. For instance, Lieutenant Colonel Sandoval himself received a Bachelor's in business administration and a Master's in finance from UNAH. Intellectual reformers would need to determine which units within the university might be amenable to curriculum reform.

Fourth, evidence-based practice scholars serious about engagement in Honduras should conceive of their project as a long-term endeavour. Institutional reform takes decades, not years. Institutional engagement by evidence-based practice scholars in Honduras would require not only appropriate manoeuvres by this relatively cohesive scholarly group, but also the maturation of the Honduran prison system itself.

Glossary

18: 18th Street Gang, one of two major gang affiliations in Honduras. The other is MS-13, Mara Salvatrucha or 13th Street gang.
Autogobierno: Self-government, i.e., the condition in Honduran prisons in which inmates control substantial operations in the prison.
CETSP: Comision Especial de Transicion del Sistema Penitenciario, Special Commission for the Transition of the Penitentiary System.
CIDH: Comision Interamericana de Derechos Humanos, Interamerican Commission on Human Rights.
Conquistador: Spanish conqueror in the 16th century.
CONADEH: Comision Nacional de Derechos Humanos, National Human Rights Commission.
Condenado: An inmate who has received a criminal sentence from a Honduran criminal court.
CPTRT: Centro de Prevencion, Tratamiento y Rehabilitacion de Victimas de Tortura, Center for the Prevention, Treatment and Rehabilitation of the Victims of Torture.
CICR: Comité Internacional de la Cruz Roja, International Committee of the Red Cross.

CIDH: Comision Interamericana de Derechos Humanos, Interamerican Commission for Human Rights, a human rights commission associated with the Organization of American States (OAS).
***Defensa publica*:** Public defender, an autonomous unit in the Honduran government, not just a specialisation in the court system, as in the US.
***Encomienda*:** A grant of indigenous people to Spanish caretakers starting in the 16th century.
***Fusina*:** La Fuerza de Seguridad Interinstitucional Nacional, National Inter-institutional Security Force.
***Hacinamiento*:** Prison overpopulation.
ICRC: International Committee of the Red Cross.
INFOP: Instituto Nacional de Formacion Profesional, National Institute of Professional Education, a national government agency promoting modern technology and management practices within government.
INP: Instituto Nacional Penitenciario, National Penitentiary Institute.
La Tamara Prison: A multi-sectioned set of prison complexes housing about 4,300 inmates, or approximately 29% of Honduras's inmate population situated one hour from Tegucigalpa.
***Ladino*:** Mestizo, or Spanish speaker of mixed European and indigenous heritage.
***Mestizaje*:** Miscegenation between European and indigenous groups.
***Ministerio public*:** Attorney general's office.
MNP-CONAPREV: Comité Nacional de Prevencion Contra la Tortura, Tratos Crueles, Inhumanos o Degradantes, National Committee for Prevention of Torture, Cruel, Inhumane or Degrading Treatment.
MS-13: Mara Salvatrucha, or 13th Street gang, one of two major gang affiliations. The other is 18th Street gang.
OCS: Officer Candidate School, a US military training programme, at the end of which successful students are commissioned as officers.
***Personas privadas de libertad*:** People deprived of liberty, inmates.
***Poder judicial*:** Judicial branch of government.
Positivism: The belief in the application of rational and scientific principles to issues of material wellbeing and public policy, influential in Central America as early as the 1850s, and derived from the thinking of Auguste Comte and Herbert Spencer. Akin to the cientificos of Porfirio Diaz in Mexico.
***Procesado*:** 'Processed' but not sentenced inmate.
***Pulpería*:** Sundries store, in La Tamara, owned by individual inmates.
***Reinserción*:** Rehabilitation.
***Sentenciado*:** An inmate with a sentence from a criminal court.
***Secretaria de Seguridad*:** Secretariat of Security, or Defence Ministry, a civilian government entity tasked with defence issues, created in the late 1990s.

SDHJGD: Secretaria de Derechos Humanos, Justicia, Gobernacion, y Decentralizacion, Secretariat of Human Rights, Justice, Government, and Decentralisation, akin to an interior ministry.

SICA: Sistema de Integracion Interamericana, Inter-American Integration System, a multilateral initiative in Central America for governments to share technical procedures and promote integration.

UNAH: Universidad Nacional Autonoma de Honduras, National Autonomous University of Honduras.

Notes

1 For information on the whird Wave, see Huntington (1991).
2 CIA World Factbook, 'Honduras'." www.cia.gov/library/publications/the-world-factbook/geos/ho.html, accessed 19 August 2015.
3 'Languages of Honduras: Extracted from *Ethnologue*, Seventeenth Edition.' www.ethnologue.com/sites/default/files/17-Report-HN.pdf, accessed 19 August 2015.
4 World Bank World Development Indicators Online, URL: http://databank.worldbank.org/data/reports.aspx?source=world-development-indicators#, accessed 19 August 2015.
5 See Table 3.4, Carga de trabajo judicial, for estimates of numbers of judges per capita.
6 Data are synthesised from Santana and Romero (2015); CIDH (2013); MNP-CONAPREV, *Informe Annual a la Nacion* (Tegucigalpa: MNP-CONAPREV, 2014); and one unpublished report. Data on the number of employees in the system came from Colonel Garcia.
7 All translations from Spanish to English are mine.
8 In fact, the military, which had only left power in 1980, still controlled police forces and effectively controlled the prison sector until 1998. See also Ungar (2011, pp. 105–173).
9 Other citations on the walls of La Tamara included Psalms 7:10, Proverbs 16:6, Proverbs 22:16, Proverbs 29:15, Genesis 22:14, and Revelation 20:1-3.
10 Professional researchers are dedicated human resources employed by multilateral organisations, such as the United Nations Development Program, or consulting firms. Academics' research agenda might overlap with that of researchers, but academics hold appointments at universities and have teaching duties.
11 Note that Cuba has produced its own criminological text, apparently in autarky, that is, without acknowledging that it replicates the efforts of others across time and space (Navarrete Calderon, 2006). Because Honduras, unlike Cuba, is an open society, it is unlikely that Honduras's academics are completely ignorant of criminological analytical traditions outside the country, but more research needs to be done to ascertain the state of knowledge in the country on these topics.
12 See Schmalleger (2013, pp. 21, 22–24) for a description of evidence-based practice.
13 This last bit of information was obtained from an interview with the ICRC on 24 July.
14 A rough estimate is that 1% of the Honduran population might be HIV-positive, and 3% of the prison population might be positive. Epidemiologists and careful analysts note there are several problems in estimating the HIV-positive population in Honduran prisons.

15 Interviews with Honduran Red Cross, 22 August 2015.
16 'Honduras: En 24 meses, mas de 5,000 reclusos seran trasladados a nuevos centros,' *El Heraldo* (13 March 2015). www.elheraldo.hn/alfrente/821969-209/honduras-en-24-meses-m%C3%A1s-de-5000-reclusos-ser%C3%A1n-trasladados-a-nuevos, accessed 20 August 2015.
17 "Operativo de Fusina: Solo una pistol decomisan en la Penitenciaria Nacional," *La Tribuna* (24 July 24), p. 102.
18 It should be noted that neither Honduras nor the prison system in general is unique in suffering this sort of tragedy. The Ycua Bolaños supermarket fire in Asuncion, Paraguay in 2005 claimed 400 lives. See "Once años del Ycua, con una misa" *ABC Paraguay* (31 July 2015). www.abc.com.py/edicion-impresa/locales/once-anos-del-ycua-con-una-misa-1393433.html, accessed 21 August 2015. To avoid pilfering and shoplifting, the supermarket had only one entry and exit point, and this proved disastrous during the fire. Such institutions can be characteristic of societies that possess low social capital, or are 'low trust' societies. See Fukuyama (1995).
19 See Norris (2018) for a description of how some prison administrations are characterised by such balance, while others are not.

Section IV

Asia

Chapter 8

Satoshi Tomiyama, Director-General of the Japanese Correction Bureau

Interviewer: Carol Lawson

Contents

Overview	127
Introduction	130
Career	130
Changes Experienced	132
Personal Correctional Philosophy	135
Problems and Successes Experienced	138
Theory and Practice	140
Evidence-Based Corrections	141
Transnational Relations	143
Role of Corrections	145
General Assessments	146
Conclusion	147
Glossary	148

Overview

Structure of the Prison System

The Japanese penal system consists of 184 institutions in all, evenly distributed across eight penal regions. These 184 facilities comprise 76 (68 main and eight branch) prisons for convicted offenders, and 108 (eight main and 100 branch) detention houses for pre-trial detainees and those on death row. The 68 main prisons are divided into two broad categories: six juvenile prisons, and 62 adult prisons. The 62 adult prisons comprise 52 mainstream adult male prisons divided into just two security classifications, Category A for 'those whose criminal tendencies are not yet confirmed' and Category B for 'those with confirmed criminal tendencies'. The remaining ten institutions are six women's prisons, and four medical prisons.

There are also 103 juvenile facilities (94 main and nine branch) nationwide, comprising 52 juvenile classification homes and 51 juvenile training schools, and a single women's guidance home. Pre-charge detention is largely outside the purview of the Correction Bureau, with suspects held in police cells historically known as 'substitute prisons'.

Japan's extraordinarily low incarceration rate, and leniency were described by Foote as 'benevolent paternalism' (1992, p. 317). The incarceration rate stood at just 41 per 100,000 at the end of July 2018 (Institute for Criminal Policy Research, 2019). Although over 1.05 million crimes were referred to prosecutors in 2017, the practice of maintaining the historical 99% conviction rate (Ramseyer & Rasmussen, 2001) by only pursuing matters where a conviction can be secured meant they declined to prosecute in 65% of cases (Ministry of Justice, 2018: 2-1-1; Table 2-2). Of the 299,319 criminal matters prosecuted, just 52,252 resulted in a custodial sentence. Over 93% of those sentences were for three years or less, and 62% were wholly suspended, leaving just under 20,000 custodial sentences imposed (Ministry of Justice, 2018: Table 2-3-3-1; Table 2-3-2-3). Further, in 2016, new legislation made the partial suspension of sentences possible (Japan Times Online, 2016c).

Current Correctional Standards

Japanese prisons are remarkably safe, with reported security incidents of all kinds at negligible levels for several decades. However, they are also inherently frugal, militaristic, harsh and industrial in nature. Reforms to the anachronistic 1908 *Prison Act* were stymied across the postwar era by a political deadlock (Lawson, 2015, pp. 134–137). However, the Nagoya Prison Scandal, which broke in late 2002, finally led to reforms after 97 years of stasis. These reforms were completed in 2006.

The Ministry of Justice reported its analysis of a million recorded convictions across the postwar period in a special feature in the 2007 *White Paper on Crime*. While the crime rate had continued to drop, it was shown that '. . . around 30% of . . . repeat offenders . . . were responsible for about 60% of all offences' (Ministry of Justice, 2007: 7-6-1). This struck a particular chord with the media, Diet (Japanese legislature) members and the public, as the percentage of those entering prison who were repeat offenders had been rising since 2004, and would continue to rise to a disturbing 59.4% in 2017 (Ministry of Justice, 2018a: Figure 5-2-3-1). It should be noted that this statistic is not a measure of recidivism; Japanese recidivism rates are low and falling.

A raft of further reforms then began under the Democratic Party of Japan's rule in 2012, and these reforms have been ramped up considerably in recent years under the second Shinzo Abe administration. After Japan was announced as the host of the 2020 Summer Olympics, the Abe government reinvigorated an existing government-wide body, the Ministerial Meeting Concerning Measures against Crime (Prime Minister of Japan, 2017) to achieve the 'soft power' objective of ensuring Japan remains the 'safest country in the world'. This has now prompted legal and regulatory reforms designed to reduce recidivism at almost every stage of the criminal justice process: policing, prosecution and probation. Two crucial results for correctional standards have been the rapid resolution of prison overcrowding, and integration of police, prosecution, prison and probation databases for the first time, so as to make Throughcare (coordinated support for an offender from the start of a sentence right through to their reintegration into society) possible. It was finally announced in late December 2016 that these reforms will extend to prison conditions as well (Japan Times Online, 2016a). From a larger perspective, the reforms since 2012 in particular signal a gradual transition away from Japan's historically retributive approach and the increase in popular punitivism noted by Johnson early in the new millennium (2007) which lead to the overcrowding in the first place, towards a therapeutic ethos in the corrections system.

Current Correctional Standards

A forceful driver behind this gradual shift away from a retributive ethos and towards the reform of prison conditions is Japan's rapidly aging population, complicated by a formal rejection of immigration. These combined factors make the full rehabilitation of offenders and their reintegration into the workforce increasingly attractive, and mean that Japanese prisons, once run by a steady supply of healthy young prison labour, can no longer operate as they have done. In 2017, 63.6% of all prisoners were aged 40 years or more, and 11.8% were aged 65 years or more, while for female prisoners these figures were worse, at 69.3% and 19.7% respectively (Ministry of Justice, 2018: Figure 7-3-4-1). Some prisons are already aged care homes in all but name (Brasor, 2017).

In concrete terms, overcrowding was resolved by enhancing already exemplary diversionary practices and increasing capacity through commissioning four private finance initiative (PFI) prisons as well as falling crime rates. The overcrowding peaked at 106.5%, or roughly 69,500 prisoners, around the time of the Nagoya Prison Scandal arrests in 2002, but, by 2007, had already fallen to under 100% of capacity, and further precipitous drops in male prisoners recently have brought this figure to an astounding 60% overall, or roughly 53,233 prisoners (Ministry of Justice, 2018: Table 2-4-1-2),[1] with work in progress to repurpose male prisons for women, and convert Nara Juvenile Prison into a hotel (Japan Times Online, 2014, 2016b).

Meanwhile, the prisoner to corrections officer ratio, which peaked at 4.8 prisoners per corrections officer in 2006, fell to 2.92 in 2016, below the 1997 level of 3.0 prisoners per corrections officer (Ministry of Justice, 2017: 2-4-1-2). At interview, Director-General Tomiyama quoted internal Correction Bureau figures showing a 10% increase in the number of corrections officers over the ten years to 2015 to a total workforce of 19,634, and a 50% increase in the number undergoing training at the Training Institute for Corrections Personnel (TICP) over the past five years. A larger staff training facility was to be opened in 2017.

Introduction

Mr Tomiyama was kind enough to engage with the interview questions across several stages in May 2016, both in writing and face-to-face. All communication was conducted in Japanese. My translation of Mr Tomiyama's responses was approved by the Correction Bureau.

Career

Mr Tomiyama was only the second career corrections officer to be appointed as Correction Bureau Director-General in Japan.[2] He entered the Correction Bureau on the 'fast track' in April 1981 after passing the Senior Civil Service Exam in his final year of university. His 35-year career demonstrated the frequent rotation to ensure thorough exposure to all aspects of an agency's work that is typical of a 'fast-track' civil service career in Japan. He served in a diverse range of managerial, policy and educational roles at Kawagoe Juvenile Prison, the Tokyo Detention House, Nagano Prison, the Training Institute for Correctional Personnel, Sapporo Regional Headquarters and the Correction Bureau Headquarters in Tokyo, not to mention an early secondment to the Probation Bureau and a senior role in the Secretariat of the Minister of Justice.

Crucially, he worked on the special project team that investigated the Nagoya Prison Scandal, which prompted the first prison reforms in 97 years after coming to light in 2002. Then, from April 2003, he began a four-year stint as a key figure in the ensuing reform process. This began with the role of Correction Bureau liaison for CARC, the Correctional Administration Reform Council, which was the body of eminent persons charged with redesigning Japan's corrections regime that met for eight months in 2003. He then oversaw all legislative personnel, as well as the drafting and implementation of the new prisons legislation that resulted: the *Act on Penal Detention Facilities and Treatment of Inmates and Detainees* (Act No. 50 of 2005). He rose to senior executive roles from 2008.

Q: What motivated you to enter corrections?
A: A criminal policy seminar I took in my third year at university had a significant impact on me. It was with Professor Tetsuya Fujimoto, a very famous criminal policy scholar, and we learned about the realities of correctional administration through activities like visits to prisons. I was particularly motivated at the time by something

that the Warden of Chiba Prison said. He'd been a trainee pilot in the Imperial Japanese Navy's pilot training course, and would have died on a *kamikaze* mission had the end of the war come a single day later. He'd lived his life feeling cowardly for having survived.

Working in penal institutions, he felt that this was the place where the dregs of this world gather. They may be at rock bottom [in society], but this doesn't necessarily mean that they're the bottom in terms of their humanity. He'd played *shōgi* [Japanese chess] with a detainee[3] the day before he was to be executed, and was overwhelmed by the man's composure.[4] Human beings can be noble and can also be depraved, irrespective of the circumstances. He said that since we were elite students from the Chuo University Faculty of Law, we may well become judges or prosecutors. But it's in penal institutions that we would find the essence of humanity; that it was a workplace worthy of a man investing his life, and that we should listen to the ramblings of an old man.

Q: Did your work prove as interesting or rewarding as you thought it would?

A: I think this work has been even more interesting and meaningful than I'd expected . . . I've grown fond of corrections officers, who struggle in a melting pot of all different types of humanity . . . they're everyday people, doing their best . . . Corrections officers tend to have a relatively low level of education . . . Currently, around half of them have a college degree, but when I was first hired 70–80% of prison guards only had high school diplomas. But they give their all to their work. I felt this was a really great workplace for me. I still feel really glad that I'm able to work with these people. So I wanted to improve this workplace, even a little . . . I feel my work has been very meaningful.

Q: Do you have any regrets about opportunities you did or did not have during your career?

A: Naturally there have been any number of things that I've had to be patient with, but I've reflected on them and accepted that I need to persevere, so have no regrets.

Q: Did the way your career developed surprise you?

One surprise, and perhaps a source of chagrin, was that Mr Tomiyama's elevation to his first senior executive role in April 2008 cut short his first appointment as Warden, at Nara Juvenile Prison, in which he had served just six days. Another came from a ground-breaking appointment in January 2013 as the first corrections officer to be put in charge of all aspects of all MoJ facilities nationwide. This opportunity brought several entirely new perspectives. The first two were the need to balance security specifications with budgetary needs, to ensure facilities were secure *enough* without excess expenditure, and the need to provide corrections officers with spacious housing and pleasant workplaces, to avoid imposing undue stress. But the most important was the potentially therapeutic relationship between prison buildings and their occupants:

A: I've had the opportunity to hear how the features of buildings can influence the way people feel in a variety of ways... To illustrate, entering a cathedral makes one feel reverence. Until then I'd primarily seen buildings and facilities from the perspective of security performance (holding capacity, the ease with which the inside of a cell can be observed, a cell door's sturdiness, the length of the movement route from cell to factory floor, the number of blind spots along the way where a prisoner could hide, availability of multiple movement routes to keep feuding prisoners apart). But gaining this perspective... has been surprising. I felt that we should communicate our needs better to architects – not in the sense of frontline corrections officers saying that they want particular types of rooms, but in the sense of communicating the kinds of correctional treatment we want to carry out, and asking what kind of building design would be best...

For example, in a particular Juvenile Training Home, they made the hallways a bit wider, created a space with a lot of light and put in a park bench. This facilitates communication between corrections officers and juveniles by offering a casual space where they can sit and talk together... Hearing this a lot, I felt as if I'd wasted some opportunities in the past.

Changes Experienced

Q: What do you see as the most important changes in the field of corrections over your career?

The Nagoya Prison Scandal reforms of 2005 produced the first substantive changes to Japanese corrections since 1908 (Lawson, 2015, pp. 144–151). Mr Tomiyama's thoughtful, candid response to this question highlights an attitudinal schism in the corrections service. In his view, this schism was behind the scandal, where eight guards were charged in the deaths of two prisoners, and permanent internal injuries to a third:

A: The most important changes... have been the Nagoya Prison Scandal reforms, which have, in a real sense, made the rehabilitation and reintegration of prisoners the primary aim of corrections for the first time. On the surface, the objectives of prisons are to rehabilitate and reintegrate prisoners into society . . . But, in reality, until the Nagoya Prison Scandal, the key priorities were secure custody and maintaining discipline and order. I don't think this is wrong thinking at all. To properly rehabilitate and reintegrate prisoners into society, you have to prevent them from escaping . . . and to provide education you have to maintain discipline and order . . .

But if the only thing in your head is secure custody and maintaining discipline and order, and you think that as long as these two conditions are met nothing else matters, that could lead to a punitive culture. If rehabilitation becomes secondary, the point of incarceration is lost . . . I think there were both rehabilitation-focused and discipline-focused corrections officers at Nagoya Prison. Everyone may have been saying that they wanted to do rehabilitation, and societal reintegration properly. But . . . corrections officers were probably split into these two camps, and there tend to be more discipline-focused officers who work on site at prisons.

Obviously, a corrections officer wouldn't do anything that might put himself or herself at risk, but this thinking gradually becomes extreme. There's been a lot of commentary in Japan, triggered by the Nagoya Prison Scandal, say on the regulations on prisoner movements from the cell blocks to the factory floor, where prisoners are made to march in step in lines, chanting '1, 2, 1, 2.' . . . The usual pattern is '1, 2, 1, 2' but the command is often given for a military pattern, '1, 2, 1, 2, 1, 2, 3, 4, 1, 2, 3, 4' . . . There was a time when people walked from their room to the factory in small groups as they liked. But . . . everyone was talking as they walked and some *yakuza* [Japanese mafia] types would swagger along ordering others out of their way. So there'd be fights and arguments, and things would get out of control. This is why first they get them to line up. And if they're chanting, they can't chat among themselves. And if they keep a certain distance as they move, no one can say someone touched their shoulder or that something touched them, and it prevents that kind of trouble-making. So . . . the marching has value . . .

But then . . . gradually, everyone starts to listen and march obediently. And then, commands turn into, 'Raise your arm from here to here – the full 90 degrees!' or 'Don't hold your fingers like that, extend them like this!' . . . Where's the value in that? It's excessive, but that's what ends up happening. [Some officers want to abolish these excessive commands but] others argue that 'It's better this way, because this way even if they slack off a bit the level is still acceptable' . . . So this meant that, at that time, there were these two different ways of thinking, and . . . well, it was like they were in opposition to one another. The Nagoya Prison Scandal was a turning point in terms of this internal difference in approach.

Q: What changes in external conditions have had a significant impact on current correctional practices and policy?

Mr Tomiyama describes the 'social panic' that gripped Japan across the winter of 2001–2002 when the Nagoya Prison Scandal broke as 'intense media and Diet [Japanese legislature] attention that necessitated a Ministry-wide response'. He then reflects on another dimension to the schism within the Correction Bureau that led to this tipping point. This was tension between the more progressive policies favoured by Correction Bureau Headquarters in Tokyo and frontline corrections officers who were resistant to even gradual change:

A: Actually, even before the Nagoya Prison Scandal happened, the Correction Bureau's Custodial Division gave instructions at prisons to stop this kind of over-the-top stuff, like these instructions of what to do with their hands – that it was unnecessary, that although it was okay to have them march, that doing this over-the-top stuff would incite rebellion . . . So they were actively making efforts like this to say: 'Let's not do this any more', you see? The thing was, as I said earlier, there were opposing forces in there too, and so they would say things such as: 'But, you see, that may sound good on paper, but here on site at prisons, things are not that easy.' Of course, we would try to tell them we used to be on site at prisons, too. Obviously things couldn't change right away, but it was clear that everyone intended to change things . . . the young officers especially . . . So, we thought that, over time, even the stubborn wardens . . . would stop after a while, and that things would probably change gradually. I suppose that you could say that what happened was that, instead, an outside force changed things all at once . . .

Q: Overall, has the quality of prisons in your country improved or declined over the past ten years?

The extraordinary focus on order, frugality and productivity in Japanese prisons gradually led to the virtual eradication of reported security incidents. Mr Tomiyama notes annual escapees reached single figures in 1971 and have hovered near zero since 1982. But he acknowledges that this was due to 'overly strict discipline', and that the challenge since the 2005–2006 reforms has been to maintain this almost perfect level of security while gradually increasing prisoners' freedoms.

He is generally sanguine about qualitative improvements in Japanese corrections over the past decade, pointing to several accomplishments, notably the rapid resolution of overcrowding, which will be the envy of correctional regimes everywhere. He also notes that the 2006 reforms led to the creation of six new prison programmes targeting drug dependency, *yakuza* [Japanese mafia] gang affiliation, sex offending and traffic offending, and teaching work skills and empathy for victims. A further three smaller programmes were added around five years ago to assist rehabilitation from alcohol dependency and violent offending, and support reintegration. Overall numbers participating have increased year on year, despite the falling prison population. The drug dependency programme is the largest, with around 11,000 prisoners involved at 75 prisons, while the sex offender programme is the smallest, with roughly 500 prisoners involved at 21 prisons (Ministry of Justice, 2018: Table 2-4-2-3).

Turning to reported security incidents, escapes, serious assaults on corrections officers, and assaults on prisoners causing death, as well as workplace and accidental fatalities, have remained near zero across the past decade. Prisoner suicides have remained stable at between ten and 25 annually, while serious assaults on prisoners have declined from 25 incidents in 2006 to single figures in recent years (Ministry of Justice, 2018: Table 2-4-3-1).

Mr Tomiyama further noted the lack of additional budgetary allocation, commenting that:

A: Although honestly we would like more money, if we start saying that there's no end...We're being looked after fairly well given Japan's harsh financial circumstances...
Q: In general, is it more or less difficult to be a correctional officer now?

Here, Mr Tomiyama describes the workplace implications of the watershed change that has begun in Japanese corrections. The existing workforce must adapt to the relative complexity of modern correctional practices.

A: My sense is that it's more difficult now. All that was required in the past was to give absolute priority to maintaining discipline and order inside the institution. Now they have to achieve the rehabilitation and smooth reintegration of prisoners as well, while giving ample consideration to other priorities like building links with the local community... They need to have a sense of balance to correctly juggle a range of different factors in their decision making.

Personal Correctional Philosophy

Q: What do you think should be the role of custodial and community supervision officers in society?
A: Obviously it's important for each custodial officer... to carry out their duties in a professional manner. And we need those who work in the community and look after prisoners after their release to prepare properly for them to work in the community. These two

roles must be closely linked. What we hope is for custodial officers to not only do their work inside the prison, but to also build trust in penal institutions through their personal attitudes and by communicating accurate information to the community . . . And we expect more . . . from corrections managers, because it's part of their job to speak to the media or in the community.

Q: What organisational arrangements work and which do not?

Japanese corrections officers are highly trained and well supervised, and Mr Tomiyama was quick to express confidence in their overall ability and the quality of leadership within the Bureau and at prisons. In his view, organisational success depends on three factors: 'robust' leaders, 'capable staff' and a 'shared sense of purpose'. He elaborated on the need, however, for better internal dynamics:

A: The most important factor is leadership – and it's also essential for corrections officers to be able to communicate their ideas freely to each other (what we call 'good ventilation') . . . If this doesn't exist, it will make things rigid and make the organisation a difficult place to belong to, which honestly I think is a problem in Japanese penal institutions. By nature, Japanese are poor at stating their opinions and have a lot of trouble telling others that they're wrong. On top of this, the organisation itself is pyramid-shaped and in this hierarchical structure it takes a lot of courage for someone to tell their superiors they think something isn't right . . .

So, I'm always saying that they need to listen to opinions, even negative opinions . . . If we can truly achieve this throughout the organisation, I think this will create more open and natural relationships with mutual understanding, and this will result in less waste.

Q: How should corrections institutions be run? What programmes should be provided, and how would you prefer sentencing laws to be modified?

Mr Tomiyama's response lays out a bold personal vision for a corrections leader in a jurisdiction noted for a traditionally retributive, rather than therapeutic, view of justice. His second proposal on reducing the full-time factory work now mandatory for almost all prisoners is clearly already contemplated by recently foreshadowed regulatory reforms to prison conditions (Japan Times Online, 2016a). Further, his third suggestion is likely to encounter little resistance in that, in effect, it proposes introducing Throughcare. This would ensure that repeat offenders who currently serve their full sentence then disappear from view are monitored and assisted to at least some degree following release:

A: The mission of penal institutions is to ensure secure custody, and to influence prisoners and juvenile training school detainees.

The secret of success is for penal institutions to work out how to realise both these aims with limited human and physical resources. The programmes we deliver have to be tailored to the individual needs and characteristics of each prisoner, and contribute to their rehabilitation and smooth reintegration to society. It's ... an extremely difficult task to actually put into practice ... Japanese correctional policy is going well overall, but my personal view is that the following reforms would be worthwhile:

1) Decriminalising the personal use of drugs and imposing compulsory treatment orders instead;
2) Combining the sentences of imprisonment with work and imprisonment without work, so that we impose a duty on each prisoner to not only work, but to also receive all treatment appropriate for that person to be rehabilitated and smoothly reintegrated into society;
3) In addition to the current discretionary parole system, automatically releasing prisoners on parole when they have served four-fifths of their sentence, except for a few exceptions (where there is a high risk of serious reoffending – in that case introducing continuing detention orders to keep the offender who poses a 'threat to society' out of the community even after their sentence is complete);
4) Increasing sentencing options, including community service orders.

Q: What services should penal institutions provide that are currently not offered?

Mr Tomiyama's first focus was on external outreach to the local community:

A: I think it's important for penal institutions to make an effort to coexist with the regional community. Prisons and detention houses exist within local society, so they can't function without gaining the understanding of, and coexisting with, the local community. For example, building ties with daycare centres and retirement homes ... The prison should be open to the public as much as possible.

He then turned to what would be a groundbreaking innovation in Japan – practical training in life skills:

A: Currently, at Japanese prisons, there is a really strong focus on providing job skills training, but I'm sure there are other elements that are even more important for daily life as a member of society ... cooking meals, doing cleaning, doing laundry ... and money management. The fact is that many prisoners can't manage money. I really think they need more assistance with this, but until now it hasn't really been done properly at a Japanese prison. Women prisoners do a little, but it's rare for men . . .

There are no spaces in Japanese penal institutions to teach life skills, especially in men's facilities. For example, there is no place to cook . . . It's something I believe will become necessary . . . so how we'll go about implementing changes will be an issue for us to consider.

Problems and Successes Experienced

Q: In your experience, which corrections policies or programmes have and have not worked well, and why?

Japan's unusual history of maintaining a corrections regime predating the First World War into the new millennium has meant its foray into 'what works' has been relatively recent. Aware of this lag, the Correction Bureau began experimenting with evidence-based programmes in 2000, before the Nagoya Prison Scandal erupted in late 2002:

A: When I was hired in 1981, we had a treatment programme in prisons for stimulant addicts, but . . . the guidance we provided didn't reach addicts where they really are . . . We'd gather small groups of 10–20 prisoners in a programme that included . . . lectures, audio-visual materials, and scientific information about the harm caused by stimulants. We called on doctors and other experts to teach the programme . . . and many prisoners commented in the completion survey that they 'fully understood the dangers of stimulants now, and would never touch them again', so it looked like an incredible success. But actually this old programme had no effect.

The programme that we sense is actually effective began from around 2000 as a trial in a few penal institutions, and is now the standard Correction Bureau programme . . . This guidance programme uses the group work technique and is led by former addicts from self-help organisations. We feel that the programme reaches prisoners where they really are, because these programme providers have actually been users and have served time in prison themselves . . . It works wonderfully well for some, but not so much for others. Seeing this, we can focus on those for whom it doesn't work, or do something else, like cognitive behaviour therapy (CBT).

Q: What would you consider to be the greatest problem facing the correctional system?

A: There are three major issues, all equally serious. The first is Japan's aging corrections facilities, the second, our fragile corrections medical system due to the shortage of doctors willing to join the service, and the third the increase in cases where the way we've always done things (having prisoners work in prison and reintegrating them by providing them with a job and a place to live on release) doesn't fit due to the aging prisoner population.

A fourth issue we're just beginning to face, which is likely to become our greatest challenge, is changes in the nature of prisoners themselves. Since the introduction of our intensive nationwide effort to prevent reoffending, we've been able to get people who can be reformed out of the criminal justice system early. We're becoming more able to secure a 'place to belong' in the community for low-risk prisoners, even those who've been in and out of prison. This inevitably means that the intractable 'hard cases' will rise as a proportion of the prison population.

Given that, in Japan, most prisoners have been fairly well-behaved, we've run our institutions to be self-sufficient, with prisoners . . . cooking, serving meals, and doing washing, maintenance and repairs. But we're already finding that prisoners suited to this . . . work are running scarce, and this trend will only worsen. What is more, our prison factories operate with a single corrections officer supervising at least 50 prisoners, who are using work tools that could easily be weaponised. If a prisoner attempts to harm the corrections officer, most other prisoners will step up to protect the corrections officer . . . This kind of positive human relationship that allows us to maintain order with few staff, and, to a certain extent, means we cultivate a healthy spirit in our better prisoners. [But there is a question as to whether] this . . . is sustainable.

Q: Which corrections problems do you find the most difficult to deal with, and which easy to change?

A: The easiest problems to respond to are those we can tackle using the command system within the corrections service, like issues around organisational culture, managerial deficiencies and corruption allegations. The next most amenable category is problems we can cope with through negotiating with external bodies like the Probation Bureau – especially if there is a rigorous command system in those bodies. Conversely, the problems that are the hardest to deal with are those where these means are not available. In short, these are problems where even the question of with whom we should negotiate in order to reach a resolution is unclear. Where community support is concerned, we need to begin by searching for the right people to negotiate with, so it's harder to tackle this issue . . .

Q: What is the most successful programme you have worked with in corrections? What is the most successful policy in regards to the positive improvements that have been made to prisons?

Mr Tomiyama's response underscores the pivotal nature of the 2005–2006 prison reforms:

A: When a prisoner comes to the prison we evaluate and examine the kind of issues they face, and what needs correcting. For typical prisoners, it takes two weeks. For young first offenders, we do a thorough evaluation, which takes around two months. This scheme has helped facilitate correctional treatment – work, guidance for reform and educational guidance – tailored to each prisoner ... There was a similar system ... under the previous legislation. However, it was more perfunctory ... and corrections officers at prisons would often take a cynical view, saying prisoners were 'Classified? Yes. Treated? No.' ... Now we finally have a system where prisoners are 'classified *and* treated'. This policy was essentially the same under the old 1908 *Prison Act*, but the awareness that correctional treatment is to be tailored to each individual has permeated through frontline corrections officers much more [now].

Theory and Practice

Q: In your view, what should be the relationship between theory and practice? What can scholars and practitioners learn from each other?
A: Practice without theory is reckless, while theory without practice is hollow. Corrections practitioners should be interested in theory and have a pioneer spirit, trialling [promising] theories. And theoreticians should be careful to not lapse into 'armchair' theories that ignore the practical realities of corrections work (like the limits of human and physical resources and the laws of inertia where policy is concerned).
Q: What is the relationship between theory and practice right now? What holds collaboration or interactions back?
A: Academics and practitioners in the criminal policy field do mix ... and this relationship is stimulating for both sides, but I don't think it's particularly broad or deep ... I don't think anything is necessarily preventing cooperation and dialogue ... The main reason is that both sides are hesitant. First, on the practitioner's side, there are many who feel that academics are not necessary. In short, they think they can do it on their own ... They feel like they can do their jobs by going through the same motions every day – there is

no need to bring in academics, it's too much trouble . . . From the academic's perspective, they might feel awkward visiting because the prison is so busy. This kind of reserve is common among Japanese people . . . I think this is the main reason. We saw that this situation needed improving and the Correction Bureau established the Correctional Treatment Policy Research Group about 20 years ago.

It's not a matter of corrections officers being told what to do but rather of engaging in an exchange of opinions after all . . . corrections officers can raise issues like the risks of 'lowering the prison walls' and how these risks can be dealt with . . . My personal view is that it would be good if we could engage with academics from a broader range of disciplines.

Q: What kind of research would you find most useful for practice?
A: [. . .] Research to verify the effect of prisoners' correctional treatment comes to mind. But I also expect that research would not only meet our perceived needs for information but also provide unexpected results as academics carry out research on topics they're interested in or concerned about.
Q: Where do you find theory-based information?
A: I read materials like specialist journals, books and reports, but am basically only reading in Japanese.
Q: Does the Correction Bureau conduct research on its own? On what issues?
A: [. . .] We send a number of staff to work at the Training Institute for Correctional Personnel (TICP) every year to do research on specific practice-related themes. They produce various outputs, including practical manuals and training texts. And in recent years we've also been doing continuous work in areas like research and development in prisoner treatment programmes, the effectiveness of the treatment programmes we now use, and reoffending risk assessment tools.

Evidence-Based Corrections

Q: In your experience, has Japanese corrections made use of evidence-based programmes? Is it best to use evidence-based practices (or 'what works')?
A: We've recently begun engaging with evidence-based treatment. The programme that has been through thorough testing is our sex offenders' programme. For a long time we'd been releasing a thick volume of corrections statistics every year, so we were gathering and releasing data, but we weren't . . . measuring the effect of each prisoner's treatment on that individual, beyond carrying out

an [exit] survey of all prisoners, and asking corrections officers for their impressions.

'The best' policy is an absolute expression and at present I can't specify to that degree, but I think evidence-based corrections is very important . . . But we do also need to consider the big picture and determine whether or not these policies can actually be put into practice. I feel that practices must be selected only after considering budget, human resources, time constraints, and all other related factors – even when the potential benefit is clear.

Q: What evidence-based practices are used now in prisons, for intermediate sanctions, or in community supervision? Do you agree with these practices? Would using more evidence-based practices be a benefit?

A: I hesitate to call this an evidence-based practice – but because our rough data analysis has shown that the most effective way to prevent reoffending . . . is to make sure they have a job, and a place to live, the Japanese correctional and probation services have for some time now been striving to ensure that prisoners learn vocational skills, secure business people in the community who'll employ them . . . and match ex-offenders with these employers.

We've also published some statistically significant test results verifying the outcomes of our sex offenders' programme, and are building on this to further expand and strengthen that programme.

When we consider corrections policy, not only must each policy be reasonable and legitimate, but we need systematic coordination overall, so that what we've done so far doesn't go to waste. I wouldn't agree with relying on evidence-based practice on its own, no matter what, but, conversely, I think it's in principle correct to give serious attention to evidence-based practice as we consider policy . . .

Q: You mentioned that for some time the Correction Bureau has been ensuring prisoners acquire job skills, securing employers in the community who will hire people they know to be ex-offenders and striving to match prisoners with these employers on release. When did these efforts begin?

A: The oldest roots of this kind of idea go back to the Ishikawa Island Workhouse of the Edo Period. A samurai of relatively high rank, Heizō Hasegawa – commonly known as Heizō the Demon – institutionalised homeless men who had been rounded up to prevent them from causing trouble. It was essentially a labour camp, with residents made to learn a trade so they could be given jobs and work in the community. Modern corrections and probation practices have followed this approach from at least just after the end of the Second World War, with the Correction Bureau cultivating relationships with cooperating employers so that former prisoners can work in the community . . .

Q: Do you read information on evidence-based practices? Where do you get this information?

A: I've read the Campbell Collaboration's research reports on evidence-based corrections, in translation. The Campbell Collaboration is an international non-profit organisation that supports properly informed decision making regarding the effect of interventions in social policy (education, criminal justice, and social welfare). It was formally launched in February 2000 at the University of Pennsylvania. The stimulus for the Campbell Collaboration was the Cochrane Collaboration, a groundbreaking effort in the field of medicine. [See /www.campbellcollaboration.org/]

Transnational Relations

Q: How have you been affected in your organisation's work by developments outside Japan?

A: Our discussions with foreign correctional services – and the embassies in Japan – help in particular with improving how we treat foreign prisoners who need different treatment to that for Japanese prisoners.

The *United Nations Standard Minimum Rules on the Treatment of Prisoners* [SMR, now the *Mandela Rules*] and German criminal law had an impact on our attempts to revise the old *Prison Act* around 1980, and before that the SMR had also triggered the overhaul of the old *Prison Act Enforcement Regulations* in 1966.

We've actually had corrections officers constantly on assignment to the UN regarding the adoption of the [revised] SMR. Let me refer you to an article by Tae Sugiyama in *Keisei* [Criminal Policy], a journal published by the Japanese Correctional Association, to inform other corrections officers of how the SMR had changed (Sugiyama, 2016). Sugiyama was posted to the UN when the final decision was made.

Japan's penal institutions are run, by and large, so as to reflect the revised *Mandela Rules*, and we're not in the situation of needing to consider an immediate response. This isn't to say that we're fulfilling every clause to perfection – in future we will no doubt examine whether or not to make changes as part of the policy revision process.

Q: Have those interactions been beneficial or harmful? What kinds of external international influences are beneficial and which less so?

A: Well, I did note that the SMR requirement for at least one hour of outdoor exercise each day would be difficult to achieve . . . While I realise that one hour is ideal, achieving this in practice is far from easy. Japan's new legislation stipulates that daily outdoor exercise should be 'as long as possible'. We comply with this law, but the actual time may be less than one hour. It would be very difficult in today's Japanese prisons to guarantee that every prisoner would get one hour of outdoor exercise each day, ultimately because we don't have sufficient outdoor facilities for exercise... And prison work naturally has to be done every day, and we have prisoners exercise in spare moments, but we just don't have the resources for every prisoner to have an hour a day.

The German penal code *Strafvollzugsgesetz* was also a significant influence on our deliberations on reforming the old *Prison Act* that began in 1986, and its influence remains strong in many aspects of the new prisons' legislation. But there were some parts that we decided not to use. One example is what is called *urlaub*, a vacation from prison where a prisoner gets to go home. We didn't adopt that concept, but we created something similar called overnight leave. We didn't agree with the concept of vacation.

The [old] *Ministerial Ordinance* was comprehensively revised [in 1966] some time after the SMR were established. Looking back with today's perspective, those revisions were only natural, but at the time it was the [1955] SMR that was the driving force behind them.

There's no question of external influences having been negative. Japanese law wouldn't have been influenced by systems we regarded as irrelevant.

Q: How have Japan's international relationships or other political influences had an impact on correctional policy or practice?

A: Japan's penal institutions are not swayed by Japan's relationships with other countries or political pressure. Historically, we've humbly accepted comments we can see are justified and made improvements, while refuting comments that we can't see in this light, giving specific reasons.

We still receive comments, particularly from western nations, that we should give greater recognition to prisoners' freedoms. However... we must strive to pay meticulous attention to not overstepping on the basis of isolated cases...

For example, embassy personnel may bring us a claim that the treatment of a prisoner doesn't seem right and request to change it... Also, there are a number of committees whose interests may include penal institutions such as the UN ICCPR Committee and the CAT. When they point out their concerns in response to reports submitted by Japan . . . we take [them] seriously . . . and make improvements where possible. And when we have reasons for doing things the way we do, then we explain our position at the next meeting. And we certainly receive opinions from NGOs, but that isn't really pressure as such. Basically, they don't have the authority to pressure us to do something, so we address their concerns by providing explanations.

Role of Corrections

Q: How do you think the public views corrections in Japan? Q: Is corrections viewed as a tool used to maintain the existing social order and power structure in your society?

A: Most ordinary members of the community think penal institutions are necessary to rehabilitate offenders and keep society safe, but don't feel connected to prisons personally. They feel we need them, but don't want them near where they live – the NIMBY [Not in My Back Yard] phenomenon. I think corrections is a means of maintaining social order (the security of the public) and preserves authority structures to the extent that maintaining public security leads to this outcome.

Q: What level of public support does the corrections service have in Japan?

A: I suspect we would have an average support level of around 60 out of 100. But I think most people have only a vague understanding of corrections . . . so when some kind of specific incident happens, public support changes dramatically. For example, public support drops sharply if there is an escape . . . and rises sharply if people hear about our . . . contributing to local communities, like by designating penal institution facilities as evacuation centres during major natural disasters, and providing our stored emergency provisions. I feel this is beneficial as an effort to counter the NIMBY effect . . . After the recent earthquake, Kumamoto Prison hosted evacuees, and provided food, water and emergency bathing facilities.

Recently, we've begun an effort to raise interest in corrections by appointing celebrities as 'Corrections Patrons', and inviting them to visit penal institutions, and to dialogue with corrections officers and local residents. We're also continuing with [having] corrections officers and their families participate actively in local events . . . I [also] feel it's important to continue to use avenues like the media and the internet to disseminate accurate information . . . We've created the MoJ Channel on Youtube . . . but we can't do anything expensive.

General Assessments

Q: Are you basically satisfied with developments in the corrections field?
A: Yes. There are so many things I'd like to do that I could go on endlessly . . . Obviously, I'd want more manpower and budget. But when I see things with a larger perspective, I understand that I can't always ask for more for my own ministry. So I think I need to make the best use of the resources I've been given.
Q: What developments are most likely in the next few years, and which would you prefer to see?
A: I think that in order to further strengthen our anti-recidivism efforts, we can expect personnel and budget increases, and expanded placement options for ex-offenders through increased resources from civil society, like social enterprises.

Employers like Okonomiyaki Chibo [a savoury pancake chain store] are increasing gradually. But not all are success stories. I've heard a story that when the shop owner finally decided a former prisoner employee had earned his trust and let him work at the cash register, the employee stole money and disappeared . . . But the shop owner still continues to hire former prisoners. I'm just so grateful to him. I believe even if you are betrayed like that, it's essential that you continue . . .

For this to work, we need to provide a greater variety of treatments for offenders in prison. It's not easy to help instil a mindset not to betray people, but we have to find a way reach them, and make sure they learn things like life skills. So when they're out, they'll be better prepared to live in society.

The deregulation of corrections physicians passed the Diet [Japanese legislature] in August of 2015 and came into effect from November. So it's been in place for six months now. Actually, we've already seen some results. In essence, the number of doctors, which had been steadily declining, has stopped declining. We haven't achieved what could be called a V-shaped turnaround yet, but, based on the number of applications from doctors coming in, we're encouraged to think that we'll have more doctors working for us. Also, because the law now permits it, doctors from private clinics can come to work for us part-time . . . So I think the effect of the law is quite significant.

I think it's actually better [to work at a prison than at an ordinary hospital]. In a mainstream prison, you have flexible working hours and don't have to do night duty; when the need arises, the doctor is just on call and gives instructions. Also, people think it's scary to work in prison, but on the contrary, it isn't at all. It's rare for a prisoner to attack all of a sudden. And if a prisoner might pose a threat, a corrections officer will be there ... and he'll be restrained. So it's much safer to work in prison than a regular medical clinic. We explain this [and] quite a few female doctors come to work for us.

Q: What is most needed now to improve penal institutions, community supervision, and the overall punishment process in Japan?

A: I think that the MoJ as a whole, and all the relevant ministries and agencies must move forward with a shared, serious commitment to reform. Japanese governance prioritises consensus, so if an entire administration has a serious desire for reform, this will compel a powerful response.

This is difficult because the MoJ is a big organisation, and there is a slight difference in degree between different bureaus. I wouldn't go so far as to say it as sectionalism, but the focus differs slightly between bureaus. We're trying to make the bureaus work together better within the MoJ, like a tag team, and to go further, to extend this collaboration to the Ministry of Health, Labour and Welfare, the Cabinet Office and other ministries and agencies in order to find a way to truly eradicate crime ... But I'm not sure whether people can become more team-focused and voice their opinions.

In other words, because each organisation is large, exchanging messages between contact persons may result in not having the messages reach the top – it could turn into a game of 'Chinese Whispers'. Indeed, to implement Throughcare, we need a system for people at the top to be able to talk with each other more freely. Right now, we're engaged in a 'nationwide effort' and things are gradually changing in that direction at last ... It's working fine within the MoJ, but we need more improvement between the MoJ and other ministries. And sharing data is also important.

Conclusion

Reading Director-General Tomiyama's candid responses against the backdrop of Japan's rapidly greying society, and the wide range of impacts this phenomenon has on prisons and criminal justice policy generally, it is clear that Japan's corrections regime is now in an inexorable transition. It is a cautious process, which adopts gradualism to the extent that the transformation may be almost imperceptible to the naked eye. But a return to the dogged resistance to change that characterised the 20th century is now unthinkable.

Mr Tomiyama's views demonstrate a keen understanding of the inherent harmfulness of incarceration, particularly under conditions where maintaining impeccable discipline and order are fetishised, and the obligation to society to provide a rehabilitative experience is forgotten. The vision he describes is unprecedented in its willingness to leave dated, retributive penal practices behind in favour of a fresh and practical blend of work and programmes designed to set offenders back on their feet on release.

Glossary

Campbell Collaboration: An international non-profit organisation that supports properly informed decision making regarding the effect of interventions in social policy.

Cognitive Behaviour Therapy: A type of psychotherapy that assists in changing counter-productive thoughts, feelings and conduct.

Correctional Treatment Policy Research Group: A Correction Bureau study group 'Kyosei Shogu ni Kansuru Kenkyukai' formed in 1999, comprising corrections officers and emerging corrections scholars.

NIMBY: Not In My Back Yard – a reference to opposition by local residents to an unwelcome or potentially dangerous development project.

PFI Prison: Private Finance Initiative Prison – a type of public–private partnership (PPP) where a private company covers the initial costs of a major public works project.

Training Institute for Correctional Personnel: The Correction Bureau staff training college headquartered in Tokyo.

Throughcare: Coordinated support for an offender from the start of a sentence right through to their reintegration into society.

***Yakuza*:** Japanese organised crime syndicates, or mafia.

Notes

1 See also Ministry of Justice (2017) for the most recent figures available in English.
2 The first Director-General in the postwar era with a corrections background was Mr Hiroshi Nishida (January 2013–December 2014). The Director-General role also involves a concomitant role as an Administrative Vice-Minister of Justice.
3 Death row prisoners are held in Detention Houses in Japan, not prisons.
4 These events occurred not long after the Second World War. In the modern Japanese corrections system, death row prisoners are not told the date of their execution. See Lane (2011).

Chapter 9

Randel Latoza, Jail Superintendent, Quezon City Jail Male Dormitory, Philippines

Interviewer: Raymund Narag

Contents

Overview	149
Introduction	151
Career	151
Changes Experienced	153
Personal Correctional Philosophy	157
Problems and Successes Experienced	158
Theory and Practice	159
Evidence-Based Corrections	161
Transnational Relations	161
Role of Corrections	162
General Assessments	163
Conclusion	164
Glossary	164

Overview

The Philippine Correctional System is considered one of the five pillars of the Criminal Justice System, which includes the police, courts, prosecution, corrections and the community. The Philippine Correctional System is composed of different agencies catering to various clients. The adult corrections system is composed of the Bureau of Jail Management and Penology (BJMP), the different provincial jails, and the Bureau of Corrections (BuCor). Both the BJMP and the provincial jails cater to inmates who are undergoing trial and those sentenced to three years or fewer. The BuCor caters to inmates who are convicted with a sentence of more than three years of imprisonment. The Parole and Probation Administration (PPA) caters to parolees and probationers. The Department of Social Welfare and Development (DSWD) caters to the needs of juvenile offenders. Both the BJMP and the provincial jails are under the supervision of the Department of the Interior and Local Government (DILG), while the BuCor and the PPA are under the Department of Justice (DoJ).

The BJMP is a unitary and highly centralised agency with a national headquarters (NHQ) office, 18 regional offices, and 80 provincial offices. Using this organisational command, the BJMP supervises 464 district, city and municipal jails scattered throughout the country. Being a national government agency, the BJMP budget is provided for by the Philippine Congress through annual budgetary appropriations.

As of February 2017, there were 140,000 inmates under the BJMP, representing a steep increase of almost 40% in jail population since 30 June 2016, or the inauguration of Rodrigo Duterte as Philippine President and the unleashing of the aggressive 'War on Drugs'. This sudden increase has created tremendous strain on jail management, as the facilities, personnel strength and resources have practically remained the same. This sudden increase also threatens to negate the innovations introduced by the BJMP in its 26 years of existence.

The BJMP is a relatively new agency created in 1991 with the purpose of unburdening the then Philippine Constabulary-Integrated National Police (now the Philippine National Police, or PNP) of its function of jail management. In its early years, BJMP was a fledgling organisation, which inherited from the police the old penological practices of running the jail through the inmate mayores, the pangkat (gangs) and very important preso (VIP) treatment systems. In this old set-up, inmates' leaders were designated custodial, administrative, and rehabilitation functions in order to augment the lack of personnel and resources. While helpful in running the day-today needs of the jail, it led to abuses and human rights violations. These informal practices currently characterise majority of the provincial jails and BuCor prisons. Through the years, the BJMP conducted efforts to modernise and professionalise the Jail Bureau, punctuated by the passage of the BJMP Modernisation Law of 2006. The Jail Bureau is now considered the leader in the Philippine correctional field and has surged ahead of the century-old BuCor and provincial jails, which continue to be plagued with corruption, drug dealing, and violence. The BJMP has also become a key partner in case management, as its jail inmate record keeping is far more advanced compared to the record keeping of the Courts, National Prosecution Service (NPS) (prosecutorial agency) and the Public Attorney's Office (PAO) (Public Defender agency).

The success of the BJMP in professionalising its ranks can be attributed to the continued inflow of commissioned officers (Inspector and above) trained in the Philippine National Police Academy (PNPA) and the continued personnel development every three years for its non-commissioned officers (Sergeants and below) trained in the National Jail Management and Penology Training Institute (NJMPTI). In the PNPA, cadets receive a four-year Bachelors' Degree in Public Safety, where they can choose from different specialisations (police, fire and jail). In the NJMPTI, cadets must first complete a four-year Bachelors' Degree and undergo six months of intensive in-house training. These training academies continue to update their curriculum as they incorporate knowledge in jail administration.

However, the nagging problems of overcrowding, lack of facilities and personnel, and the presence of informal practices, such as reliance on gangs and inmate leaders, continue to be a festering issue for jail management. Additionally, the delay of case disposition by the courts and the lack of coordination among the five pillars of the criminal justice system continue to hamper effective jail management practices. These issues provide the backdrop on the challenges faced by the jail wardens and other managers.

Introduction

In this interview, Warden Latoza relates his personal experiences, philosophies, and the challenges he faced as a commissioned jail officer. He also relates his observations on the strengths and shortcomings of the Jail Bureau and his vision on how to proceed.

While majority of his thoughts presented here were captured in a two-hour Skype interview conducted on 13 February 2017, previous discussions and conversations with the Warden were also incorporated. In the summers of 2015 and 2016, the interviewer (referred to by the Warden in this interview as the 'US-based academic') implemented a series of training programmes for the staff of the Quezon City Jail, which was eagerly supported by the Warden.

Career

Q: Tell us a little bit about your career: length, organisations worked in, movements, specialisations, trajectories in your career that might differ from those expected, etc.

A: I finished a Civil Engineering degree in 1995. Immediately after college graduation, I entered the Philippine National Police Academy (PNPA). I initially wanted to become a commissioned police officer. The PNPA is the premier institution in the Philippines that produces the commissioned officers for the three Bureaus (police, jail and fire), which are all under the Department of the Interior and Local Government (DILG). Upon graduation in the Academy in 1997, we were given the option to choose which of the three Bureaus we wanted to join. Surprisingly, it was my first time to hear of the Bureau of Jail Management and Penology (BJMP, or the Jail Bureau). It never dawned on me that I would become a jail officer. But I had a classmate in the Academy that persuaded me to join the Jail Bureau. We both joined. My motivation was simple: there were fewer commissioned officers joining the Jail

Bureau (as compared to the Police and Fire Bureaus) and so our career progression looked better.

But, to be honest, I knew very little about jail work at that time. Most of our training is on policing because the PNPA is a police academy. What is funny is that when we were in the academy, what they taught us was about prison work and the instructors were from the Bureau of Corrections (BuCor). BuCor is a different Bureau, which is tasked to handle convicted inmates. This is quite different from the Jail Bureau, which is tasked to handle inmates who are undergoing trial. There were no teachers from the BJMP back then. The BJMP was created only in 1991.

Frankly, I experienced difficulties in my first few years with the Jail Bureau. I felt that we were not fully trained and we were ill prepared for the job. Admittedly, I was at a loss and confused. I was assigned to the BJMP National Headquarters, doing almost nothing, wondering what should I do. I was very idle. Because of this, I initially regretted joining the Jail Bureau.

[This lasted] until such time that I was given an assignment as a warden in a small jail in Naic, Cavite. That jail in Naic had fewer than 100 inmates. But dealing with jail staff and inmates directly gave me the opportunity to appreciate the importance of my work. I saw the need for rehabilitation. I realised that inmates' lives should be reformed, that they should be following the law. I also gained important managerial skills, like coordinating and asking for help from the local government. As you see, the BJMP is a national agency with a limited budget and so we had to rely on the local governments for financial assistance. I learned how to engage the City Mayor in jail issues. I was able to solicit help from non-governmental organisations (NGOs) and other socio-civic organisations. And with the resources I mobilised, I was able to transform the jail physically and operationally. I introduced many reformation programmes. I felt satisfied as I saw the results of my efforts directly. So, my initial plan of transferring from the Jail Bureau to become a police officer dissipated soon after that.

Then, I was promoted to become warden to bigger jails. I assumed bigger responsibilities. I tried to document all the innovations I introduced in the jails I was assigned to. Not to brag, but I was the first to introduce the biometrics system of inmate booking in most jails. This systematised the inmate records and documentation. I streamlined the operational procedures in each area of jail management: security operations, admission of newly committed inmates, mess operations, and visitations. I developed manuals for these and now it has been replicated in other jails. The innovations I introduced, modesty aside, had been deemed as best practice.

Because of my innovations, I received the Dangal ng Bayan Award in 2007 (the most prestigious award given to a government employee). I was also awarded an Outstanding Alumni of the PNPA in 2015.

For me, despite the challenges, it has been a rewarding career! I had ups and downs in my career as a jail officer but it has been worth it. I am now fully committed to the jail service.

Changes Experienced

Q: What do you see as the most important changes that have occurred in the field of corrections over the course of your career (philosophies, organisational arrangements, specialisations, policies and programmes, equipment or technologies, methods of rehabilitation, methods of community supervision, intermediate sanctions, personnel, diversity, etc.)?

A: There have been a lot of developments in jail management since the BJMP started in 1991. Some pertain to our efforts to improve inmate services; other reform efforts centred on personnel development.

In terms of inmate services, we now have paralegal units in all the jails. The paralegal unit monitors inmates' cases; they make representation to the courts, especially on cases that are delayed or long overdue. This started in 2001. Prior to that, inmates rot[ted] [sat] in jail for as long as five, ten, 15 years, and they were not convicted yet. This delay of case disposition leads to jail overcrowding, which plagues most of our jails. And with jails being overcrowded, this leads to problems of jail violence, poor public health, and general low regard or unfavourable view of the jail agencies. With the paralegal unit, we can coordinate with the courts, prosecutors, and the Public Attorney's Office (PAO). We inform them of the case backlogs. We identify inmates who had been languishing in jail and let the judges know of their situation. We report slow performing judges to the Supreme Court. So we train our jail paralegal officers on how to follow up cases in courts, how to make legal manifestations, and how to determine whether inmates had already served the minimum portions of their sentences. With this innovation, case management improved. The profile of the jail bureau among other criminal justice agencies has improved as well.

Additionally, we now have the inmates welfare division (IWD) in all the jails. This started in 2003. The IWD is the unit that introduces educational, livelihood, educational, spiritual and other programmes to inmates. The IWD runs the therapeutic community (TC) in each of the cells. The TC is a holistic programme that incorporates behavioural and cognitive changes among inmates. With the IWD, we are able to systematise and coordinate our rehabilitation programmes. We now have procedures on how to accredit organisations providing services to the inmates. We make sure that the programmes they offer are consistent with our overall rehabilitation plans. We also see to it that the programmes are offered to inmates who really need it. Prior to the IWD, we did not have integrated rehabilitation programmes. When inmates were committed to our jails, we sent them to their cells, and that was it! They were idle – doing nothing but counting the bars. There were no specific personnel tasked to develop and implement inmate programming. Some of the bigger jails offered programmes but the programmes were not well thought of and were poorly implemented. Our programmes were topsy-turvy. We had no guidance. We simply allowedNGOs and religious groups coming into the jail to introduce programmes. We were not able to determine whether the programmes were effective or not or whether it was offered to the right people. We were too dependent on the NGOs for programmes and sometimes they interfered with our jail security. They became a source of our problems. Sometimes, the NGOs competed against each other. But with the IWD, we are slowly gaining knowledge on what programme works and how to implement programmes properly.

And finally, we now have a better health service. The BJMP is now provided with Php 5 per day per inmate budget. That is not much, but [is good] compared to previous years, [when] we didn't have a budget allotted for inmate medicines at all! As a consequence, many inmates died in our jails. In my own jail with 2,800 inmates, around 40 inmates died each year. But with our better health service, we were able to reduce that to 20 [inmates dying], which is still high, and we are doing all we can to reduce it further. We also now have more medical and health personnel assigned in our jails.

All these changes (paralegal, rehabilitation, and medical) bode well for the inmates. It is a manifestation that the BJMP strives to improve the services it provides to the inmates. We aspire to provide humane safekeeping and meet international standards. It is still a long way to go but we are on the right track.

In terms of personnel development, there are also great strides that were introduced. This started with the Modernization Law of the BJMP in 2006. All new personnel must now have a college degree. It used to be that high school graduates could work in the Jail Bureau. With a more educated workforce, it is easier to introduce new technologies and systems. We also instituted merit-based hiring and promotional systems. Admittedly, there were issues of favouritism and political patronage before. It was chaotic. Many personnel were demoralised due to discretionary promotions. That has been greatly diminished. Now, we match our hiring process with the personnel needs of the Bureau. We are now able to attract skilled personnel like psychiatrists and psychologists. We have a continuing professional development for the personnel as well. They go for additional training every three years, which is prerequisite for promotion. Personnel remuneration has also improved. Salaries are distributed on time and in a consistent manner. As such, personnel morale is high. Corrupt practices among the guards had been reduced, not completely yet, but at least not at the level it used to be.

Additionally, we introduced a major change in jail management. It used to be that inmate food management was done through private concessions. Since these private concessions incurred additional operational costs and needed to make profits, food quality was quite poor. Inmates complained of the poor food quality and, unfortunately, it was the jail wardens who suffered from poor food management. Inmates held protests and wardens were booted out of office. In 2003, food management became an integral responsibility of the wardens. The wardens are [now] given discretionary control over the food budget. They are given leeway on how to reduce the operational costs. This has led to better jail operations. Wardens are held accountable for actions in which they are directly involved.

Despite these key developments, there are also challenges faced by the Bureau. This is tied particularly to the two waves of 'drug wars' initiated by the national government. The first drug war was a legislative action, when the lawmakers introduced the draconian *Republic Act* 9165 in 2002, which prohibited bail release for inmates charged with drug dealing. This law led to the increase of the national jail population from 30,000 to 60,000 in just three years. After a decade of this law, all our jails hold more than double their capacities.

But the situation has worsened tremendously in the past year with President Duterte's drug war. The police were ordered by the president to aggressively arrest low-level drug users and dealers. The jail population, which was already strained, got even more strained. The national jail population now stands at 140,000 inmates. However, our jail space capacities have not increased a bit. The overall jail crowding is now over 400%, but some jails experience 1,200% over-congestion. The Quezon City Jail is only built for 280 inmates but now accommodates 2,800 inmates!

Thus, the major problem is jail overcrowding. The construction of new jails is slow and dependent on local government funding. If local governments do not have the funds, then jails are extremely overcrowded. We are lucky that the Quezon City government is supportive of our jail. The Quezon City Council committed to help us in constructing a new jail. Though we cannot say that of all city governments, as very few city governments help their local jails.

Our personnel strength is slow in catching up with the inmate population increases. Though we had been recruiting quality personnel, the quantity is lacking. By law, we should have a custodial ratio of one custodial officer for every seven inmates; in actuality, our ratio is 1:80, and with some jails having a custodial ratio of 1:120. So that places tremendous strain on our personnel. Many of our personnel had to work overtime without pay just to meet their daily obligations. Many people don't realise this, but our personnel are volunteering their time and resources to support the jail service.

Though our paralegal units are doing their best to fast-track the release of inmates, still more inmates are coming in than are being released. So we are doubling our coordinative efforts with the courts and the defence lawyers for the speedy disposition of cases.

Overall, I would say that it is easier to be a jail officer now than it used to be. The BJMP now has more than 26 years of experience as an organisation and the top leaders now have a better appreciation of the nature and quality of the jail work. Our bureau is much more professionalised, our operations are now formalised and standardised, and our hiring, retention and promotion have become more merit based.

Having said that, the major source of the problem is the lack of resources given to the Bureau. As mentioned, we lack space, facilities, personnel and what I call other 'structural deficits'. These structural deficits led us to develop 'coping mechanisms' that became part of the jail's operational dynamics. For example, due to lack of personnel, we utilise inmate leaders to co-manage the cells. Due to lack of space, we allow inmates to construct their own *kubols* [makeshift beds] and living spaces. These are informal coping mechanisms that we allow just to keep the jails afloat. It has been an age-old practice we inherited from the police. Now, these pose problems, as these coping mechanisms are not allowed according to our formal operational manuals. They are, in fact, prohibited. So the national headquarters would issue directives to the local wardens ordering them to dismantle the *kubols* as it is sometimes used for illicit purposes. But if we dismantle the *kubols*, where would inmates sleep? Inmates' conditions would further worsen. And that is the current situation: we now have developed formal rules and standards to manage the facility, but the attendant resources needed to meet the rules and standards are not yet in place. This places jail wardens in a tough bind: they want to follow the formal directives but are forced to use informal mechanisms to keep the jail operations afloat.

Personal Correctional Philosophy

Q: What do you think should be the role of prison, jail, and community supervision officials in society?
A: Jails play an important role in the Philippine Criminal Justice System. Since we are the ones in charge of inmates undergoing trial, we should coordinate with the courts in the speedy disposition of their cases. Unfortunately, many inmates stay longer in our jails due to case delays. Many inmates end up serving their sentences in jail. And so the jail must also incorporate rehabilitation programmes and make inmate time productive. Thus, we assume the functions of the Prison Bureau.

My personal philosophy in jail management is to make lives of the inmates bearable while undergoing trial. They are still presumed innocent. I emphasise approaches that meet the basic standards of human rights and human dignity. I try as much as possible to minimise pain and suffering. This, I believe, will strengthen the public good.

So, for example, in the jails I try to improve mechanisms to provide sufficient food to all inmates and to improve their living conditions. I try to hear feedback from inmates and personnel and incorporate their suggestions. I try to explain to the inmates and their leaders why certain policies are to be implemented. I use 'soft power' like dialogue and open communications rather than 'hard power' like force and intimidation. For example, the national directive on the dismantling of the *kubols*: some jail wardens have implemented the policy with the custodial force; this has led to inmate protests and jail disturbances. In my jail, I explained to the inmates the pros and cons of the *kubols*, and having convinced them, the inmates themselves dismantled their own *kubols*. I appeal to the inherent dignity of the inmates, and they do respond.

I believe that if you treat the inmates as human beings, they will be receptive to the reformation programmes. And that is the reason why the inmates are supporting our educational programmes.

We have inmates who serve as auxiliary teachers. And inmate leaders make sure our inmate participants attend the programmes regularly. And outsiders eventually notice these successes. When the TESDA (a government training agency) heard of our livelihood-training programme, they came here and adopted it. Now, it is being replicated in many other jails. It all started with a humane treatment of the inmates.

Most of the inmates are charged with drug offences. Almost 70% of our inmates are charged with drug related offences. I understand that the current Philippine president is serious about the drug problem and I support efforts to eradicate drugs. However, there should be programmes to be implemented for these drug dependents in our jails. The [current] policy is simply to put them in jail and hope that this will serve as a deterrent to other offenders.

As a jail warden, I am forced to develop my own programmes to deal with the needs of the drug dependents. Thus, I directed my rehabilitation officers to train with the city's drug prevention units so they may be properly equipped. I tasked them to develop our own classification, programming, and housing protocols for the drug dependents. We need to do these ourselves because the national government does not have any resources. The national government, through the police, simply dump the inmates in our jails and then we are tasked to rehabilitate them without attendant resources.

Problems and Successes Experienced

Q: In your experience, what policies or programmes have worked well, and which have not? Can you speculate for what reasons? What would you consider to be the greatest problem facing the correctional system at this time?

A: One big and ongoing problem we face as an institution is corruption. And here, there must be a holistic understanding of why corrupt practices happen so that it can be placed in context. As I mentioned, the Jail Bureau is one of the least prioritised agencies of the national government. We perennially lack resources to run our jail facilities. We are short-staffed. We lack facilities and space. All these structural conditions put a strain on our capacities. Inmates' living conditions are admittedly below the acceptable standards for humane treatment. Now, in order to address this, there are coping mechanisms that we informally allowed in the jail management, and this becomes a 'grey area'. For example, inmates are formally prohibited from bringing money and food inside the jail facilities. But we all know that if we implement this rule to the letter, inmates would be more hungry and restless considering the limited food budget allotted to the bureau. So, despite this formal prohibition, we informally allow our jail officers to exercise their discretion when they allow inmates to bring money and food inside the jail. This informal set-up becomes a 'slippery slope' and opens the floodgates to corruption. Some jail guards can use this informal power to generate additional income. Aside from bringing money, inmates can now bring contraband inside the jail, like cigarettes, alcohol, and drugs.

Now, I must say that there have been efforts to reduce corruption. One project initiated by the Regional Director is the *Matyag-Mata* where personnel from the Regional Office are assigned to the jails and they frisk the jail guards before entering the jail premises. Even the wardens are not exempted from the body search. This has tremendously reduced the amount of contraband smuggled inside the jails.

However, for this to be sustainable, the structural deficits need to be addressed as well. There is a need to improve the food budget for the inmates, improve jail conditions, and the working conditions of the personnel. Unless these are addressed, all these target-hardening activities will be palliative and short-term interventions. It does not address the root causes of the problems.

Theory and Practice

Q: In your view, what should be the relationship between theory and practice? What can practitioners learn from studying and applying theories, and what can those who create theories of punishment gain from practitioners?

A: Correctional theories are important. We need theories to guide our work. Fortunately for us, there are many institutional partners helping us learn about theory. For example, the International Committee of the Red Cross (ICRC) has been helping us in jail architectural designs. We have been trained in the importance of creating architectural briefs as a prerequisite for constructing new jails. Here, we incorporate theories on rehabilitation, security and administration in the design of a functional jail. Lately, we had training from a US-based academic on the principles of effective jail management. Here, we discussed theories on inmate classification, housing and rehabilitation. On a personal level, I try to read books on correctional management and best practices from successful wardens all over the world.

However, there is one big problem that we commonly encounter when we implement the theory that we learned. That is, we perennially lack funds. For example, jail management theories suggest that inmates need to be classified based on risks, needs and responsivity (RNR). And the classification of inmates will inform where they will be housed and what programmes they will undertake. These are all good principles: the problem is, it takes resources and facilities for this to happen. But our jails are overcrowded, so how can we classify and segregate inmates?

Thus, sometimes, theories become ideals that we can only aspire to implement. In reality, we come up with programmes that are incompatible with the correctional theories. For example, we classify inmates based on membership in the *pangkat* (gangs) and group inmates according to their *pangkat*. The *pangkat* are provided with their own cells and brigades. There could be as many as 300 to 500 inmates in one *pangkat*. The *pangkats* have their own set of leaders and rules and regulations. We informally deputise the inmate leaders as co-managers of the cells and brigades. These inmate leaders are in charge of maintaining the cleanliness and orderliness inside their cells and brigades. We allow them to mediate their own conflicts. We make sure that the leaders are role models and they follow our official BJMP rules. Of course, these coping mechanisms are all against the correctional management theory that suggests inmates should not exercise supervision over other inmates. But this is what we found working in our jails. Without the inmate leaders, our jail will collapse.

I believe that research is also important. Research plays a key role in determining which of our programmes work or not. I had been a big proponent of research. That is why I sent my officers for graduate studies. Out of my own pocket, I sponsor their studies. I just had an officer who finished his Masters' degree and came back to the jail. His thesis investigated the factors related to recidivism in our jail.

With research, we can be informed on the appropriate programmes to introduce. For example, based on my officer's Masters' thesis, he found that most of our recidivists are, at most, high school graduates only. So, lack of education is related to recidivism. From this finding, we featured the educational programmes as a key component of our rehabilitation. Our current recidivism rate is 40%. We intend to reduce it by half. I also believe that, with proper evaluation, we can do away with programmes that are not really helpful and effective. So, our baseline data will help us determine if we are implementing the correct programmes.

And this is what I had been telling my higher-ups in the Jail Bureau – the need to prioritise research. Unfortunately, we are also hampered by the lack of budget. The BJMP has very limited amount allotted for research purposes. Additionally, our Research and Development Office lack personnel with the skills to conduct scientific and rigorous research. I had been an advocate of sending our best personnel for graduate studies here and abroad so we can develop appropriate research and evaluation skills. Without these investments, we are incompetent to do research and evaluation. As such, we are not particularly sure which of our numerous programmes are effective and which are not.

Evidence-Based Corrections

Q: In your experience, has your county's correctional system made use of various evidence-based programmes? Do you feel that it is best to use evidence-based practices (or 'what works') or that this focus is not important?

A: As I said, I am a big proponent of evidence-based practices. I try that in my own jail. I usually create working committees to develop the operational manual of a programme and see if the programme is implemented based on the operational manual. And then, I direct the working committees to determine if the programme achieves its stated goals. And then we use this as evidence to determine whether we continue the programme, tweak it, or discontinue it. This way, we have an empirical basis to determine the viability of the programmes. Having said that, it does not mean our evaluation mechanism is scientific and rigorous. Again, remember, most of my staff members are recruited as jail officers with limited backgrounds in scientific research.

The Jail Bureau, as a whole, is slowly learning the importance of evidence-based practices. We now require jail wardens to submit reports on their performance based on certain metrics. We now start to collect data on the number of participants in the different programmes, the type of programmes offered, the number of completers, and other programme outputs and outcomes. This way, we can compare and determine which programmes are working and what type of inmates are most likely to benefit in a programme. Of course, we are still in the preliminary phase of implementation. Many top leaders of the Jail Bureau are still used to the anecdotal and 'hunch' way of determining success. But the new breeds of jail officers are more receptive of evidence-based practices.

Transnational Relations

Q: How have you been affected in your organisation's work by developments outside the country (human rights demands, universal codes of ethics, practical interactions with corrections officials from other countries, personal experiences outside the country, programmes developed by other countries, new sentencing laws, political strife or war in your or neighbouring countries)?

A: The *United Nations Standard Minimum Rules for the Treatment of Prisoners* and the *United Nations Universal Declaration of Human Rights* are the key documents that personally influenced me on how to conduct my job. The conditions inside the jails, admittedly, are deplorable, and so I try my very best to reduce pain and human suffering. I go beyond the limitations of my Bureau and find mechanisms to improve the lot of the inmates. For example, with the limited budget, I solicit help from the local government, NGOs and other socio-civic organisations. I maintain a very visible profile so the issues of the jail can be discussed publicly. I usually seek help from the media so the inmates' conditions can be openly discussed. I usually frame my engagements based on the need to fulfil the basic human rights obligation of the state and the society to the least of its members – the inmates.

Role of Corrections

Q: How do you think the public views corrections in your country/community?

A: Unfortunately, with the current 'war on drugs', we Filipinos have a very punitive view of offenders. Police have implemented thousands of arrests in the past eight months, bloating the jail population, but Congress has not addressed the bulging jail population. Many Filipinos see the offenders as deserving of being placed in our overcrowded jails. I don't foresee any improvement of this in the near future.

However, despite the current political climate, we in the Jail Bureau are doing our best to mitigate the impact of the drug war. We try to develop good working relationship with our service providers. For example, due to the sudden increase of inmate population, the food budget for the inmates was already consumed by October of 2016. For the months of November and December 2016, we ran out of food budget. As wardens, we need to devise mechanisms on how to feed our inmates. We need to develop good working relationships with our food suppliers. We sought loans and credits. We begged assistance from the local government. Formally, these are not our tasks, but we do it anyway.

On the other hand, NGO support to the local jails had been continuous. They provide additional resources and volunteers to the jail. Without their assistance, jail work would be very difficult.

General Assessments

Q: Are you basically satisfied or dissatisfied with developments in the field of corrections?

A: One of the exciting things happening in jail management is the one-*carpeta* system. This innovation intends to link the *carpeta* (legal documents) of the inmates from the police, courts, jails, prisons and probation and parole offices. This is a cloud-based file sharing technology where all the agencies involved use a similar platform. This is a game changer. This will improve document sharing among the agencies, reduce delay in the processing of cases, and should lead to the reduction of jail and prison populations. Additionally, there will be a better coordination between the Jail Bureau and the Prison Bureau. Inmate data and behavioural history in the jail will be transmitted to the Prison [Bureau], which can be used for their classification and programming purposes. Indeed, this will hopefully make the criminal justice system efficient.

Overall, I am optimistic in the development in the Jail Bureau. Far from the 'lowly jail guards', we are now viewed as a professional bureau with dedicated personnel. Judges, prosecutors and defence lawyers now see us as their 'equals' in the justice system. In the correctional field, the Prison Bureau and the parole and probation offices view the Jail Bureau to be innovative and a leader in introducing reforms. We used to be recipients of their training; now, we are the ones training them. The BuCor is learning from our best practices and they replicate it in their prisons.

Of course, like other agencies, we are plagued with limitations. We are overworked and underpaid, which increases the strains that lead to corrupt coping practices. And, when unchecked, corruption becomes a way of life in a jail facility. To address corruption, we need to introduce a holistic intervention: one that addresses the structural, organisational, and cultural components of corruption. As mentioned earlier, we need to provide additional resources, personnel, facilities, salary improvements, and overall improved working conditions. But this structural change should be complemented with organisational change. That is, jail personnel should be equipped with theory-based knowledge on how to run the jail facilities. Personnel should understand the importance of classification, programming and housing and the need for research and evaluation. One may have the facilities but if the jail is managed in the old set up of *pangkat* and inmate *mayores*, then the structural improvements may be for naught. Then, finally, we need to have a cultural change, a change in world-views and ways of doing things. We had been plagued before with favouritism and patronage, such that meritorious personnel are not promoted. There should be value formation programmes, ethical trainings, and gender-sensitivity trainings so we can have a more empowered Jail Bureau.

This is a mouthful and it cannot be done overnight. It takes everybody's commitment in the Jail Bureau to make this work. But, with my 20 years of engagement in the Jail Bureau, and seeing all the past developments, I believe this is attainable.

Conclusion

Warden Randel Latoza provided an honest assessment of the current state of the Bureau of Jail Management and Penology (BJMP). He correctly identified the structural, organisational, and cultural factors that affect the efficacy of jail management in the Philippines. Being a long-term observer of Philippine corrections, I concur with his incisive insights. He utilises this knowledge to introduce holistic and multi-component approaches to jail reforms.

More importantly, Warden Latoza's integrity and humility has earned him a reputation of credibility within the agency. Outside of this interview, I was able to observe him deal with inmates, jail volunteers and jail staff. He articulates his visions clearly and inspires everyone to action. He indeed deserves his latest accolade as an outstanding jail warden.

Glossary

BJMP: Bureau of Jail Management and Penology, one of the three adult correctional agencies.
BuCor: Bureau of Corrections, the first and oldest correctional agency of the Philippines.
CO: Commissioned officers.
***Dangal ng Bayan*:** Outstanding Public Officers and Employees, a prestigious government award.
DILG: Department of the Interior and Local Government.
DoJ: Department of Justice.
DSWD: Department of Social Welfare and Development.
IWD: Inmates welfare division.
ICRC: International Committee of the Red Cross.
***Kubol*:** Inmate cubicles.
***Matyag-Mata*:** A surveillance programme introduced by the Regional Director of the BJMP-NCR to eradicate contraband smuggling inside the jails.
***Mayores*:** Inmate cell leader.
NCOs: Non-commissioned officers.
NGOs: Non-governmental organisations.

NHQ: National headquarters.
NJMPTI: National Jail Management and Penology Training Institute.
NPS: National Prosecution Service, the prosecutorial agency of the Philippines.
Pangkat: Inmate gang.
PAO: Public Attorney's Office, the public defender agency of the Philippines.
PNP: Philippine National Police.
PNPA: Philippine National Police Academy.
PPA: Parole and Probation Administration.
TC: Therapeutic community.
QCJ: Quezon City Jail.
VIP treatment: Very important preso, a system where inmates are allowed to bring their money and resources inside the jail to mitigate their living conditions.

Chapter 10

Nathee Jitsawang, Ex-General Director of Department of Corrections, Thailand

Interviewer: Dittita Tititampruk

Contents

Overview	166
Introduction	167
Career	167
Changes Experienced	168
Personal Correctional Philosophy	170
Problems and Successes Experienced	171
Theory and Practice	172
Evidence-Based Corrections	173
Transnational Relations	174
Role of Corrections	175
General Assessments	176
Glossary	176

Overview

The corrections work relating to the care of adult inmates in Thai prisons is under the responsibility of the Department of Corrections, Ministry of Justice. However, the supervision of youth offenders is under the responsibility of the Department of Juvenile Observation and Protection, Ministry of Justice. In addition, the treatment of offenders in the community and probation of both child and adult offenders is under the responsibility of the Department of Probation, Ministry of Justice. Accordingly, the Ministry of Justice has three departments that are responsible for the care of both child and adult offenders, and the detention facilities and community corrections. Furthermore, the Ministry of Justice includes the Thailand Institute of Justice (TIJ) that serves as a supporting unit to promote and propel compliance with international standards regarding inmates, especially the *Nelson Mandela Rules* and the *Bangkok Rules*, including correctional reform. In general, the officials who work in these four organisations work in an interrelated and mutually adaptable way because the nature of the work is similar.

Introduction

Mr Nathee Chitsawang is a specialist in correctional work in Thailand and is internationally renowned. He served as the Director General of the Department of Corrections twice, and was the Director General of the Department of Probation. Currently, he is the Deputy Director of the Thailand Institute of Justice (TIJ), responsible for driving prison reform forward in accordance with international standards especially the *Nelson Mandela Rules*[1] and the *Bangkok Rules*.[2] Mr Nathee is highly associated with, and experienced in, the correctional service over 40 years.

Career

Q: Tell us about your career in corrections.
A: My personal interest in corrections began when I was an undergraduate student at Chulalongkorn University, where I had a chance to study criminology and penology. It could be said that, at that time, I did not even think to pursue my career in the correctional sphere – it was only my general enthusiasm. At a later time, I was awarded the Royal Thai Government Scholarship to further my Masters' degree in Criminology at Florida State University (FSU). Under the conditions of the scholarship, after graduation, I must come back to work at the Department of Corrections. Because of this turning point in my life, my occupational focus had changed to correctional staff instead of being a legal officer, as per my academic background, the Bachelors' degree in Law.

At FSU, I enhanced not only my profound knowledge but also my love of corrections. I started to collect textbooks, journals and many articles, for the reason that, during that time, this area of study was neither popular nor widespread in Thailand. In fact, there were only a few people undertaking this subject seriously. Once finishing my postgraduate study, I came back to Thailand to commence my vocational journey at the Department of Corrections in 1977. By recognising the importance and expectation of being a former scholarship student, I clearly intended to work very hard with strong determination. My job title had started as penologist and later changed to legal officer, researcher and the Director of Correctional Staff Training Institute, consecutively. It is worth mentioning that at the latter position, I could fully capture the essence of prison and correctional studies by sharing viewpoints and exchanging experiences with all levels of students, ranging from the newly recruited staff to the prison directors. At the same time, in this position, I also found out the core characteristics of Thai correctional work: 3Ds and 1L, standing for 'Difficulty, Dangerous, Dirty and Low Salary'.

Later, when I gained promotion to work as an executive in the Department, starting from the Deputy Director General and being promoted to the highest rank, the Director General, I applied all the knowledge, together with experiences I had acquired from all training course participants, to develop the Thai prison system, especially the introduction of a change in general attitude towards the 3Ds of Thai correctional work. By doing this, interestingly, there were both success and failure stories.

In my opinion, one of the success stories was the advancement in almost all aspects of inmates' lives, starting from shifting thinking about a prison so that it could be a 'home of development' with the aim of transforming the twilight or dark zone behind the prison walls to be a school developing people. On top of that, I launched the campaign to open prison gates to the outside world on the grounds that Thai society was encouraged to support the released inmates and acknowledge their capabilities, as well as to perceive prison work as an invaluable task for Thai people. On the other hand, there was, however, a duty that I could not accomplish: the attempt to overcome the prison overcrowding crisis. Instead of reducing the number of prisoners, during my reign as the Director General, the total prison population increased from 160,000 to 300,000 within 15 years, due to large increases in the number of imprisoned drug-related offenders. Although I did introduce various diversions and alternatives to prison measures, the problem clearly remained. Shortly after I had tried my best to overcome this hard-to-conquer problem, I was appointed to be Director General of the Probation Department and Deputy Director of the Thailand Institute of Justice, consecutively.

Changes Experienced

Q: What do you think are the most important changes that have occurred in the field of corrections over the course of your career?

A: From my point of view, the correctional work these days has changed dramatically, different from when I started working at the Department of Corrections. In reality, change can occur all the time, but normally it proceeds rather gradually. The massive change in various areas of Thai corrections actually occurred in the last 15 years. At first, I noticed that the characteristics or profiles of prisoners were different. In the past, when I began my work, most of the inmates were poor, uneducated and underprivileged. Contrastingly, in present days, inmates tend to be rich, well educated, and influential. They tend to be politicians, businessmen and large-scale drug dealers. I found that the shift in the characteristics of inmates has made prison work much more difficult. Besides, because of the prevailing trend towards human rights and the goal of protecting the rights of inmates, our prison officers could not fully exercise their custodial power over inmates, since some prisoners keep complaining to various outside agencies and media.

Due to the complaints, correctional officers were quite afraid to manage prisoners strictly. In addition, the rise in democracy and the collapse of socialism influenced the ideas of auditing and monitoring government agencies from the external sector, such as political parties, public and private sectors. All of these factors could contribute to the growing challenges in performing prison work. To properly deal with these, several measures are necessary to be introduced, that is, the emphasis on a prison's physical settings and the introduction of high technology equipment to assist correctional duties by replacing manpower in doing custodial tasks and to avoid the potential risk in provoking serious confrontation between prisoners and prison staff. More importantly, it could prevent the frequent complaints from inmates because of an increase in systematic and standard operations, rather than using personal discretion case by case.

Another decisive factor responsible for the changes in the prison environment, especially when I was the Director General, is the advance in technology, in particular the mobile phone and the internet. While the size of mobile phones became so small that they could be easily smuggled into prisons, our prison authority at that time did not have sufficiently advanced technology to prevent and block the telephone signal. Accordingly, some prisoners could still commit further crimes by using smuggled mobile phones to do drug dealing behind bars.

Moreover, it is very important to bear in mind that the prison population still kept growing. In fact, when I joined the prison service, the figures were only 70,000, but now there are approximately 300,000 inmates due to the spread of illicit drugs and increase in drug crime. It should be noted that the number of prison officers has not been radically modified, as there are about 11,000 prison staff these days, rising from 7,000 officers previously under the situation of overcrowding prison population. At the same time, only 20 correctional facilities were added, and these are still not enough for the number of inmates, as the total capacity is for only 200,000. Hence, prisons are overcrowded and the prison population exceeds the space inside the prison walls.

In a nutshell, I personally believe that the prison administration in Thailand is now facing more challenges and difficulties. The countermeasure is to find diversion schemes and alternatives to imprisonment to reduce the prison population and to enable the prison authority to perform its mission, both custody and rehabilitation, more effectively.

Personal Correctional Philosophy

Q: What do you think should be the role of prison, jail and community supervision in society?

A: I have my personal viewpoint on corrections. Throughout my career, I had the very firm belief about correctional work that it was to improve people and assist their reintegration. Undeniably, the focus on custody must come first, before rehabilitation, as prison is a place to incarcerate and detain criminals. Most importantly, it should be noted that effective rehabilitation will not succeed if the inmates are not imprisoned securely and safely. Having said that, from my own experience, the efforts to rehabilitate and change people behind bars could come to nothing unless the community outside is willing to support their return. In essence, Thai society still perceives ex-prisoners negatively, due to continuing media attention given to recidivists. Thus, most released inmates must conceal their identities in order to work and live well in society. In the worst case, some Thai people do not even want to support rehabilitation and treatment programmes for inmates inside prisons. As a result, the Department of Corrections becomes the only agency playing the principal role in giving treatment or rehabilitation programmes to inmates.

Although I believe that a prison should be an institution for improving people, it does not mean that all offenders must be detained behind bars. In other words, prison should undoubtedly be used as the last resort. To clarify my viewpoint, in Thailand some offenders should not be sentenced to imprisonment in the first place, on the grounds that they were first-time and unintentional offenders committing only minor crimes. Nevertheless, the criminal justice system at that time did not have other proper options, such as the implementation of intermediate sanctions. Further, many Thai people demanded the sending of all criminals to prison, no matter how serious [the crime] and what type of criminal behaviour they committed. The consequence of this was the phenomenon that both serious or professional offenders and less habitual criminals were mingled inside overcrowded prisons.

Therefore, it seems to be an appropriate and perfect time to reform the penal system in Thailand. By doing so, the unintentional criminals should be offered a second chance to return to society, while the serious or habitual criminals must be incarcerated within the prison walls for a long time to protect society and to provide them with rehabilitation programmes; serving time until the prison authority is confident that they are not dangerous for society any more. However, the complicated problem is that habitual criminals tend to receive shorter sentences for lesser crimes, namely robbery and burglary, which will normally receive less than 3–5 years of imprisonment. At the completion of these prison sentences, this group of inmates tends to reoffend after release.

Thus, it seems to me that the relevant laws should require offenders who are real criminals and repeat offenders to face longer sentences in order to protect society at large from being future victims. Also, other offenders who did not intentionally carry out crimes should be given the opportunity to be in the outside world by serving community sentences.

Problems and Successes Experienced

Q: In your experience, what policies or programs have worked well, and which have not?

A: During my entire career at Department of Corrections, one of my achievements was the change in the mindset of prison staff to increasingly focus upon rehabilitation. There were various types of rehabilitation programmes which I decided to launch: for instance, 'Prison as a Home of Meditation', 'Prison as a Home of Sport', 'Prison as a Home of Education', and 'Prison as a Home of Development'. By running all of these, prisoners could be improved at all stages of corrections: intake, rehabilitation, pre-release and aftercare periods in the community. Additionally, prison work was gradually transforming to be positively recognised by Thai society, which started to understand not only prison authority, but also prison staff. Most importantly, our prison officers were particularly proud to be part of correctional work.

Concerning unsuccessful stories, as mentioned previously, this was the failure in overcoming the prison overcrowding crisis. Although the Department of Corrections tried to apply alternative measures, such as parole, overcrowding continued. Its root cause was the serious drugs problem that occurred in Thai society. Inside Thai prisons, about 65% of all inmates have committed drug-related crime. On top of that, the Thai criminal justice system did not implement many effective alternatives to imprisonment. As such, many offenders were sentenced to prison, whereas the Thai Department of Corrections itself did not have many options to release prisoners before the end of their sentence.

Theory and Practice

Q: In your view, what should be the relationship between theory and practice?

A: I fully realise that prison work needs the right combination of both science and art. To put it simply, prison work requires not only theoretical knowledge, namely criminology, penology, law, behavioural science, management and research, to deliver performance behind bars. Prison work also requires practical knowledge in terms of experience, intuition and cleverness to work well in prisons. If officers employ only theories or what is written in textbooks, and command other prison staff to follow them, that would be a genuine mistake because the prison authority will not be able to accomplish it. As a result, staff working at the Department of Corrections must be, to some extent, the academic scholars who understand theories and also emphasise practical work. Likewise, the practitioners themselves must not leave theories behind.

Interestingly, my work at the Department of Corrections needed some research and studies as the keys to answering numerous enquiries. To illustrate, research was needed when the Department of Corrections was criticised for releasing inmates too soon, or when offenders did not spend as long a time in prison as they should do because of the system of reducing the initial prison sentence (e.g., through Royal Pardons or other types of remission). To investigate, I decided to do a study to explore whether inmates were spending relatively shorter time in prisons or not. In other words, I did research to find the average time served in Thai prisons. One of my findings was that prisoners did not actually serve short times behind bars, as other people had assumed.

In addition, there were many studies conducted to resolve management or administration ambiguity. From my perspective, study and research are indispensable for supporting the key decisions, especially the assessment and evaluation of the rehabilitation programmes in order to assist the executives to understand and make the right decisions as to whether to continue or stop running the programmes.

I once carried out an evaluation on the 'Rising Star Inmates Going to the Olympics' project, which, in my opinion, clearly showed how successful ex-inmates were in becoming national team athletes. Moreover, it was considered a successful outcome-orientated project on the grounds that about 2–3 inmates could develop themselves to join the national sports team and reach national competition levels. Some people suggested that these outcomes were satisfying while other parties, on the contrary, believed it was not cost–effective. Therefore, this project, which was run at Thonburi Remand Prison, was terminated.

Evidence-Based Corrections

Q: In your experience, has your country's correction system made use of various evidence-based practices?

A: According to my work experience within Thai corrections, it could be said that the evidence–based approach was rarely applied, although it could offer many benefits. The most concerning aspect, or typical pattern, when running the projects was that they must be in compliance with various legal frameworks, as well as the top-down orders from higher level people. Additionally, there were many new campaigns launched but they were not properly evaluated and not evaluated consistently. One of primary reasons was that the Thai prison system was undergoing the development of more effective inmate databases and statistical systems, which were fundamentally important for valid assessment. Furthermore, I believe that the number of academic scholars or researchers at the Department of Corrections was still insufficient. Thus, some regulations were amended recently to allow lecturers and scholars working in academic institutions to conduct evaluation studies of projects and put the research findings into practice.

Apart from that, the progress in internet technology obviously facilitated the access to research, data and evidence-based studies of correctional agencies in other countries by enabling journal searches of articles and research archives which had never happened before. This encouraged the Thai Department of Corrections to highlight and promote evidence-based study.

For example, in the case of considering private prisons, there was a comparative study of private prisons in other countries to explore advantages and disadvantages and also to examine the future possibility of establishing private prisons in Thailand. In fact, due to the findings, the Department of Corrections decided to drop the plan of introducing private prisons.

Among various successful projects, the meditation programme for inmates proved to be highly successful in terms of outcomes. Also, education training courses, particularly, the university degree programmes have been provided to many graduate students behind bars. Nevertheless, it is worth noting that the outcomes of these initiatives has not been fully evaluated yet and there is a need to follow and monitor participants' lives longer after release to determine whether they have reoffended or not following programme participation. Undeniably, one of the factors preventing evaluation was the lack of an effective inmate database.

Transnational Relations

Q: How have you been affected in your organization's work by development outside the country?

A: About 40 years ago, at the beginning of my career at the Department of Corrections, heroin remained remarkably widespread among Western countries. Thailand became the supply route, transferring illicit drugs from the production site to third countries. As a result, many foreigners were arrested, charged and sentenced for drugs trafficking across borders. Once they were sent to prisons, the foreign inmates were likely to complain about the living standards, in particular those who could not adapt to life in Thai prisons: food, weather, sleeping culture and language.

As a consequence, the Department of Corrections was under intense pressure after receiving complaints from many embassies, consulates and international human rights organisations. However, this has changed in recent years, as Thailand's Department of Corrections tried to improve the plight of foreign and all prisoners by enhancing and improving prison standards to be in line with UN standards. Also, when some foreign prisoners had been transferred to their home countries under Prisoner Transfer Treaties, these complaints were gradually reduced. These days, less pressure exists from the human rights agencies, but they still keep asking to frequently visit and monitor prisoners' standard of living behind bars.

The adjustment problems experienced by foreign prisoners in Thai prisons is partly due to the dissimilarity in culture, as such adjustment problems for foreign prisoners are found in other Asian countries. To deal with this, there was a gathering of correctional agencies in Asia and the Pacific to organise a correctional administrators' conference to discuss and exchange experiences among the attendees. This conference, which has been held annually up until now, is a great opportunity for all parties to develop correctional work in Asian and Pacific nations by means of official visits, training, and conducting research together. The Thai Department of Corrections has gained many benefits from this forum, particularly strengthening good relationships instead of facing intense pressure from neighbouring countries.

Role of Corrections

Q: How do you think public view corrections in your country?
A: It is undeniable that, in the past, public opinion of corrections was largely negative. The stereotyped view was that prison was a scary place, full of dangerous criminals, dirtiness and uncivilised punishment. Nonetheless, this opinion has become more positive. One of the key factors is the campaign called 'Opening Prison Gates to the Wider Society', which promotes prison products or services provided by inmates to the public. 'The Prison Product Exhibition and Fair' has been hosted in Bangkok for a week to gather and sell various types of products made by prisoners from correctional facilities all over the country. Apart from this, many prisoners could undertake public work outside the prison walls. To illustrate, some inmates were trained to sing in the choir, and one female prisoner won the Women's World Boxing Championships title while she was still in prison.

It could be suggested that Thai prisons have been more exposed to monitoring by outside groups, such as consular representatives, reporters, students and human rights agencies who come to visit quite regularly. More importantly, the Department of Corrections encouraged prisons to invite prisoners' families and relatives to participate in the 'Family Visit Day' event inside prisons. By doing this, the inmates could stay closely connected with their families by having the great opportunity to meet and have a meal together. On top of that, their families and relatives could observe the prisoners' lives in the prison world, including the living standards and activities provided.

Another example of an important event is the commencement ceremony for inmates where prisoners' families are usually allowed to attend and congratulate the prisoners on graduation. Owing to these changes, wider society and prisoners' families started to have better views about the prison system, which were different views from those they had initially imagined or held based on watching TV series or films.

Currently, I am quite positive that our society, both public and private sectors, is likely to offer support to Thai corrections at the highest level. Thai people tend to accept the custodial and rehabilitative needs and roles of prisoners, although there are some terrible news stories. However, it seems to me that the good stories have outweighed the bad ones. In fact, these days, many private companies are willing to help prisons in various areas, not only the provision of budgets to support the vocational training of inmates, but also assistance with many other activities in prisons.

General Assessments

Q: Are you basically satisfied or dissatisfied with developments in field of corrections?

A: In terms of satisfaction in the development of Thai correctional work, I think it has progressed from the past, with developments in facilities, higher levels of training for professional staff and a more effective throughcare system since the development of the prisoner intake system, correctional training, pre-release preparation as well as post-release supervision of the correctional staff. Society accepts corrections and has a better image of correctional work. As a consequence, they admit inmates more than in the past. This is the result of the openness of the prison to society and the creation of a participatory society.

However, many problems are not entirely solved yet, especially prison overcrowding. Overcrowding greatly affects the control and training of inmates. To be more specific, the congestion of inmates in prisons is a result of Thailand's lack of the implementation of both alternative measures and intermediate sanctions. Inevitably, misdemeanour perpetrators in minor cases are sent to prison and socialised with other, more serious, offenders. However, many parties are currently trying to promote alternative measures, such as house arrest and the Detention Centre with Intensive Supervision. Above all, proposed drug law reform may reduce the number of imprisoned drug offenders. The amendment to drug law aims to punish the drug offender after investigation of the offender's behaviour and background, and setting the punishment by taking behaviour and background into account, rather than only considering the quantity of drugs as the key factor in sentencing. If this implementation is successfully achieved, the number of imprisoned drug offenders, which currently stands at 65%, will be significantly diminished and this should lessen the congestion in prisons. As a final point, reducing overcrowding in Thai prisons will lead to an efficient treatment of inmates in the future.

Glossary

Bangkok Rules: *United Nations for the Treatment of Women Prisoners and Non-Custodial Sanctions for Women Offenders.*
BJMP: Bureau of Jail Management and Penology.
BuCor: Bureau of Corrections.
DILG: Department of the Interior and Local Government.
DOJ: Department of Justice.

DSWD: The Department of Social Welfare and Development.
Nelson Mandela Rules: United Nations Standard Minimum Rules for the Treatment of Prisoners.
PPA: The Parole and Probation Administration.
TIJ: Ministry of Justice includes the Thailand Institute of Justice.

Notes

1 United Nations (UN) General Assembly, *United Nations Standard Minimum Rules for the Treatment of Prisoners (the Nelson Mandela Rules)* January 2016, A/RES/70/175. Retrieved from: www.refworld.org/docid/5698a3a44.html
2 United Nations (UN) General Assembly (2010), *United Nations for the Treatment of Women Prisoners and Non-Custodial Sanctions for Women Offenders (the Bangkok Rules)* December 2010. Retrieved from: www.penalreform.org/priorities/women-in-the-criminal-justice-system/bangkok-rules-2/

Section V

South Africa

Chapter 11

Mr Johan Ellis Le Grange, Prison Leader – South African Department of Correctional Service

Interviewer: Anni Hesselink

Contents

Overview	181
Introduction	182
Career	183
Changes Experienced	185
Personal Correctional Philosophy	189
Problems and Successes Experienced	191
Theory and Practice	201
Evidence-Based Corrections	202
Transnational Relations	205
Role of Corrections	206
General Assessments	206
Conclusion	211
Glossary	211

Overview

The interview process for this chapter involved eight electronic communication interviews conducted with the interviewee and South African Prison Leader, Mr Johan Ellis Le Grange, over the period of July to October 2018. Due to the distance (of approximately 1,434.5 kilometres) between the author (who resides in Gauteng province) and the interviewee (who resides and works in the Western Cape at the Helderstoom Correctional Management Area), one-on-one personal interviews could not be conducted. It was also deemed necessary in the development of this chapter to direct three follow-up communications with the interviewee to clarify answers and to probe for more information in order to provide an accurate and clear picture of Mr Le Grange's views, experiences and working life in South African corrections.

The following interview addresses the unique correctional environment and intricacies of South African Corrections. For the purpose of this chapter, Mr Le Grange will be referred to as 'the interviewee', 'Mr Le Grange', or 'Le Grange'.

Introduction

South Africa is a democratic country with a diverse and soaring population estimated (in 2018) at 56.32 million people, which exhibits 11 official languages, nine provinces and a living space of 1,221,037 square kilometres, rating South Africa as the 24th largest country in the world.

Many people associate South Africa with Mr Nelson (Rolihlahla) Mandela – South Africa's first black president (1994), President of the African National Congress (ANC) from 1991 to 1997, Nobel Prize winner and activist against apartheid (Editorial Staff, 2018). Mr Mandela was sentenced to life imprisonment for sabotage and he served 27 years in various South African prisons, of which Robben Island is the most famous. Nelson Mandela's imprisonment was perhaps one of the first and most prominent exposures of South African prisons and prison conditions to the outside world (Nelson Mandela Foundation, 2019).

The South African Department of Correctional Service (DCS) is responsible for 243 correctional centres, of which only 235 centres are active (Department of Correctional Service, 2018). During March 2017 and March 2018, the DCS housed 160,583 offenders in approved bed space for 118,723 offenders. The overcrowding conditions, coupled with the country's high unemployment and crime rates, are a reflection of the socio-economic and socio-political environment, where South African prisons serve as microcosms of what is happening in society and in this country (Chabalala, 2019; Daniel, 2018; Department of Correctional Service, 2018; Felix, 2018; Stober, 2016).

During the 1970s and up until the early 1990s, the DCS boasted of being one of the best government departments in South Africa with an exemplary staff force, educated officials and excellent staff morale (Coetzee, Loubser & Krüger, 1995). However, at this time, the department was not without problems, evident in reports of detaining accused persons for long periods without trial, being held in solitary confinement without being sentenced, incarceration of offenders of different races in different prisons and prisoners' rights violations (i.e., interrogation) (Van Zyl Smit, 1987). Years later, the department was tarnished with issues of corruption, overcrowding, inadequate prison conditions, violence, gangsterism, inadequate mental health services, low staff morale and ongoing human rights violations (Chabalala, 2019; Daniel, 2018; Felix, 2018; Sekhotho, 2018).

Although the DCS refers to its incarceration facilities as 'correctional centres', the media, officials from the criminal justice system (i.e., police and court officials), and national and international literature refer to these facilities as correctional centres, prisons and jails interchangeably. Likewise, the terms 'inmate', 'offenders' and 'prisoners' are utilised interchangeably in this chapter when referring to incarcerated persons in South African prisons.

Career

At the time of the interview process, Mr Johan Ellis Le Grange was 58 years old with a 40-year service record at the DCS, South Africa. Mr Le Grange grew up on a small farm in the Klein Karoo, Western Cape, South Africa. Two weeks after he wrote his last subject in Grade 12 (Matric), he started his career on 5 December 1977 as a 17-year-old boy in the South African Correctional Services (then known as the South African Prison Service). He decided to join the then Prison Services because they offered interest-free loans to officials who were interested in studying further.

The candidate's employment timeframe, positions and major duties (although not complete due to space limitations) within the South African correctional environment are outlined in Table 11.1.

Due to Mr Le Grange's diligence, he was promoted from Sergeant to Warrant Officer. As a recruit, Le Grange was assigned to the Training Centre's financial office and he was awarded a trophy for 'best financial conduct' – an accolade associated with the 'most savings' and for the 'best candidate in the subject of financial management'. He enrolled for a Diploma in Public Finance and Accounting and this qualification was followed by a Bachelor of Arts degree in Administration (with Public Administration and Industrial Psychology as major subjects), obtained *cum laude*. He also received honorary colours and the Faculty's prize (a medal) for the highest achievement in a Bachelors' degree at the University of South Africa (UNISA), Pretoria (Gauteng province).

Table 11.1 South African prison leader's career path

Timeframe and position	Corrections profile and responsibilities
Timeframe: 1977 to 1995 Positions: From probation officer to Colonel	Finance clerk, basic training period and club treasurer Supervisor of salaries and accounts, prison statistics, facilities and finance Budget and resource management Personnel provision, assessment and utilisation Affirmative action
Timeframe: Middle 1995 to 2019 Positions: Deputy Director and Director	Provincial Head: Personnel, labour relations, resource management, community corrections, corrections division, risk assessment, policies, rehabilitation paths of offenders, quality assurance and security Area Commissioner: Overberg (Western Cape province) Management of: Strategic leadership, programmes, security, humane conditions, treatment of offenders, offender well-being, social reintegration, remand detention systems, parole, supervision, overcrowding, assessment procedures, and resource and risk management

While working at his first prison, challenging tasks such as carrying the keys of the finance office, managing the debt register, banking duties, payment of special salaries and balancing the prison's logistics and finances were entrusted to Le Grange. As a probation officer in corrections, he was assigned to train personnel in the administration of prisoner cash.

In 1985, Mr Le Grange was promoted to the rank of Lieutenant and appointed as Manager of Prison Services Projects at Head Office. In this role he was responsible for various committees and projects, including uniform for offenders, building of new prisons, training of staff in prison cash and warrants and budget management of the Prison Services. He established a system of financial accountability in every post in the Prison Service and for the first time, monthly financial meetings were held, and he developed a document stipulating the purpose of each financial activity that could be purchased. To date (2019), this document is still in use (with amendments through the years) and is known as the 'Activity Delimitation Document'. In 1986, Le Grange was promoted to the rank of Captain (from 1980 to 1994, the minimum period for promotion was two years) – making him the youngest Captain in the Prison Service at that time. The then Deputy Commissioner, Prison Services, requested Le Grange to be his Administrative Officer. In 1989, Le Grange was promoted to the rank of Major and he was placed in the Human Resources Directorate at Head Office, where he was leading 'Human Resource Utilisation' (HR planning, recruitment, transfers and promotions).

In 1992, Le Grange enrolled for a Master of Commerce degree in Personnel Management and Industrial Psychology at the University of Pretoria (Gauteng province) which he obtained *cum laude* (degree obtained with distinction) with honorary colours. His thesis was titled 'The development of a Culture Change Model for Correctional Services'. After his industrial psychology internship (focusing on decision making, consultation, management change and negotiation skills), Le Grange registered as an industrial psychologist. In 1994, Le Grange arranged a work session for all the provincial heads and the Commandment Office heads of personnel to clarify the new Behaviour Anchor Rating Scale (BARS) performance system and to discuss other challenges such as recruitment and promotions. During this work session, the General instructed that Le Grange be promoted to 'Provincial Head: Human Resources' in Gauteng province, where he established various recruitment, labour relations and utilisation procedures. Also, during this time, Le Grange was tasked to travel around South Africa to recruit potential black officials to be appointed as assistant directors, deputy directors and directors.

During 1999, Le Grange was appointed by the National Commissioner to lead a team to eradicate corruption and criminality that prevailed at the Johannesburg prison and, in 2014, he was appointed as Area Commissioner of the Overberg area (Western Cape province) – a position he still holds.

Regarding his career, Le Grange admits, 'It does not matter where I was placed, I tried to make a difference in the lives of people and I applied and developed departmental policies and procedures.'

Changes Experienced

Shortly after South Africa became a Union in 1910, the Department of Prison Services was established under The Prisons and Reformatories Act (13 of 1911). For the first four decades, the Department of Prison Services was strict on security, punishment and hard labour. Punishment methods such as corporal punishment, reduced diet and solitary confinement were maintained for offenders. A Prison Board was assembled to assure effective and humane treatment of prisoners, better detaining conditions and implementing remission of sentences subject to good behaviour.

A milestone was achieved in 1998 when the *Prison Services Act, 1959* was replaced by the *Correctional Services Act 111* of 1998. The government instructed that all state departments be managed according to business principles. This proclaimed policy removed many limits on the use of prison labour and during this time the *Criminal Procedure Act* was amended to constrain the imposition of the death penalty.

With the introduction of the *United Nations Standard Minimum Rules for the Treatment of Prisoners* in 1955, the policies of the old Prison Services had to be amended to fit into the trends and requirements of the Western world. This gave rise to the abolishment of the *Prison Services Act* (8 of 1959), which upheld racial segregation and incarceration as punishment (warehousing of offenders) while rehabilitation of offenders was ignored. Adequate standards regarding bedding, hygiene, clothing and food for offenders were instituted, and although international organisations such as the Red Cross visited prisons, other parties, such as the media and non-governmental organisations (NGOs), were not allowed to work in the prisons or to interview offenders or warders.

For the past 40 years, Correctional Services in South Africa endured a series of changes from apartheid to a democratic society. A philosophical change occurred in the late 1980s that embedded an imprisonment culture of rehabilitation and a name change from Prison Services to Correctional Services occurred in 1991, according to the *Correctional Services Act, 1991*. Designated top correctional managers visited Australia and the USA to study these countries' correctional systems. This led to the introduction of community corrections (enabling opportunity for parole or supervision in the community) and unit management, with both serving to diminish the overcrowding rate in prisons.

Another profound impact on corrections occurred with the release of Mr Nelson Mandela and the acceptance of the previously prohibited African National Congress (ANC) in 1990. This brought about intensive efforts to transform from an apartheid-orientated to a democratic country. The official language in the public service changed to English and this presented challenges, as English was (and still is) a first language to a small proportion of individuals in South Africa. During this transformation phase, an amendment was made to the *Correctional Services Act* (1991) to eradicate corporal punishment, reduced meals and solitary confinement as forms of punishment for institutional transgressions of offenders. The recall of apartheid policies resulted in the integration of self-governing states, such as Transkei, Bophuthatswana, Venda, Ciskei (TBVC) and Kwazulu-Natal (KZN) into the South African system, where one policy was adopted for all offenders in South African prisons. This amalgamation resulted in surplus staff in these states, compared to the South African ratios, and problems arose with decisions on whom to transfer to provinces where there were staff shortages. While negotiations were in process, a large number of officials were promoted without the necessary qualifications or experience, leading to them earning higher salaries than other officials in similar posts. This practice was reported to Parliament and the President of South Africa appointed the 'White Commission' to investigate and correct the irregular appointments, promotions and rewards that took place. Large-scale corruption and maladministration also occurred that prompted investigations into these irregularities.

Furthermore, a middle-management course for Majors before being promoted to Lieutenant Colonel was introduced to bring into line with the middle-management courses of the Defence Force and the Police Service. Financial management, team work, leadership, public speaking and other subjects that could assist the managers at the higher level of management were incorporated in the course.

The Reconstruction and Development Programme (RDP) of 1994 outlined the principles according to which transformation would occur. The RDP emphasised the implementation of non-racial and non-sexist principles, human rights and the rehabilitation of offenders. Transformation within the department was mainly understood as 'racial transformation of the staff force' and the forerunners of this process embarked on an organised campaign to ensure control of management and key positions. Widespread corruption and a culture of lawlessness was galvanised within the DCS.

In 1994, the department announced the 'White Paper on the Policy of the Department of Correctional Services' in the new democratic South Africa. The aim was to enhance debate on correctional matters and to prioritise and facilitate the transformation process of South African corrections in terms of a constitutional state with freedom and equality as underlying principles. The first five years of democracy within the department were associated with substantial changes to the management and personnel, in particular with regard to representation. Broad-minded efforts were aligned according to international best practices in corrections and an independent body (an inspecting judge) was introduced to oversee and investigate DCS's activities (i.e., human rights violations).

Labour unions (i.e., the Police and Prisons Civil Rights Union (POPCRU)) were acknowledged in 1994. The leaders of POPCRU were directly connected to senior comrades in the ANC and members of parliament and, through the unions and its political links, changes in corrections were established after 1990. POPCRU had its base in the Police Service as well as in the Prison Services and was a militant organisation that focused its powers on disruptions, use of firearms, hostage taking and in mobilising black prisoners to reach its goals. Le Grange was removed twice from his post to be replaced by a comrade in POPCRU.

During this period, a lack of interest in the staff's well-being by managers had a detrimental impact on staff morale and motivation and this resulted in the reduction of members interested in practising sport and a decline in dedicated correctional sportsmen and women. The decision to halt correctional sport championships had a devastating effect on a once fit and proud correctional staff corps. According to Le Grange, correctional officials' high work stress levels and exposure to a dangerous environment increased medical and psychosocial conditions such as depression, high blood pressure and alcoholism.

During 1997, minimum sentencing legislation was promulgated that prescribed minimum periods of imprisonment for first, second and repeat offenders (with the rationale to curb violent crimes). By the turn of the millennium, parliament was informed that the state had lost control over the Department of Correctional Services and the Jali Commission of Inquiry (2001) was established to investigate and report on maladministration and misuse of powers. Overcrowding became an increasing challenge and regular meetings were held within the justice, crime prevention and security (JCPS) cluster to reduce the number of persons awaiting trial(remand detainees) within the correctional system. Currently, approximately one-third of the inmate population in South Africa consists of persons awaiting trial. Efforts were made from Correctional Services and the courts to reduce the number of persons awaiting trial, a structure was put in place at Head Office, and policies were finalised to efficiently manage and centralise all remand detainees. Cabinet approved the submission and a 'White Paper on Remand Detention' was approved in Parliament.

The White Paper on Corrections (known as the 'Bible' of correctional practices and policies) was approved in 2005 and, in the same year, community gang members shot at correctional officials while they guarded an offender at the hospital. This incident led to questions from parliament regarding what the department was doing about the growing gang problem in prisons. Because of this, an 'anti-gang strategy' was implemented in the Western Cape province. A 12-hour shift system was implemented to reduce the cost of paying officials for overtime work and to provide 'hands' to carry out additional functions in prisons. This resulted in half of the staff being on duty and on some weekdays, due to staff shortages, limited services were rendered inside the prisons. To date, this is still a challenge, as there are not sufficient staff to do the work that is required by law: for instance, supplying offenders' supper in the evenings.

During 2011, the *Correctional Services Act* was promulgated to implement new legislation on the management of persons awaiting trial (remand detainees) and for them to wear uniform. The then Minister of Correctional Service, Honorable Nosiviwe Masipa-Nqakula, indicated that 18,430 posts would be created to implement the establishment of a seven-day week, but nothing came of this. The main intention was to prolong the 'inmate day' to create more time for rehabilitation and to address the lack of staff and security risks associated with a limited staff corps. Up until 2009, the department embraced a five-day workweek and a two-day weekend off period – this was much cheaper and more efficient than the seven-day week. The implementation of the seven-day week disrupted services at many prisons because of a lack of consistent shift patterns. Some correctional centres developed their own shift patterns, which resulted in staff working either too many or too few hours per week.

With the number of posts decreasing and an increasing inmate population causing additional work, the department appointed unemployed young persons (who did not necessarily have a passion for the correctional environment) and many of the new recruits did not make any effort to improve their qualifications or skills. Hence, they did not display a rehabilitation-orientated attitude towards offenders. Another change was the appointment of female officials. An inmate population of around 165,000 (of which approximately five per cent were female offenders) was in contrast with the pressure to appoint 50% male and 50% female officials. It was also important to have a system where administration officials worked the same hours as those that are centre based and that they be required to work inside the centres over weekends to understand the processes inside the centre.

Le Grange attended the first Imbizos (public gathering of communities) in his management area (as Area Commissioner), as some communities still complained about parolees being released into society. Le Grange initiated a social reintegration forum (SRF) that worked closely with key persons and decision-making bodies in corrections, members of the Community Police, a police official, home affairs official, representatives from the schools and churches, social workers and NGOs that would discuss high-risk parolees (i.e., with a history of substance abuse and gang involvement). Social auxiliary workers were appointed to trace victims of crime and to prepare the victims with the assistance of social workers. Victim–offender dialogue (VOD) as a restorative justice initiative ensured that the offender, victim, families and the community participated in the mediation process for the purposes of repairing the harm created by the crime. This is still a growing service, but it cannot produce the expected results in the absence of resources.

Concerning finances, no capital funds were received for the replacement of vehicles, and these have been breaking down on the road while transporting staff and offenders, causing serious security risks. As part of cost containment, the government implemented a process to limit stock (i.e., toiletries, etc., for offenders) on the shelf and this had caused discontent because sometimes there were no soap, toothpaste or jam for the offenders. Offenders also have to wear their own shoes because the workshops that manufacture the shoes are not operational and there is no money for external contractors. Further containment included the travelling of managers, which was reduced to 500 kilometres per month. When a centre in the management area is 300 km away, then it becomes a challenge to attend to all the needs of the centres and to attend meetings with other departments.

Personal Correctional Philosophy

The Finance Department of the DCS became a closed specialised group in 1983 and Le Grange requested to be transferred to the Prison Services branch, where he was appointed to consolidate and analyse the monthly and annual national prison statistics. He recalls an incident where Mrs Helen Suzman (freedom activist and the leader of the opposition in parliament) mentioned in parliament that the prisons are overcrowded because of 30,000 black persons being in custody for not carrying their passbooks (identity documents) – a law applicable to black persons during the apartheid regime. The Minister of Justice ordered an audit and every prison had to certify the number of inmates in custody related to the passbook law. The Minister reported to parliament that only 3,300 black persons were in custody for not carrying their passbooks. Mrs Suzman replied that he was lying to parliament. Furious, the Minister ordered another audit with an instruction that even a 'nil return' (zero per cent statistic) must be certified within two days. Back then, communication occurred through facsimile (fax) or a telegram. Some heads of prisons were called after hours at home to send their statistics by fax immediately. A small prison in KwaZulu-Natal did not certify their statistics and it was already late at night. The statistics had to be on the General's table the next day. Le Grange contacted the Head of Prison who informed him that he was booked off (due to illness) and at home. Le Grange then requested to speak to the Acting Head, who was also at home. However, the Acting Head did not have a phone at home and correctional officials were despatched to the Acting Head's home to transport him to the prison for him to provide the required statistics. When asked why he did not reply to the prison's statistics, the Acting Head stated that the prison did not house any passbook law detainees at the time. The Acting Head furthermore stated that the prison was far from the nearest town and the only available fax machine was at the police station (which is situated in town, about five kilometres from the prison). The Acting Head was requested to travel to the police station to fax the nil return certificate as the General was waiting for statistics from all the prisons. Before he complied, the Acting Head stated, 'Serge, I do not have a car, and how will I get to the police station at this time of the night?' Le Grange explained to the Acting Head that no matter how this happens, the certificate must be faxed through within the next hour – which then happened.

When the democratic dispensation (1990) started in South Africa and Nelson Mandela was released from Victor Verster prison, POPCRU was the main union in Correctional Services and their political support drove affirmative action. Le Grange and other officials were trained to negotiate and POPCRU came with a demand that they wanted promotion for black officials, whose qualifications must be condoned. After much preparation on how to approach the union and what to say according to policy, the negotiation team was instructed by the then General that 'this matter is non-negotiable.' The Union representatives were arrogant and demanding. When the negotiators from the Department explained why policy cannot be changed without the Department of Public Services and Administration's approval, they were belittled as 'rigid racists'. There was no support from the top management, except instructions that the policies must be enforced. These were trying times and one had to absorb these insults.

Le Grange, the Manager of Human Resource Utilisation at Head Office, realised that the department must fast-track the appointment of black people to higher ranks, but that there had to be a balance to make the white officials feel that they were acknowledged for their achievements. He then instituted programmes to enhance the managerial skills of non-whites to enable them to become managers, and for interested white officials with managerial potential to provide them with an opportunity to excel. Le Grange travelled through the country to motivate the staff to improve their knowledge and qualifications and for the mentors to lead the mentees. Within the DCS (1998), there were many inexperienced but potential managers, including officials from the TBVC states in senior ranks who were in serious need of training. However, Le Grange's removal from Human Resources in 1999 led to the programmes being discontinued.

At the end of 1998, Le Grange was called by a POPCRU representative who informed him that they were moving him from this post to Offender Control, as they needed his Human Resource post for a comrade of the union. Thus, in January 1999, Le Grange was moved horizontally in the organisation to the post of Provincial Head Offender Control – a post he had no knowledge or experience of. The functions of the posts included, *inter alia*, the monitoring and evaluation of administration related to inmates and overcrowding was, at that stage, only an *ad hoc* matter that you attended to when being asked to do so.

Concerning Community Services, Le Grange was privileged to be in the posts at Head Office and Regional Offices where he was in touch with the top management of other departments. This position assisted him to continue improving relations between the different departments and municipalities. He became known as a nodal person to iron out challenges. Part of his responsibility was to make contact with the mayors of the four district municipalities and he assisted them with support in the fight against drugs, safety in the community and the use of parolees to serve the community by cleaning streets and rivers, painting bridges, and cleaning schoolyards. Le Grange also participated in various safety and empowerment fora.

Under Le Grange's management, various rural public schools services were rendered, such as the cutting of trees and bushes, cleaning gardens, establishment of vegetable gardens, provision of vegetables for soup, painting of classrooms, building ramps for disabled children, replacement of window panes, provision of stationary, uniforms, shoes and winter clothes. Wheelchairs were handed to 36 persons and children and a house was renovated where both the wheelchair-bound children and unemployed mothers were assisted.

Le Grange and correctional officials from his management area also got involved in rural safety. Adding to this, Le Grange reasons:

> It is important to inform the rural safety committees about offenders that are to be released and to gain information from the community on crime trends and the behaviour of parolees. This is a win–win situation to get the community's buy-in and to keep them informed. Sadly, due to the economic situation in South Africa, these communities are not attended to on a monthly basis and it has many times resulted in the communities being upset about 'the police not doing their work' in combating crime and in assisting with criminals in the communities.

Problems and Successes Experienced

Through Affirmative Action, a memorandum was submitted to the Executive Management Board, where Le Grange negotiated for the condonement of qualifications in cases where officials qualify for the Officers Course. In 1995, many experienced Warrant Officers were nominated to undergo the Officers' Course. However, most of them were already in their late 40s and 50s and found it difficult to learn and sit examinations. Some had to sit the examinations twice or more before they passed. At the Officer's Course and Middle Management Course, Le Grange and psychiatrists assisted with career development and team building with the officials. *À propos* this, Le Grange postulates:

History proves that the condonement of requirements for a certain group will be regarded as unfair by the affected group and perceived as fair by the other. Even in a militaristic environment, the relationship between manager and subordinate should never be that authoritarian that the official cannot approach the manager with an open mind. There is a sensitive relationship between a manager and a shop steward where the manager does everything that he/she believes is in the interest of the organisation and being mindful of time and funds restrictions, while the shop steward does everything in the interest of the staff, regardless of red tape and funding. During the reign of President Zuma, it became customary to shout at another in parliament, showing no respect. This, unfortunately, spilled over to the unions and the staff doing the same while the manager must listen while being undermined or pilloried.

Le Grange further reflects:

In South Africa, citizens learned that when they submit their grievances to the politicians or administrators, nothing happens. To get the desired results, they strike, burn tyres and offices, and use violence and vigilantism – only then do politicians listen and money becomes available. This notion triggered the unions to strike to get results. South Africa needs managers that uphold the policies of the department and a top management that is independent from unions and that can support managers at local level when they are approached with demands on matters that cannot be changed by the manager. It becomes a serious indictment when senior managers join a union to protect their own positions and they disregard the position of the state, namely, to ensure that the policies of parliament are complied with. Senior managers, at least from Assistant Directors upwards, should not be allowed to belong to a union, or a union that represents those in lower ranks. They should be independent, so that they can ensure that the standing policies and procedures are complied with regardless of the skin colour, gender or affiliation of the official. Unfortunately, this did not happen between 1994 and 2004 and it caused major damage – effects that are, in 2019, still hampering the efficiency of the department.

During the late 1990s, about 20 investigations were completed into irregularities and abuses within the department. Le Grange elucidates: 'If the recommendations from some of these commissions were implemented, it would not have been necessary for the Jali Commission of Inquiry.' In 2001, the Jali Commission was assigned to investigate extensive allegations of corruption, maladministration, violence and intimidation in the DCS. Although senior managers preached rehabilitation, it was not the top priority in the department. Rehabilitation was ineffective and hampered by overcrowding, gangsterism, corruption and the attitude of staff, which was still cemented in security. The Jali Commission compared the conditions in South African prisons with that of a war zone, with extreme levels of violence where prisoners were tortured, assaulted, insulted, traumatised, and spat upon while in the care of the department. So, too, were many employees distressed and emotionally damaged by witnessing the rights of prisoners being dishonoured – all of which hampered effective rehabilitation efforts of that period.

With the new democratic dispensation in South Africa, the government has attempted to incorporate human rights values and international principles in the provision of correctional services and one of the initiatives that set out to accomplish this goal was the drafting and implementation of the new Correctional Services Act in 1998. Two specific matters that were embraced in the new legislation were: detaining all people in safe custody while ensuring their safety; and promoting the social responsibility and human development of all prisoners (Section 2 of the *Correctional Services Act 111* of 1998).

In 2000, it was reported to parliament that 'the State had lost control of the Department of Correctional Services' (Audit of Department of Correction Services, 2000). The inspecting judge system was still finding its feet, as it was only proclaimed in 1998 in the new *Correctional Services Act*, 1998. The Jali Commission did a thorough investigation into practices and policies and some of the findings include (Bouzaglou, 2006):

> *Gangs*: Prison gangs alleviate boredom, institutionalisation, idleness, sexual frustration and powerlessness. They are an ongoing threat to the functioning of prisons and it was found that some prisons were even managed by gangs. Thus, gangs play a pivotal role in corruption and violence. The Commission revealed that there is a direct link between street and prison gangs and that they work together to reinforce drug smuggling in prisons. Le Grange opines that:
>
>> prison gangs and gang involvement will escalate if it is not limited with strict control. The low level of education, lawlessness, joblessness, influx of hopeless people from other African counties and the notion to take what you did not work for, are contributing to gangsterism in South African prisons.

He further notes that:

> when these people are arrested for crimes, they continue with their practices inside the overcrowded and understaffed correctional centres. The main medicine for this ulcer lies in education of the society, which in itself is difficult in gang-stricken areas where children are at shot at while walking to school.

DCS staff members: Many correctional officials took bribes and 'turned a blind eye' to sexual abuse, thefts, and gang violence and they were sometimes complicit in these activities. Evidence illustrated that some members of staff even belonged to prison gangs. The Commission revealed that a 'culture of lawlessness' was synonymous with the department and that it was common practice for staff members to be forcibly removed from their positions and for unlawful actions to happen with exemption. This culture was enhanced by the benefits that resulted from unlawful activities. The Commission recognised that staff members were appointed on the strength of their influence within the union and management and those who did not enjoy union protection were intimidated. Many of these members resigned and those who persisted had to 'toe the line' or be forcibly removed. The union was no longer acting in a lawful manner in the department and appointments (even that of a Commissioner) were subjected to union approval.

Super-max prisons: Institutions of solitary confinement were found to be counterproductive to rehabilitation; instead they were known as institutions of torture.

Sexual violence: Members of staff ignored or supported sexual violence in prisons and some exhibited a lack of empathy and sensitivity to the sexual violence that 'plagues' prisons. The Commission noted a case where a young prisoner in KwaZulu-Natal reported to a warder that two offenders sodomised him. Instead of receiving support, he was sodomised by the warder, apparently the first of many such incidents. Furthermore, it was found that the department ignores the fact that sexual violence is rife in prisons and this may lead to prisoners being exposed to unprotected sex, HIV/Aids and in imposing a death sentence on helpless prisoners.

Overcrowding: This problem aggravates maladministration, corruption, violence, sexual violence, and gangs and it has a detrimental effect on rehabilitation. According to the Commission, up to 60 prisoners had to share one toilet, sleep two in a bed, while others slept on concrete floors, sporadically, with one blanket to share. In some prisons in the Eastern Cape, prisoners slept in shifts, constituting a 400% overcrowding rate. Overcrowding in some prisons were associated with mismanagement. This was in vast contrast to a prison 80 kilometres away (from the aforementioned prison) that was only seven per cent full.

In emphasising this, Le Grange points out that:

> overcrowding has, all through the years, been a matter of concern and the parole policy was mostly manipulated to get offenders out of prison earlier in order to reduce overcrowding until Community Corrections

was implemented (1991). The number of lifers [offenders sentenced to life imprisonment] escalated from 400 (1994) to more than 11,000 in 2013. In my post in the Western Cape, I became known in the JCPS cluster as 'Mr DCS' (Department of Correctional Services) as I had to address severe overcrowding in the Western Cape and interact with senior post incumbents of the sister departments in the province. From the meetings, a process was put in place to speed up cases in court, get children out of prison, and referral of bail cases back to court to reduce bail or to place them out in the community under probation. Several systems were put in place to decrease overcrowding, like monthly meetings where Correctional Services presents the statistics and overcrowding tendencies to the JCPS cluster. As a result of the successes in the Western Cape, these processes were rolled out nationally for implementation during 2004. These procedures are still in place and are monitored from Head Office as well as the Regional Offices. Besides, the mandate of minimum sentences (prescribed minimum sentences for certain scheduled offences) offers false hope to society that something is being done about overcrowding, while it is not the case, as South Africa is still one of the most violent and crime-ridden countries in the world.

Sexual harassment and abuse of power: A senior official made suggestive comments, sexual advances, inappropriate sexual contact and kissed three female employees of the DCS. This official was never disciplined; he was promoted shortly after the plaintiffs laid their charges. Instead of receiving support, the females were exposed to severe trauma both during the investigation of their complaints and in their working environment. One of them resigned, another was boarded on medical grounds while the third female remained at the department. This female was exposed to disciplinary action and was dismissed by the department.

Lax security services: The Commission received proof of prisoners who disappeared from prison, or escaped 'for a fee'. Staff members who aided in this were not severely punished. In the Eastern Cape, a prisoner escaped on six occasions – assisted by members of staff. This prisoner was nicknamed 'MacCyver' based on the television series in the 1980s.

The Commission recommended a prison ombudsman to prevent corruption within the department although it always had an anti-corruption unit, albeit not functioning effectively.

The department was fully aware of the findings of the Jali Commission while it was writing the White Paper on Corrections. In this regard, the hearings and submissions to the Jali Commission had a positive influence on the principles and policies accepted in the White Paper. The Jali Commission put pressure on the department to establish policies and procedures to place rehabilitation at the centre of its operations. Having been aware of its own trouble, which was pointed out in at least 20 investigations, a number of appearances before the Parliamentary Portfolio Committee and qualified audits, the department commenced in 2001 to write a 'Green Paper on Corrections' that should guide it towards rehabilitation. In 2005, the 'Green Paper on Corrections' became the 'White Paper on Corrections' and the department took full responsibility for correcting offending behaviour in a secure, safe and humane environment.

The White Paper on Corrections was finally prepared and ready for approval in Parliament at the end of 2004. Le Grange anticipated that the new Act would bring new challenges for which the department was not geared up. Being the Provincial Head of Offender Control, he started to implement processes and tools to enhance compliance to the new legislation, such as the assessment of offenders upon admission, compiling a 'Correctional Sentence Plan' to guide the rehabilitation of the offender, and risk assessment of offenders at admission and thereafter. This was the start of the risk and comprehensive assessments, Correctional Sentence Plans, Inputs to the Parole Boards and social reintegration of offenders that was put in place on a national basis.

In 2000, the new *Firearms Control Act* was promulgated with the aim to reduce the number of firearms in the possession of citizens. It also made it difficult for members of Correctional Services staff to obtain an accredited certificate because there were only a handful of trained assessors and a few shooting ranges that were accredited. Another challenge was that the students were trained in 'business shooting' (shooting with a range of firearms in a number of positions) instead of competency shooting (knowing when and how to use a firearm). Within the department, every competent official must reapply for their licences every five years. Extension to reapply for firearms licences was provided to the department, but financial constraints and practical realities, such as those mentioned above, hampered the department's compliance. This resulted in days when offenders had to be transferred to court or between correctional centres and there were not enough officials with firearms licences to escort these inmates.

Given this circumstance, Le Grange explains that:

> politicians are clueless where information comes from and what must be done to get the information. They believe that everything is available at the press of a button. Unfortunately, it does not work that way in South Africa. It takes sometimes weeks to gather the information they want, which looks like 'only for the sake of interest' because no improvement follows. South Africa is far behind the Western world with the computerisation of information. The computers are old and obsolete, the programmes were last updated in 1998 and new programmes are too costly to implement. Meanwhile, information is handled manually, which occupies officials with paperwork instead of security or rehabilitation.

In search of future managers, the department then took a radical step in 1997 to create 50 senior posts additional to those that were earmarked for Affirmative Action appointments. The idea was to appoint the 'cream of the crop' in higher ranks and give them the opportunity to grow at that level before they are moved to posts such as heads of correctional centres. Being an industrial psychologist since 1994, Le Grange was given the responsibility to travel through the country to interview potential senior non-white officers and to make recommendations to the National Commissioner. A psychometrist assisted him with the interviews, tests and reporting of identified and interested potential candidates for the posts. Over almost eight months, 1,623 applicants were interviewed. In Cape Town, one of the applicants, being a junior in rank, was so arrogant that he interrogated the panel and asked their views on Affirmative Action. Fortunately, Le Grange was well versed in Affirmative Action and the applicant accepted the reply. The applicant informed the panel that a Deputy Director's post is earmarked for him and that his interview 'is just a formality that whites introduced to select their preferred candidates'. The applicant furthermore warned that if he does not get the Deputy Director's post, he will know that Le Grange obstructed his appointment. Considering this, Le Grange indicates:

> It was only later established that the junior [applicant] was promised the post through POPCRU and that the National Head of Human Resources was waiting for the memorandum to appoint him regardless of the recommendation. Irrespective of the psychometric tests' outcomes, candidates were recommended for posts that they did not qualify for.

Further rounds of interviews followed, but by 1998, after the first recommendations and after the investigation into the irregularities of the first round, the leadership of POPCRU was not satisfied with the candidates that were recommended and blamed it on subjectivity and the use of the psychometric tests. By the end of 1998, the department recalled the use of psychometric tests and only relied on a short 30-minute interview. On this point, Le Grange says: 'this was a mistake, but the tests that were administered at the time were compiled on data from the USA and British participants, which of course are not applicable to the South African population and scenario'.

Before demilitarisation, the department, as part of the security forces, adhered to a military structure with ranks equal to that of the South African Police and the Defence Force. Medals and decorations were handed over on parades and even formal officers' functions were in place. Le Grange reflects:

> When an official in uniform and a rank walked in the streets, he or she was acknowledged. When one arrived at a public office, you were attended to first. You felt important. In prison, a similar situation prevailed. An offender might challenge the authority of a Lieutenant, but

the word of the Captain was law. The only time when prisoners got to see the Colonel was when they transgressed and when returned, they went to the single cells, with a restricted diet. Even today, years after demilitarisation, ex-offenders and many offenders call an official with a rank, Captain.

In mid 1995, the then Minister of Correctional Services, Dr Sipho Mzimela, announced that the DCS would demilitarise on 1 April 1996. According to the Minister, demilitarisation would improve the psychological effects of imprisonment on inmates, personnel and the whole country. He reasoned that the department assists offenders to change their behaviour and, thus, cannot be a military institution. Putting this in context, Le Grange adds that:

> This announcement was received with shock and joy. Those with ranks like Generals, Brigadiers, Colonels, and Majors were perceived as 'nothing' (a 'nobody' – a person without status). All staff of all the ranks wore the same uniform without any insignia, there was no parade in the morning and the unstructured routine resulted in chaos. Some officials bundled together, others ignored the morning gathering, the warders did not wear ranks, but they were mostly happy about this because nobody could see that they are at the lowest ranks. Those who previously enforced a structured and orderly workplace felt a collapse in the discipline in the department. Suddenly, the offenders disregarded the heads of centres because they had the same rank as a warder. Officials perceived the decision by the state to demilitarise the department as a blunder, as no system was put in place to gradually transform to a new dispensation. The effect of sudden demilitarisation of the structure and the loss of control led to an overflow of a large number of high-ranking officials in 1997. Hence, many of these officials took early retirement.

The decision to demilitarise was politically driven and it did not promote efficiency in the department. Insignia, similar to the military and Police Service, were implemented in 2003. For instance, an official would wear insignia that represents a Colonel, but will be addressed as 'Sir', holding a Deputy Director's post. The department did not refer to the term 'uniform' for officials, but to 'corporate wear'.

Le Grange clarifies that:

> although correctional officials cannot be regarded as soldiers, every correctional official is, in fact, a policeman and has the authority to arrest criminals. The Police Service underwent the same demilitarisation process, but they moved back to the use of military ranks and practices. In fact, the department should form part of the security cluster (police and

military) as their work is also to ensure that everyone in South Africa is safe. Our task is to rehabilitate offenders to live a crime-free and productive life that contributes to safety and productivity in society.

Efforts were made to move the department back into the security cluster, but to date this has been unsuccessful.

Next, challenges in Le Grange's career are outlined. The interviewee notes that:

> My correctional career is marked by a few disappointments. First, in 1997 a Director's post – Provincial Head: Human Resources – was advertised in the office of the Provincial Commissioner, KwaZulu-Natal, for which I applied. Interviews were conducted, and I was recommended as the best candidate by the panel. The National Commissioner at that time deleted my name from the list and replaced it with a black official's name. Three months later, the official could not cope with the position and he requested to be removed from the post. This matter was submitted to the Department of Public Administration and an investigation into irregularities in appointments in the department occurred. In those days, it was customary for a white person to be recommended as the best candidate for a post, but then a black person, who did not come out as the best candidate, was appointed.

The second hitch in Le Grange's career occurred in 1998, when several POPCRU affiliated officials were appointed as directors and some of these officials were not even officers at that time – most of them missed ranks. Le Grange admits that 'This was a big shock to me as I worked hard to get where I was in rank while it was not the same for the promoted officials and I felt disadvantaged.'

The third setback occurred when Le Grange received a call in 1998 from the Gauteng POPCRU leader (who was five ranks below Le Grange). Le Grange states:

> He informed me that I must vacate my post of Provincial Head of Personnel because he needed my post for a comrade. The next day I told the Provincial Commissioner about this, who just said we must accept that this is in line with Affirmative Action. I can help you to take early retirement if you do not agree.

A shop steward of POPCRU who was four ranks lower was then appointed in the post. Le Grange opines that:

> Many white officials were intimidated like this and no correction was made because top management was conspiring with the union and

fought for their own retention. I stayed in the department because my motto in life is that you cannot allow other people's attitudes and wrongdoings to derail you. You must be like a cork [i.e. of a wine bottle] – when you are pressed down in one place, you must pop up higher at another place.

Another challenging situation occurred when allegations were made of inconsistency, nepotism and victimisation (suspension without good reason) by officials. Because of this, a disciplinary action was brought against Le Grange's predecessor – the Area Commissioner of Overberg Management Area, Western Cape province. POPCRU representatives occupied the Area Commissioner's office and demanded results. The Regional Commissioner approached Le Grange and asked him to take responsibility for the Overberg Management Area and to restore working relationships. In accepting this position, Le Grange enhanced confidence and consistency in decisions and he applied the same treatment for everyone, regardless of position or affiliation, and as stipulated by the policy.

Another defeat occurred in 2015 – five years before qualifying for pension – when Le Grange applied for the post of Chief Director (Deputy Regional Commissioner) in KwaZulu-Natal. Le Grange was recommended by the panel as the best candidate for the post, but the National Commissioner decided that the preferred candidates were not requested during the interview to indicate how they would handle the politically unstable situation in the province. So, the post was re-advertised in 2017, and Le Grange did not apply.

While still in Gauteng, Le Grange initiated the 'down-management' of overcrowding, which at that time was 200% in the Johannesburg Management Area, meaning that for every bed space there were two or more inmates to be accommodated. Meetings were arranged with the Department of Justice, some of the staff of the South Gauteng Judge President, Magistrates and the Police Service to reduce the number of persons awaiting trial in prisons. This proved to be difficult because the police were of the opinion that they made efforts to get the criminal behind bars and the magistrates stated that their decisions are independent and if Correctional Services refers a detainee awaiting trial back to the court to reconsider bail, they interfere with their judicial independency. So, in one of the meetings, Le Grange brought along photos to show the impact of overcrowding on the drains and sewerage systems, water supply, hygiene, hot water systems, kitchens and staff. Le Grange purports that: 'all present at the meeting were shocked, as they did not realise the impact when you lock up 3,600 offenders in a place that was built for 1,600 inmates.' Gradually, success was achieved when all the departments worked together to reduce the number of prisoners awaiting trial through placement in the community under probation, reduction of bail to an amount that the person could afford, or to increase the court cycle time (for reappearing in court).

Theory and Practice

Due to the escalation in the number of inmates in prisons and the realisation that the country cannot build itself out of overcrowding, the department approached parliament in 1981 to approve drastic measures to reduce the prison population. A committee recommended the introduction of supervision and investigation into alternatives to imprisonment. The probation system in the American state of Georgia and a literature study of penal systems in Europe led to adopting the term 'probationer' as being in line with the *Standard Minimum Rules* accepted by the United Nations. This change led to the establishment of Community Corrections in 1991. The imposition of supervision of minor offenders assisted in offenders continuing with work, earning a living for their families and with reducing overcrowding. This adopted theory proved to work well in practice in South Africa, as alternative measures to imprisonment for first-time offenders for minor offences contributed to the reduction of the inmate population, family cohesion, and the economy, in so far as these offenders continued with their employment in society.

However, the communities where offenders were released questioned the remission of sentence, claiming that offenders are not prepared for release. Furthermore, regular amnesty was given to large numbers of offenders to alleviate overcrowding and the Department implemented a system where offenders were rewarded for good behaviour and completion of rehabilitation programmes. Accordingly, offenders earned credits for progress in rehabilitation and they could be considered earlier for placement on parole in the community.

During 1988 to 1994, Le Grange attended various external conferences on Human Resources and this enabled him to assist with introducing Affirmative Action in the department. He had to compile a list of non-white officers who performed well on their merit assessments to be earmarked for senior managerial posts. The results were not quick enough and POPCRU claimed that the department must put a plan on the table as to how it was going to transform to being more representative of the broader population. Meetings were held with union representatives. On the one hand, POPCRU perceived transformation as the appointment of black people in higher ranks, while, in contrast, the Public Servants Association supported appointments based on merit and prescribed requirements for transformation. The first meeting between POPCRU, the Public Servants Association and designated members of the DCS was unruly and aggressive, with demands to appoint black persons to senior posts regardless of potential or ability. One of the historical challenges was to overcome the qualifications gap. Only a handful of non-white persons obtained post-school qualifications. Suggestions that were tabled were the condoning of qualifications, number of years in the service, a promotable merit classification and training programmes. The policy concerning the number of years in a rank before one can be promoted to the next rank was condoned for black persons, so that an official could miss ranks. However, as much as transformation is important in the department, this incident proves that when theory (i.e., working hard, and being promoted to higher positions on merit) and practice (i.e., demanding higher positions without the necessary experience or qualifications) are not intertwined, that opportunities for maladministration and corruption can occur to the detriment of the department's efficiency and morale.

Electronic monitoring (EM) was introduced in 2013 as a further effort to reduce overcrowding. Tagging of offenders allowed for parole and for them to be monitored more effectively. The then Minister of Justice and Correctional Services, Mr Jeff Radebe, announced that 5,000 offenders would be released under EM. This never materialised because of the additional burden that EM placed on the already overburdened staff force and a technically insufficient control room. In 2017, this system was discontinued due to allegations of corruption and maladministration.

Evidence-Based Corrections

During 2002, Le Grange and other officials drafted a programme to enhance offenders' insight and understanding into their behaviour. They compiled manuals and workbooks that catered for literate and illiterate offenders. Officials were trained to facilitate the programme and, to date, this is still a prominent programme within the DCS. From 2004 onwards, rehabilitation became the underlying principle and every correctional official was perceived as a rehabilitator, regardless of the person's post. The government broadcasted that offenders' families are the primary level of correction of behaviour and community (i.e., schools and churches) the secondary level of correction, leaving the state as the driver and facilitator of correction of offending behaviour. Furthermore, 11 corrections programmes were operational in Le Grange's management area and these programmes focused on life skills, decision-making skills, self-reflection, sexual offences, economic crimes (theft and fraud) and behaviour modification for gang involvement. More programmes could have been presented, but, up to 2018, there were no posts for officials.

Concerning team building, one of the needs at Johannesburg Correctional Management Area (Gauteng province) was to have a team-building session for the management and the unions. Le Grange facilitated the team-building and strategic session where 'new life' was pumped into the officials. According to Le Grange,

> In Correctional Services one might be lucky to get approval for a team-building session for three to five days, but not for a follow-up. The challenge is always to get [non-attending] staff to do the work of those who are attending the team-building session. Another challenge is to get the staff who work directly with offenders to a team-building session, as they need it the most – it is difficult.

In his current position, Le Grange arranged with the Emergency Support Team to assist staff from lower levels to attend team building. But, he then confirms that 'in the large centres, where you lock up 1,000 and more offenders, this is not possible.'

In 2000, Le Grange and colleagues embarked on the President's Awards for Youth Empowerment (internationally known as the Duke of Edinburgh's International Award) through the Fish River Canyon in Namibia. The programme offers young people the opportunity to discover themselves and to grow on three levels (bronze, silver and gold). It covers areas such as sport, skills of choice, community service of choice and an expedition.

While in his current post, he contacted the President's Awards for Youth Empowerment, suggesting that it should be implemented in the Western Cape. Le Grange says:

> It was easy to connect the programme with offenders, but how do you allow offenders to go out for three to five days on an expedition or hiking trail? Initially, the offenders were taken out during the day and came back to sleep in the prison. Then I thought, if we want to make a change to the beliefs of the offenders, then we must show that we trust them. I met with the prison staff and we planned together to allow the offenders to sleep in tents. Security was arranged at a distance so that the offenders were not aware of the guarding, except for the two officials that accompanied them on the hike. This was widely accepted, although most of the heads of centres could not believe that it is allowed.

According to the President's Awards, the Western Cape is still leading the awards in South Africa. This was a breakthrough in the way offenders were rehabilitated.

Opportunities were created for offenders to play sports against external teams and they could attend graduation ceremonies to receive their degrees. Two offender soccer teams play rugby at league level against teams of the towns in the area. Le Grange further notes that 'the offenders displayed excellent discipline and it brought calmness to the centre. This is a wonderful way to rehabilitate offenders, as they learn to behave well to continue with sport.' Le Grange also made it compulsory for these offenders, as well as those doing other sports and activities, including choir, to improve their education as a prerequisite to being permitted to partake, as 'this assisted the offenders to improve their level of education while they enjoyed what they do (sport).'

Regarding victim empowerment, victims of crime, where agreed upon (according to the victims' availability and willingness), are included in the rehabilitation paths of offenders. This restorative process promotes offenders' sense of accountability and remorse for crimes committed. Furthermore, the damage and harm caused to the victims and their families are recognised, the victims are given 'a voice', and both the victim and the offender receive the chance to understand each other's point of view, circumstances and suffering. In this regard, Restorative Justice as an approach was accepted in 2001 with the aim to bring together the offender, the victim, families and the community in mediation to repair the harm created by crime. In line with the National Crime Prevention Strategy, the Victims Charter (2004) was implemented in the department (2012) to search for victims, prepare offenders to face their victims and to bring the parties together. Since the launch of the victim–offender dialogue (VOD) programme (2012), 85 VOD sessions were hosted and 1,342 DCS officials were trained across the country on the VOD implementation guidelines in the first year. Due to severe staff shortages, social auxiliary workers were appointed to trace and prepare the victim at the Community Corrections offices. This is still a growing service but will not produce the expected results in the absence of resources. NGOs are also involved in tracing victims, but they are not remunerated for any expenses. On this point, Le Grange reasons that 'the State should support [remunerate] them, at least for their travelling expenses.'

Unit management ensures that prisons are divided into smaller, manageable units, managing smaller groups of offenders (direct supervision) and this system also increases participation in rehabilitation programmes with less time for gang activities and earlier readiness for parole. In the light of this, Le Grange states, 'Unit management is a wonderful system, but in South Africa it never came to its full potential because the post establishment did not include posts needed for unit management.' The department did not see progress with the system and instructed that 'Centres of Excellence' must be identified to start to implement unit management and to have this system implemented in at least 80% of all the centres. Le Grange played a pivotal role in the training of unit management staff and he explained to them:

> It is not necessary to have a pool of programmes and a classroom for presentations before you can start with rehabilitation. Rehabilitation programmes must come from the soul of the official. Officials can help the offenders to prepare for interviews for a job, or to use eating utensils properly. The programmes can be conducted under a tree or in the cell. These all become lessons learned. But, it was quickly learned that success depends on the level of overcrowding and the attitude of the Head of Centre towards unit management, and in some prisons the Case Officers were responsible for 90 to 120 offenders instead of 30.

Most of the correctional centres are overcrowded and most of them were built with large communal cells to house between 18 and 22 offenders, but they actually house between 22 and 60 inmates. According to Le Grange,

Unit management is a workable model in any correctional centre where you have the required resources; the model is perfect to enhance rehabilitation on condition that you have sufficient staff and that the staff are actually rehabilitators and not security officials in being.

Transnational Relations

While a probation official, the induction training of six months was focused on semi-military principles. Le Grange explains: 'Strict order, discipline and obedience was drilled into us. What the "boss" said was law and no one argued against it.' Since the 1970s, developments in participative management, unionism, equal rights and democracy started to grow worldwide. In the 1980s, this was incorporated in curriculum at universities and articles were published in journals. The younger generation with qualifications that included the new developments became middle managers and received the chance to put their knowledge into practice. In this regard, Le Grange assisted with the implementation of Affirmative Action. It took him two years to convince top management to commence with special actions to promote females and persons from the under-represented groups.

In 1998, Le Grange was invited to the President's Awards (known as the Duke of Edinburgh Awards for the Development of Youth) conference in Cape Town, where the development of youth was discussed. The conference was attended by many countries in Africa, including Mauritius and Madagascar, as well as the Duke of Edinburgh himself, Prince Philip. Le Grange recalls:

> Interesting facts came out, like in some countries the windows in the walls of prisons are only open holes. When we asked whether they experienced escapes, the answer was 'no' because just outside, the prison guards with AK-47 firearms were guarding the prisoners. So, the prisoners knew if they climbed through that hole that they will be killed.

All participants at the conference were highly committed to start with the development of youth. Le Grange initiated the process and took offenders out of the prison, allowing young offenders to sleep outside the prison in tents.

One of the programmes that is still practised in New Zealand is the Control and Restraint course. This training was given in 1983. Of those officials that were trained, only one is still in service and he provides training on an *ad hoc* basis. When Le Grange was appointed as the Regional Head: Corrections in the Western Cape, he requested the trainer to train the emergency support team (EST) members because there were constant complaints by offenders that they were assaulted when the EST conducted special searching at centres. When he became Area Commissioner in this province, Le Grange identified the need to have his security staff trained to reduce the number of assaults, which decreased from 27 in 2013 to only five in 2018.

Role of Corrections

The public's view of corrections soon became clouded with allegations of corruption, intimidation, maladministration and misuse of power in the department. Several reports were tabled by the Auditor General in parliament reflecting the misuse of powers, intimidation, maladministration and murder in the department. The turning point was when a female colleague (the Regional Head, Human Resource Management in KwaZulu-Natal province) was murdered by correctional officials. This colleague was shot through a window in her house on the prison grounds and two senior correctional officers were convicted and sentenced to life imprisonment for her murder. The court heard that the assassination was planned after the deceased refused to consider the employment of the fiancée of one of the convicts because of a fraudulent job application.

As already mentioned in this chapter, the corruption and maladministration was so severe that the President of South Africa appointed Judge Jali (2001) to lead a Commission of Inquiry into all allegations of corruption, nepotism, maladministration and misuse of power in the department. While complaints were laid about the misuse of power and intimidation, no finger was lifted to support the victims. In fact, most of the managers in the late 1990s were affiliated to POPCRU. They were, thus, 'untouchable' because they were interlinked with politicians and members of the ruling party (ANC). Currently, similar reports have come to light where it is alleged that high-powered managers are involved in actions of corruption, intimidation, maladministration and misuse of power (Chabalala, 2019).

General Assessments

One development that contributed to the climate of chaos in South Africa is the implementation of Affirmative Action, which POPCRU used as a driving force for transformation. Race became an overriding concern and they tried every possible disruption to enforce their will in the appointment of managers. Violence and intimidation to reach their goals were the order of the day. It was so bad at one stage that they even had to be consulted for the appointment of the National Commissioner, stressing the injustice pertaining to the appointment to posts on the strength of their influence and not according to the merits of the applicants. The aggression with which POPCRU leaders enforced their will, regardless of the policies and procedures, left many senior managers disillusioned. The Jali Commission summarised in its report that the department was marked by lawlessness, intimidation, and dubious and sinister actions that were entrenched in the department. Because of the lawlessness, pressure and chaos, many managers resigned, leaving a vacuum in experienced leadership and a collapse of order and discipline in the department.

During 1999, Le Grange was appointed to lead a team to eradicate corruption and criminality that prevailed at Johannesburg prison. Allegations surfaced of offenders paying warders to bring in guns and ammunition to assist them to escape, of mistrust in managers and corruption by some officials. An action plan was compiled, and everyone was assigned actions to implement, to be reported on a weekly basis. For instance, the unions had to gain information on corruption, managers hadto implement morning parades, and to monitor the staff that came on duty. As expected, the union representatives did not make progress, but the managers took responsibility. During inspection at the married quarters, it was discovered that the member of staff living next to the Head of Security belonged to a car theft syndicate.

Because the number of posts decreased under an increasing inmate population, additional work was assigned to officials. One of the ways Correctional Services believed would address overcrowding was to build more prisons. In 1994, the then Minister, Dr Spho Mzimela, prior to joining the department, lived for several years in the USA where he gained experience of the operations of the American penal system. The Minster accentuated the importance of adapting to the systems that are working in other countries, namely the running of prisons by the private sector. A team visited the US and the UK to determine different models. Through public–private-partnerships (PPP) the state could react quicker to alleviate overcrowding through the building of more facilities. The private sector would then fund the capital cost and administer the facility and the state pays a fee per offender per day (over a period of 25 years). Two private prisons were built. One was the G4S Mangaung Maximum Centre in Bloemfontein (the Free State province) – managed by Group4Security, a British-based company. The second private prison was the 3,000-bed Kutama Sithumule Maximum Centre in Louis Trichardt (Limpopo province). The reason for allowing the two contractors to build maximum security centres was because of the minimum sentencing legislation, which increased number of long-term sentenced offenders. South African prisons were initially built to house minimum and medium classified offenders and not maximum-security offenders, so private prisons became the 'golden opportunity' to get the serious criminals out of the state-run prisons. However, the cost of repayment increased with inflation each year and the Minister informed parliament that it became too expensive for the state to continue with the PPPs. By 2004, some kitchens at large prisons were privatised to determine whether this could be cheaper and to try to improve the quality of food. Notwithstanding this, offenders are still used in the prison kitchens and vegetables and meat are still provided from prison farms, which assists in reducing some of the cost.

Offender-on-offender assaults, offender-on-official assaults and official-on-offender assaults are a worldwide challenge and are difficult to manage in gang-infested and overcrowded centres. The number of assaults in the country's correctional centres reduced from 12,018 (in 2014) to 7,800 (in 2018) per approximately 165,000 inmates. Le Grange summarises:

> I implemented several strategies to diminish the assaults. For example, inmates' complaints were solved within a seven-day period and the inmates received feedback; investigations into assaults were completed within 30 days after the assaults and disciplinary actions were finalised within the next 30 days. Offenders in the medium security centre started to play soccer and rugby and they could play against town teams, which significantly reduced frustration and tension inside the overcrowding centres. Officials were made aware of gangsterism and they were trained to be observant of gang activities. The behaviour of offenders who assaulted others was addressed and they had to show remorse for their wrongdoing – this had a positive effect on the rest of the inmate population.

Departmental decisions were taken in the past to have an ultra-maximum centre in each of the provinces, but there was never funding for this. In the Western Cape, Le Grange managed to divide one section of the Helderstroom Maximum Centre into an ultra-maximum unit. In September 2016, six officials were assaulted by eight offenders at the Helderstroom Medium Centre with padlocks placed inside socks. Le Grange soon realised that:

> high-risk offenders regarded as a flight risk or as high-profile offenders by the courts, or offenders who assault [officials or other offenders] must be housed in the ultra-maximum unit which consists of three phases. In the first phase, the offenders have limited freedom with no radios or television and they are not permitted to smoke – something that most of the offenders do. The cell door is locked, the offenders are cuffed when they move outside their cells and escorted by officials to the showers and exercising cubicles. These offenders are also formally assessed on a three–monthly basis. Every time the offenders misbehave, the period housed at this unit starts afresh (counting as day one). When they show remorse for their deeds and abide by the rules, discipline and order in the centre, they move to Phase II, which can be anything from six months to 12 months. In Phase II, the cell doors are open during the day with only the grill being locked. They can smoke, but still no radio or television is allowed, and they undergo corrections and therapeutically orientated programmes. After 12 months in

this phase, they are moved to Phase III, where the other maximum offenders are housed, and they are accommodated in a communal cell where a television and radio is allowed. In this phase they can exercise in a large area with other maximum offenders and they may be considered for performing labour, like cleaning of the rooms or passages. This process proved to be so successful that heads from other management areas and provinces are sending their high-profile offenders to Helderstroom, as offenders who went through this process do not want to be subjected to these discipline phases.

According to the current Head of the Maximum Centre, who has been in post for 12 years, this initiative is the best rehabilitative process that he has seen.

Le Grange reports:

> the maximum rehabilitation phase is working well, as over 220 offenders passed through Phases I and II during the past 18 months, of which 51 were classified as 'mediums' and functioning without any problem at the medium centres. It is still early to decide, but from the evidence, the ultra-maximum unit actively contributes to the rehabilitation of the hardened criminals.

Regarding the future, South Africa is in a unique situation to apply Western practices within an African context. In terms of overcrowding, much has to be done to reduce the inmate population. Currently, there is only accommodation for 111,000 sentenced offenders. The shortfall of 50,000 beds will cost about R50 bn to erect and billions of Rands more to operate. Le Grange opines:

> If it comes to a point to build facilities, South Africa should move away from building 3,000-bed monstrosities and rather build 500-bed centres in towns where the offenders are closer to their families. It is, however, not likely that South Africa will build itself out of overcrowding. More will have to come from the courts in terms of alternative sentencing options like house arrest and probation instead of incarceration. Investment should take place in security equipment and technology like cell phone and drug detectors, which are currently lacking in the country.

Le Grange furthermore notes:

> Offenders must be allowed to go out to play in rugby and soccer matches against schools and towns to improve their physical abilities as this opportunity to have more freedom, and a form of recognition (in terms of compliance and good behaviour) have proved to contribute to rehabilitation and reintegration of the offenders. They must also

improve their vocational training, apprenticeships, and go out for training to enhance their employability. Education and rehabilitation should include access to the internet that is currently a 'no-no' in South Africa. E-learning (online learning) must be allowed for offenders to improve their level of education at tertiary institutions. Offenders should be actively involved in their own rehabilitation by completing programmes to qualify for parole. In this case, we can even adopt the UK model, where, for instance, offenders and students are attending the same criminology classes. The internet has developed worldwide, and it is foreseen that where families are now driving up to 300 kilometres to visit an offender, that they [will] instead go to the nearest correctional centre, police station or church to Skype or video call the offender.

According to Le Grange, the breakthrough for the involvement of criminologists in assessing offenders and planning their rehabilitation path is very close. He states that an announcement was made that criminologists must have a seat on the Parole Boards, which will assist in sound decisions when placing offenders on parole. The interviewee recounts:

> More emphasis should be placed on restorative justice programmes and, where possible, attention should be given to the severity of the crime and the victims' needs. Offenders should rather compensate victims than be incarcerated. Victims must be registered on a database at court to inform the victims of the rehabilitation progress of the offender and victims must be actively involved in the decision process of the offender's parole.

Le Grange postulates that the data systems of Correctional Services, Police Service and the courts should be integrated and linked with the database of Home Affairs to link criminal actions with criminals in order to be more effective in fighting crime and to better research recidivism. He argues:

> More offenders must be sentenced to supervision or probation and they should be placed under community corrections rather than being incarcerated. Halfway houses are still in infant shoes in South Africa, but they can play an important role to house those offenders without families. Although unemployment is almost 28% in the country, more should be done to prepare offenders to secure employment after placement under parole or when released.

Electronic monitoring was implemented in 2013 and halted in 2017 due to alleged large-scale corruption. The interviewee says: 'This system can work, and it can reduce pressure on the state coffers if it is properly researched and implemented.' Last, South Africa's National Development

Plan's Vision for Community Safety, drawn up in 2012 as a blueprint for eliminating poverty and inequality and due to be implemented by 2030, promotes the safety of South Africans and aims for them to feel safe with no fear of crime. In this regard, 'The DCS must ensure that we deliver justice for victims, and offenders should make restitution to society, to their victims and leave correctional centres with better skills and prospects'.

Conclusion

South Africa has a complex correctional system that is perforated with a history of apartheid, where racial segregation and discrimination were practised in society and in the prison system. This era is marked with immense human rights violations and disrespect towards people from other races and gender. The release of Mr Nelson Mandela provided hope for many people in South Africa and we became a democratic and free country where race did not determine the area where you can live, the quality of education you can obtain or the type of employment you qualify for. However, with the new dispensation, the acquired positions of power created opportunities for corruption, misuse of power, unrealistic demands, maladministration and engagement in illegal activities. This time (currently), there are just different and more opportunistic types of illegitimate engagements than the human rights violation-orientated operations that occurred during the apartheid era.

These activities are shamefully outlined by the Jali Commission of Inquiry and some of the same activities (i.e., corruption, mismanagement and maladministration) are currently repeated by the Bosasa saga that is dominating the political and criminal justice areas in South Africa. These allegations and findings have a detrimental effect on the emotional well-being and morale of both the (diligent) correctional officials and the offender population, whose rehabilitation is in the hands of many corrupt and criminal correctional officials and managers. This aside, South African corrections can, with the assistance of right-minded and passion-driven leaders, become a global leader in corrections again.

Glossary

Affirmative Action: Also known as positive discrimination. Affirmative Action refers to the practice or procedure of favouring individuals belonging to groups that were previously disadvantaged and discriminated against.

Apartheid: Apartheid was introduced in 1948 in South Africa and is an ideology reinforced by the then National Party (NP) that called for racial segregation of different races (white versus non-white) in, for instance, social integration, quality of education, employment possibilities, living areas, inter-marriages and development of all spheres of life. Apartheid in South Africa is synonymous with gross human rights violations and racism.

Correctional Services Act 111 of 1998: This legislation replaced the *Prison Services Act* of 1959 and it embarked on a modern, internationally acceptable prison system, designed within the framework of the 1996 Constitution.

Department of Correctional Services (DCS): This department is a sub-department responsible for managing the prison system in South Africa. As with the police and military, it has its own flag and badge. The department hosts minimum, medium and maximum offenders as well as detainees awaiting trial (unsentenced persons). A political head, the Minister of Justice and Corrections, Advocate Michael Masutha, heads the DCS. The headquarters is situated in Pretoria, Gauteng province. In May 2014, the department was combined with the Department of Justice and Constitutional Development and renamed the Department of Justice and Correctional Services.

Jali Commission: The Jali Commission was founded in 2001 after widespread allegations of corruption, maladministration, violence, human rights' violations and acts of intimidation within the department (including the prisons). The Commission was named after the chairperson, Judge Thabane Jali.

Justice, Crime Prevention and Security Cluster (JCPS): The JCPS consists of all the ministries within the government in working towards a safer and secure South Africa and in building partnerships with the private and public sectors.

White Paper on Corrections: The White Paper on corrections that was promulgated in 2005 is derived from the Constitution of 1996, the *Correctional Services Act 111* of 1998 and from the integrated justice system. This dynamic and strategic document aligns correction with transformation objectives in South Africa and it drives the management and service provision of the department over the next 20 years. It reinforces values of human rights (education, religion, security, health care, and children's rights) while rehabilitation remains the core focus.

Chapter 12

Reflecting on Leaders in Corrections

Philip Birch, Mark A. Nolan, Martha Henderson Hurley and Dilip K. Das

Reflecting on all ten interviews with correctional executives from eight different countries, these correctional leaders' commitment to reform and their willingness to embrace the complex challenges this form of work entails is obvious. Again, the nature of this volume, and the expert interviewers' skills and knowledge of the jurisdictions discussed, has provided the reader with a unique collection of descriptions of challenges in contemporary and historical correctional management and of the successful and unsuccessful solutions to those challenges. Many wishes and plans for future evolution of correctional systems are clearly articulated by interviewees, providing a stimulating road map of options for future correctional leaders. Similarities in experience and professional orientation exist, which is the true emergent value of comparative work of this nature. In particular, the interviews conducted in languages other than English and presented here for the English reader in English, makes a highly valuable contribution to comparative analysis in correctional leadership worldwide. The following summary of emergent features of the interviewees' responses, taken as a group, follows the main headings and question themes utilised by the interviewees, which structure the report of each interview in the foregoing chapters.

A preliminary comment is that the various systems from eight countries presented in this volume can be grouped or distinguished in at least four dimensions: (i) responding to national independence relatively recently (Lithuania and the Slovak Republic), (ii) responding to significant prison scandals (Honduras, Japan and South Africa), (iii) responding to severe overcrowding, especially due to tough on (drug) crime policies of national governments (Philippines, Thailand), and, (iv) responding to demands for private prison providers (Texas, USA). Only one chapter in the volume was solely focused on a juvenile system (Chapter 4) and it was, interestingly, documented as a county system in the USA's decentralised approach to corrections rather than a national level of executive administration. Despite these unique pressures, there are emergent similarities under the headings below. That is even the case in the now militarised management of corrections in Honduras.

Career

A number of the interviewees had enjoyed, or are still enjoying, extremely lengthy stints in correctional or public service leadership, even if the correctional aspects of their careers were unexpected from the vantage point of their early careers or core training. For example, Mr Nathee Jitsawang (Thailand) spent more than 40 years in the correctional service system; Mr Johan Ellis Le Grange (South Africa) is still in corrections after 40 years, while Colonel Garcia (Honduras), from a military service background, was unexpectedly called upon to direct a national correctional system and has close to 40 years' experience.

In terms of disciplinary career changes and intriguing pathways into corrections, we see the following range of career movements. Živilė Mikėnaitė was initially trained in mathematics and IT before police training, legal training (to Masters level) and academic work before becoming the first woman to lead a confinement institution in Lithuania. For Martin Lulei, from the Slovak Republic, the move was not so unexpected after university studies and work experience in mediation, probation, criminal law and social work and victim support. This mirrored the apt study and training for Danny Pirtle, from Dallas County, Texas, USA, whose university study, culminating in doctoral study in juvenile justice, saw him leave academia and lead juvenile justice service units before returning to teaching and academia. The interview with Danny Pirtle reveals strong, clear and candid reasons for returning to academia from correctional leadership, despite him thinking he 'wanted to finish his career in the field'. The interview also records his view that his academic work and teaching is greatly enhanced by correctional system leadership, and, that he 'would not trade' the field experience he had in juvenile justice for anything. Similar related university-level training in criminal justice was completed by Tomiyama, from Japan, before he commenced a career in corrections, and Jitsawang, from Thailand, was a law graduate but also held positions titled penologist, legal officer, researcher and Director of Correctional Staff Training before becoming a Deputy Director-General and then Director-General of the Department of Corrections.

More unexpected career moves included that of Adonay Davila, from Texas, who wanted to be a police officer but waited three years for a police academy invitation following slow security clearance procedures due to his juvenile traffic fines record; just enough time for him to catch the correctional service bug completely and to refuse the eventual offer to train as a police officer. In the Philippines, it is now required that all correctional staff have a university degree. Randel Latoza's was in civil engineering before training at a police academy and making the unexpected discovery that he could work in remand facilities by joining a jail department rather than a prison department once he set his sights on correctional service.

There are standout examples (e.g., Tomiyama from Japan and Davila from Texas) of the rare situation of highly experienced low-ranking correctional officers eventually being promoted to become correctional system executive leaders able to structure system-wide policy and procedural changes from the perspective of grass roots practice and much lived experience on the ground in prisons. Adonay Davila is in the rare situation of having a highly distinguished career in public corrections before working in private corrections, facilitating rich comparative comments between those two systems in his interview. From these criminal justice correctional jobs, he has also ended up in executive positions in immigration detention facilities, another telling and pressing comparison many countries also have between criminal and administrative detention regimes. What is intriguing about these highly experienced correctional officers becoming executives is their familiarity with the lot of those they lead; Davila, in particular, experienced significant and extreme stress and challenge in highly violent correctional facilities and prisons with high rates of mental illness and use of segregation as a younger correctional officer.

Other leaders (e.g., Pirtle from Texas, Chapter 4) have decided to move back into academia having served some time as a correctional leader at the coalface of correctional management, suggesting that links made between theory and practice can shape mobile careers and movement between leadership and advocacy roles from both within and outside of executive teams working in prisons and correctional departments.

Changes Experienced

As the reader learns of the positive and negative system and practice changes the correctional leaders catalogued, it is clear that there are some rather unique jurisdictional politics, history and social changes contextualising the evolution of each correctional system. In the relatively new and independent nations of Lithuania and the Slovak Republic, a raft of new and constantly amended correctional and criminal legislation has posed many challenges for correctional leaders, and, in the case of the Slovak Republic, is further shaped by the regional compliance demands of EU membership. For those systems responding to scandal (e.g., 362 deaths from a fire started by a prisoner igniting his mattress in Honduras and aggression by correctional officers leading to one prisoner's death and one with permanent disability in Japan), the drastic changes witnessed by the relevant correctional officers are motivated by a need to recover public confidence in corrections. For those systems facing crushing overcrowding due to tough on (drug) crime political agendas (e.g., the Philippines at 400% overcrowding and a 40% prison population increase since 2016, and Thailand with 65% of all inmates still incarcerated for drug crimes), the ability to change much at all is remarkable and the leaders lament how their hands are somewhat tied as managers by the pressures of overcrowding. Those jurisdictions like Texas, that has seen four private prisons in 1989 (housing around 2,000 prisoners) swell to 16 private facilities with 12,908 beds in 2015, have witnessed probably the biggest change, and surrendering of private trust in correctional administration, of all the jurisdictions considered in this volume. As Adonay Davila notes, privatisation requires contracting governments to negotiate well with private providers in a highly detailed fashion if comparable prisoner experience is to be guaranteed in both public and private prisons in the one state.

Further examples of the changes noted by the interviewed correctional officers range from the realisation that true rehabilitation and reintegration success post-release only flows from individualised case management and throughcare, rather than 'one-size-fits-all' oppressive confinement and programming (Lithuania, Japan, the Slovak Republic), via an embrace of the utility of probation (the Slovak Republic), therapeutic communities and residential drug programmes in prisons (Dallas County), and greatly improved officer to prisoner ratios from the unworkable 228:1 ration once tolerated in some Texan facilities prior to the legal decision in *Ruiz* v. *Estelle* (see Chapter 4). It also requires understanding that new facilities must be built to prevent overcrowding and new correctional staff training academies are needed to develop the professional or occupational identity of correctional officers (Honduras), the provision of (para-)legal services in remand jails to avoid some remandees spending a decade or more in custody pre-trial (the Philippines), and, some notable demographic changes in prisoner profile, from poorer and less educated to wealthier and better educated perpetrators (Thailand).

Personal Correctional Philosophy

Many of the leaders stated that correctional philosophy must move away from punitiveness (South Africa), isolation (Lithuania), compulsory work (Japan), and strict security concerns (Thailand) *only*. In their place, the most favoured correctional philosophies espoused by these highly experienced and some newer correctional leaders were shaped by realisations that individualised justice is paramount if re-entry and reintegration is to succeed. In turn, that success depends on the adoption of apt correctional cultures and philosophies centred on rehabilitation and improving prisoners as people (Texas, South Carolina, Honduras, Thailand), dignity/human rights and treating prisoners as human beings (Philippines), challenging the rationale for current practice (Dallas County), and, even contemplating better separation of violent and non-violent prisoners (Texas).

In the case of Honduras, specific dimensions of rehabilitation are currently articulated as goals based on vocational, educational, spiritual, and occupational engagement. Further subtlety in correctional philosophy was conveyed by Tomiyama (Japan), who emphasised that professionalism and training of correctional staff working within well-supervised and open and non-defensive work cultures is key to implementing the other aspects of desirable correctional philosophy. This Japanese leader, heavily involved in investigating and responding to the 2001–2002 Nagoya prisoner maltreatment scandals, notes that the implementation of any correctional philosophy must result in societal trust of correctional authorities. Again, more subtlety exists for Tomiyama in demanding teaching of life skills and not just vocations as part of any rehabilitation programme focused on criminogenic needs etc., acknowledging that many offenders without core life skills need to be habilitated as they cannot just rehabilitate if they never had those skills prior to offending.

Problems and Successes Experienced

The level of specific detail given in the reflections on successes and ongoing problems for correctional leaders is a trove worth considering by any new or incoming correctional leader. Not only would digestion of these summaries by the interviewed correctional leaders assist others to prevent 'reinventing the wheel', but there is possible reassurance here that tough decisions and innovative approaches do produce both desired as well as unintended consequences and that both of these can be managed with humility and honesty. Taking such decision-making risks, such as introducing new programmes and being provocative as a correctional leader, seem worth it for good correctional leaders who must respond to pressures and demands from many directions. Many of the problems and ongoing systemic deficiencies identified by these eight leaders may seem like intractable systemic concerns; however, attempts to tackle these are the dimensions upon which all correctional leaders are judged and they are the motivations for such work.

Examples of problems noted by the interviewed leaders included poor and failing infrastructure (Lithuania), adverse impact of actuarial and other risk assessment tools on minorities, leading to harsher and more incarceration of minorities (Dallas County), high correctional staff turnover rates (Dallas County), lack of management and leadership training for correctional leaders (Dallas County), overly hasty abandonment of immature programmes (Texas), still attempting to manage prisons and lead correctional staff through fear alone (Texas), setting up programmes for failure (e.g., returning graduates of a gang renunciation programme back into a gang-structured general population of a prison (Texas), lack of prisoner classification assessments (Honduras), lack of security technology (Honduras), escalation of inappropriate control methods via excessive rule imposition (e.g., marching when moving in Japanese prisons), aging prison populations (Japan), corruption (the Phillipines, South Africa), and the need for diversion programmes, especially for drug offenders (Thailand).

Examples of successes proudly related by the interviewed leaders included implementing individual case management systems and dynamic security approaches to understand each prisoner better as an individual (Lithuania), a gardening project that assists in beautifying aging infrastructure too (Lithuania), cooperation between prisons, academics and NGOs to improve educational opportunities (the Slovak Republic) and wider partnership working (South Carolina), justice reinvestment initiatives that provide community programmes as alternatives to incarceration (Dallas County), graduation pride in vocational programmes (Texas), training correctional staff in the links between trauma and offending (e.g., under Federal US schemes such as PREA, Dallas County), more manageable case manager to client ratios (1:25 instead of 1:50, Dallas County), use of youth diversion courts (Dallas County), improving food (Honduras) by making wardens directly responsible for food quality rather than outsourced providers (the Philippines), targeted prison programmes (e.g., for drugs, gangs, sex offenders, traffic offenders, and perpetrators needing to develop empathy with their victims, Japan), deregulation of health services in prisons to encourage more doctors and allied health professionals to work in prisons (Japan), searching corrections officers before shifts and cells to reduce weapons and other contraband in prisons (the Philippines), and elite athlete development programmes (Thailand).

Theory and Practice

The clearest example of the value given to the 'vital' (Lithuania) nexus between theory and practice by the interviewed correctional leaders is the commitment to lifelong learning and higher education shown by the leaders themselves. Some leaders powerfully and simply acknowledged that 'practice without theory is reckless' (Tomiyama, Japan), especially when designing and evaluating programmes. Predictably, years of executive leadership give each leader a sharp critical edge to their engagement with theory and academic critique of correctional systems and correctional practice. However, most leaders believed that a connection between theory and practice is crucial and will usually provide mutual benefit between the communities of correctional leadership practice and the academy, realising the core *raison d'être* of professional associations such as IPES.

Examples given of successful integration of theory and practice included higher education courses for correctional officers, especially in law and psychology (Lithuania), and internships (the Slovak Republic).

Biggest obstacles to a better integration between theory and practice were noted as follows: a lack of some core disciplinary experts in some jurisdictions (e.g., lack of criminologists in Honduras, instead, being guided in policy decisions by reports written only by lawyers, priests and/or human rights activists), academics being overly critical of correctional officers instead of correctional officers being engaged in equal discussions with academics (Japan), language of the published theory (often only in English and few larger works translated from English (Japan),

Evidence-Based Corrections

Following on from the overwhelming support for fostering the nexus between theory and practice is an endorsement that evidence-based corrections is the way of the future. However, many leaders lamented that correctional system staff are poorly trained to understand the evidence base and to implement its findings (Thailand). Furthermore, many correctional systems do not fund, or cannot adequately resource, evaluative studies of programmes or other system innovations to engage in evidence-based correctional practice (the Slovak Republic, the Philippines). It is clear from the interviews that contemporary correctional leaders must utilise evidence-based evaluations and the fruits of evidence-based research. This is probably clearest in the discussion of the increased use of risk assessment tools provided by the burgeoning literature on these and their implementation. Despite the clear benefit evidence-based risk assessment has had in correctional assessments, some leaders still sounded warnings about these tools not being foolproof and false positives and other errors still resulting in the incarceration of the less dangerous or the overrepresented (Dallas County).

Transnational Relations

It is clear that correctional leaders work in a globalised world and that they learn much from each other, despite some apparent differences in systems. Not only does meeting and learning from correctional leaders from other jurisdictions educate correctional leaders deeply and seem highly valuable, but such mutual assistance is the most concrete way to allow international norms and best practice to spread around the world. When this happens, the correctional leaders are reassured in their decision making that they would be vindicated and judged more fairly against regional or international norms of best practice. Examples included the EuroPris network of 20 European countries discussing ethics, human rights, and best practice as well as hosting educational tours and cooperative training sessions (Lithuania). Other leaders spoke of support from particular historic or contemporary development allies (e.g., the Czech Republic supporting the Slovak Republic; Dominican Republic as a model for Honduras) and some were assisted by standard diplomatic engagement regarding foreign prisoners' experiences and extradition requests (Japan, Thailand). Some examples of transnational cooperation shone light on particular correctional challenges (e.g., support from the Letot Centre to increase understanding of the offending and rehabilitation challenges for juvenile victims of trafficking, as mentioned by Danny Pirtle, Dallas County). Even though some correctional leaders concluded that their system was unique and could not adopt some of the practices and innovations successful in other places, knowing of the options others have tried and succeeded with (or not) seemed to be acknowledged as the cornerstone of contemporary correctional practice.

Role of Corrections

Of those leaders who developed statements of correctional philosophy into broader views about the society role of corrections, the following points were made. Živilė Mikėnaitė from Lithuania stated that society is 'more interested to condemn rather than extend a helping hand' to prisoners, explaining the tension over the question of the role of corrections in that society that often plays out in the media or in policy and practice debates. Martin Lulei, from the Slovak Republic, expresses the role of corrections as being to instil a sense of responsibility in offenders but to provide them with 'health and dignity' and the skills to re-enter society. Danny Pirtle, from Dallas County, simply quips that if the role of corrections is not being debated in the media, then correctional leaders are clearly doing a good job! Tomiyama, from Japan, notes the paradox of Japanese society valuing corrections only if the correctional institutions and parolees are 'Not in My Back Yard!'. Randel Latoza, from the Philippines, takes issue with political campaigns such as President Duterte's 'war on drugs' which confuse the role of corrections within society and lead to unmanageable overcrowding. Nathee Jitsawang, from Thailand, describes that the best way the Thai correctional leaders found to promote rehabilitation as a core role for corrections was to hold community fairs and presentations. These events provide an opportunity where prison industries and prisoners achievements are described and the public can see the fruits of rehabilitative orientations within corrections for themselves as an anti-stigma campaign. More broadly, all of the interviewees presented in this third volume of *Trends in Corrections* believe in the positive role that corrections can and does play in society. While there are improvements to be made in the delivery of correctional practice, there is global evidence of positive change occurring within the sector.

General Assessments and Conclusions

This summary and overview of the views of the correctional leaders as a group, defined by many similarities but also some differences, ends with a few choice quotes from the interviews when interviewees were asked to make general assessments of the correctional system they work or worked in. These questions in the interviews tended to serve as summarising hopes and dreams about the future of corrections in each system. Most, but not all, of the interviewed correctional leaders responded clearly to this invitation by interviewers.

A general view from the Lithuanian leader was that a general goal must be to increase the level of individual case management of prisoners but to also remember to provide safe conditions for everyone within prisons and in the society to which prisoners return, concluding that leaders must witness an increase in funded research and collaborative activity. A general comment from the Slovak Republic included the paradox that society is punitive and demands uncompromising punishment of adult criminals but still has a somewhat humane and reintegrative view about the fate of juvenile offenders. A wish here is that greater use of intermediate or alternative or diversionary options will be possible into the future. Danny Pirtle, on retreat from Dallas County juvenile correctional leadership back into academia, laments that correctional research is often of quite a high standard and done appropriately at the right times on the right questions, but the implementation of that research is still poor and correctional leaders are often not supported in their desires to implement our scientific evidence-based knowledge of what works. This position, in part, is reflected in Fred Lux's chapter; however, in this chapter, in which Major Anderson is interviewed, a more optimistic view of corrections is presented, in that it is heading in the right direction in terms of evidence-based knowledge informing practice.

Brian Norris comments that the radical militarisation of the Honduran corrections system suggests that, when all else failed, the Honduran government and the Honduran people trusted the military to lead reform and control of corrections. Satoshi Tomiyama, from Japan, makes a practical and clear general point: employers must commit to supporting the employment of ex-prisoners in Japan to facilitate their reintegration and provide a protective factor against recidivism, especially when 94% of Japanese sentences of imprisonment are for three or fewer years. Randel Latoza, from the Philippines jail system, hopes that jails and prisons in his jurisdiction collaborate more so that insights about managing sentenced prisoners can flow to educate leaders managing remand facilities. He does comment that he is pleased that judges and lawyers now seem to respect correctional officers in the Philippines more as equals now. Echoing many comments from many leaders interviewed for this volume, Nathee Jitsawang from Thailand, one of the longest serving correctional leaders interviewed for this book, reflects on his 40 years of work and states that future correctional leaders will have to prioritise throughcare and making even more of a bridge between incarceration and re-entry into the community if the efforts of correctional leaders around the world are to find favour with many. Drawing the interview chapters to a close, Ann-Mari Hesselink presents the final interview, from a South African perspective, in which the importance and effect of affirmative action is illustrated. Since the release of Nelson Mandela from prison in the mid 1990s, the South African Corrections Department has experienced a shift in correctional practice, one where there is better treatment of prisoners and where racial segregation does not occur.

Final Thoughts

By drawing together the themes of the interviews presented in this third volume of *Trends in Corrections* the importance of both agile and responsive leadership in corrections is evidenced. As noted earlier, in Chapter 1, the need for corrections to be up to date with innovative policy and contemporary practice is a requirement for those in leadership and management roles. There is a need for these positions to be theory driven and evidence based. From examining the interview data presented in this volume, there are a number of trends affecting the future context of leadership within corrections, including shifting demographics, changes in community expectations and rapid technological advances, to name but few. These trends are all interrelated and together they are driving complexity and change at unprecedented rates, which corrections services around the world are already experiencing. The impact of such trends and changes involves technological innovations, for example, with the management of offenders, as well as growing social diversity within the system, such as ageing prisoner populations. As a consequence, future correctional organisational structures need to be more efficient in terms of cost and flexible enough to cope with greater innovation. Corrections leaders must, therefore, remain responsive to local needs as well as being capable of remotely coordinating and leading the work of prison officers. However, these leaders also need to exercise sufficient influence with partner agencies in the collaborative delivery of services such as education and training. Corrections leaders are responsible for driving their organisation forward and, while a clear strategic direction is required for any organisation, it becomes no more than a paper exercise if it has no achievable goals and direction. Clearly, corrections executives need to drive an organisation to achieve their strategic goals and the leadership role involved in ensuring that the values of the organisation are shared across it is imperative. Often the effectiveness of the individual leader and their management team can be measured simply by examining the 'buy-in' of the personnel to the organisational goals. The degree of 'buy-in' will frequently be determined by the demonstrable relevance of the strategic direction to the external environment and the integrity, commitment and persuasiveness of the individual leader in the promotion of these interconnected components. Therefore, leaders within corrections must stay agile and responsive to current and future changes and challenges, bringing all those who work in the organisation along with these changes and challenges, the importance of which is reflected in the work of Dunoon (2002) who considers 'Learning Centred Leadership'. The approach of Learning Centred Leadership creates a transformational environment in which to 'reframe issues and opportunities and identify viable pathways for action' (Dunoon, 2002, p. 9). The changes and challenges that face corrections leaders in the 21st century, in large part, could not have been imagined by many of those interviewed in this volume decades ago when they joined corrections. However, their ability to enhance and evolve their knowledge and skills over their career is reflected in the accounts of those interviewed and has been central to their success, at both an individual and an organisational level. It is this ability to evolve that has also allowed those interviewed to respond to the problems that have emerged over the course of their careers. As such, the future of corrections lies within the leadership of these organisations and their ability to respond to, and effectively manage, change and challenges, both individually and organisationally.

International Police Executive Symposium (IPES)

The International Police Executive Symposium (IPES) brings police researchers and practitioners together to facilitate cross-cultural, international and interdisciplinary exchanges for the enrichment of the policing profession. It encourages discussions and writing on challenging topics of contemporary importance through an array of initiatives, including conferences and publications.

Mission

Founded in 1994 by Dilip K. Das, PhD, IPES is a registered not-for-profit educational corporation. It is funded by the benefaction of institutional supporters and sponsors that host IPES events around the world.

Dr Das has years of experience in police practice, research, writing and education. A professor of criminal justice, former police chief, founding editor-in-chief of *Police Practice and Research: An International Journal*, Dr Das is a human rights consultant to the United Nations. Dr Das serves as president of IPES and manages the affairs of the organisation in cooperation with an appointed group of police practitioners, academia members, and individuals from around the world.

IPES Annual Meetings

The International Police Executive Symposium's major annual initiative is a four-day meeting on specific issues relevant to the policing profession. Past meeting themes have covered a broad range of topics from police education to corruption. Meetings are organised in conjunction with sponsoring organisations in a host country. To date, meetings have been held throughout North America, South America, Europe and Asia.

The IPES' annual meetings bring together ministers of the interior and justice, police commissioners and chiefs, members of academia representing world-renowned institutions and many more of criminal justice elite from over 60 countries throughout the world. The meeting facilitates interaction, and the exchange of ideas and opinions on all aspects of policing. The agenda is structured to encourage dialogue in both formal and informal settings. Meeting participants are requested to present a paper discussing the meeting's theme from their country's perspective. Compilations of selected papers from each meeting have been published, or are in the stages of preparation for publication. IPES advocates, promotes and propagates that policing is one of the most basic and essential avenues for improving the quality of life in all nations, rich and poor; modern and traditional, large and small as well as peaceful and strife-ridden. IPES actively works to drive home to all its office bearers, supporters and admirers that, in order to reach its full potential as an instrument of service to humanity, policing must be fully and enthusiastically open to:

1. Collaboration between research and practice.
2. Global exchanges among the police of all nations in the world.
3. Universal dissemination and sharing of best practices.
4. Generating thinking police leaders and followers, reflecting and writing on the issues challenging to the profession.

Through its annual meetings, hosts, institutional supporters and publications, IPES reaffirms that policing is a moral profession with unflinching adherence to the rule of law and human rights as the embodiment of humane values.

For further information: https://ipes.info/

Call for Authors Guidelines for Interviewers: Trends in Corrections, Volume 4

We are currently recruiting authors to write chapters for Volume 4 of the *Trends in Corrections: Interviews with Corrections Leaders Around the World* series. Information will be presented on several countries using the personal views and experiences of a correctional leader in that country. Corrections scholars/researchers will be asked to conduct a comprehensive interview of the experiences and thoughts of a high-ranking corrections official in their country. The scholars/researchers will edit the interviews to emphasise personal experiences, ideas, and detailed examples of issues (both positive and negative) in their country's correctional system. The relationship between theory, evidence, and practice will be highlighted. An important objective is also to present personal profiles of the corrections leaders, their core values, visions, frustrations, temptations and joys in their careers.

Brief Description of the Proposed Book

The main goal of the interviews is to capture the views of correctional officials. The scholar/researcher role should not be to be to criticise or interpret what the officials meant to say, but to write as accurately as possible what the officials told you. The chapter will be based on their views, experiences and thought processes. We know what scholars/researchers think about corrections, but we know less about what the people who work in the corrections field think about and how they evaluate trends, developments and issues in corrections. The basic reason for doing the interviews is that we firmly believe that corrections officials possess a wide variety of information about the field and that practitioners can make significant contributions to our insight into the issues and problems of current correctional practices. The knowledge these individuals possess is not easily captured, but our goal is to describe their personal information for this book. The practical reason that we are asking scholars/researchers to conduct the interviews is because leaders in the field of corrections do not have the time to write and reflect on their experiences, views, opinions and perspectives. We think in-depth interviews are one means to depict the knowledge of correctional practitioners, and it is why we are requesting scholars/researchers like you to record their views.

Guidelines for Interviewers

Goals of the Interviews and General Information

The general goal of the interviews is to present the views and interpretations of the developments, crises, and current issues in the correctional system by experienced practitioners.

Example questions include:

Corrections Questionnaire

- What do those directly involved in the corrections profession see happening in the correctional system in their countries and internationally?
- How do they evaluate or interpret developments (either positive or negative) in corrections?
  - There are many books and articles that analyse and interpret the state of current correctional policy, programmes and prisons by scholars and policy makers from outside the correctional system.
  - What we would like to have are views and interpretations from within correctional organisations.
- What do leaders in the field of corrections who work in the jails and prison systems see happening in corrections?
- What are the issues they consider important?
- What changes do they see as successes or failures?
- What aspects of the system are likely long lasting versus those policies or programmes they see as more transient?

We want to emphasise one major point. We do not want the official rhetoric (or the official success stories) that high-level people sometimes fall back on during interviews; we want their personal views and thinking. If you have the sense that you are getting the formal language and official views on correctional policy and issues, see if you can get the officials to go beyond the official story and push them for their own views. The interviewer should seek to get the person being interviewed to move beyond simple answers, and get them to analyse and reflect on their experiences, ideas, and knowledge. Our trust in your interviewing skills is why you were asked to do the interview.

Topic Areas To Be Covered During the Interview

In this section we discuss the desired content of the interviews. In some situations there may be areas of importance in your country or community that are different than the questions posed below. In those cases, you should focus on these areas more completely and ask about these issues in addition to the questions listed. For example, questions for correctional leaders in transitional countries will likely deal more with changes in correctional philosophy and in organisations than questions for leaders in stable democracies. Even in stable democracies, however, a particular area or locale can be in a state of prison crisis, and we hope that these specific issues will be addressed as well. Being familiar with the correctional policies and situations (such as any lawsuits) in your country will enable you to tailor your questions toward the dominant local issues which have had to be dealt with by the countries' leaders. Be creative while sticking to the main issues at hand.

We have listed a number of general and specific questions that should be covered in the interview. Please try to cover the topics mentioned below as the flow of the interview dictates. Please add, elaborate, and use follow-up questions as you see is necessary to clarify points, expand on ideas, or pursue an insight offered. All the topics below should be asked, but the specific questions listed for each main area are suggestions. Interviews have their own dynamics. Follow them down their most productive paths. Since each of you will be interviewing officials within different organisations, the list and sequence of questions will have to be adjusted for each interview. How you word each question is up to your own preference. When asking follow-up questions, please try to get specific examples or details of any generalisations made by the official. (Specific examples of overarching problems or situations in the leader's country are probably among the most useful and interesting pieces of information to readers.)

Eight Topic Areas (and Suggested Question Wording) for the Interview

1 *Career*: Tell us a little bit about your career: length, organisations worked in, movements, specialisations, trajectories in your career that might differ from those expected, etc.
   - What motivated you to enter the field of corrections?
   - Did the way your career developed surprise you?
   - Did your work prove as interesting or rewarding as you thought it would?
   - Do you have any regrets about an opportunity you pursued or chose not to pursue during the course of your career?

2 *Changes Experienced*: What do you see as the most important changes that have occurred in the field of corrections over the course of your career (philosophies, organisational arrangements, specialisations, policies and programmes, equipment or technologies, methods of rehabilitation, methods of community supervision, intermediate sanctions, personnel, diversity, etc.)?

- What changes in external conditions (support from communities, legal and legislative powers, relations with minority communities, resource provision, political influence, etc.) have had a significant impact on current correctional practices and policy?
- Overall, has the quality of prisons, jails, and community supervision in your country/community improved or declined over the past ten years (such as number of personnel per inmate ratio, amount and type of training offered, programmes offered to inmates, rehabilitation strategies and the amount of money available to implement these programmes, what percentage of inmates are able to have access to programmes, how recidivism of both technical violations and new criminal activity has been affected, interagency cooperation, the effectiveness of top management providing quality control and directing managing and line personnel, inmate and staff safety, and inmate suicide rates)?
- In general, is it more or less difficult to be a correctional officer (or supervisor, warden, regional management) now than in the past?

3 *Personal Correctional Philosophy*: What do you think should be the role of prison, jail, and community supervision officials in society?

- What should be their job, functions and responsibilities? What should be left to other people or organisations? What about line staff such as corrections officers? Prison/jail/community supervisors and wardens?
- What organisational arrangements work and which do not?
- What policies does your country have in regard to relations with the community, political groups, and other criminal justice organisations? Do these policies work well? What hampers cooperation with other agencies and groups?
- How should corrections institutions be run? What programmes should be provided, and how would you prefer sentencing laws to be modified so as to have prisons and jails include the individuals most deserving of incarceration? What are the best correctional strategies to ensure the safety and security of the inmates, staff, and community? What services should prisons and jails provide that are currently not offered? What services are provided that you believe should be cut?

- How should supervision post-prison or post-jail (or in lieu of prison or jail) be dealt with? Is the procedure used in your country working, or do you see an increased recidivism rate due to issues those supervised in the community experience? How would you improve this problem or why is this process working in your country?
- Do you feel that your country uses appropriate intermediate sanctions when needed, or is there a lack of such sanctions? Are intermediate sanctions such as treatment programmes, intensive supervision, or electronic monitoring utilised, and do they reduce recidivism while keeping those in the community safe? If not, what do you feel is the problem?

4 *Problems and Successes Experienced*: In your experience, what policies or programmes have worked well, and which have not? Can you speculate for what reasons?

- What would you consider to be the greatest problem facing the correctional system at this time?
- There is a concern among some correctional officials that the global economic downturn initiated by the financial crisis that started in 2007 has significantly changed the nature of work in corrections. What consequences have the correctional system in your country/community experienced? Overall, how has the economic crisis impacted correctional practices in your country/community (for example, have specific steps been taken to improve operating efficiency, to change release practices as a result of economic hardships, or to change to salary structures or benefits)? Are more people seeking careers in corrections?
- What problems in corrections do you find are the most difficult to deal with? What would be easy to change? Internal problems (culture of the organisation, managerial deficiencies, allegations of corruption or gender-related problems) or externally generated problems (resources, community support, parole or probation procedures, or lack thereof)?
- What is the most successful programme you have worked with in corrections? What is the most successful policy in regard to the positive improvements that have been made to prisons, jails, or community supervision?

5 *Theory and Practice*: In your view, what should be the relationship between theory and practice? What can practitioners learn from studying and applying theories, and what can those who create theories of punishment gain from practitioners?

- What is the relationship between theory and practice right now? Does it exist? Does it work? What holds collaboration or *interaction* back?

- What kind of research, in what form, and on which questions would you find most useful for practice? If not very useful, what could or should creators of theory do to make their ideas more useful to you?
- Where do you find theory-based information? Where do you look: journals, professional magazines, books, publications, reports?
- Does the department of corrections you work for conduct research on its own? On what types of issues or questions?

6 *Evidence-Based Corrections*: In your experience, has your country's correctional system made use of various evidence-based programmes? Do you feel that it is best to use evidence-based practices (or 'what works') or that this focus is not important?

- What evidence-based practices are used now in prisons, jails, for intermediate sanctions, or in community supervision? Do you agree with the use of these practices? Do you feel that using more evidence-based practices would benefit the correctional system?
- Do you read information on evidence-based practices? Where do you get this information? If you do not have this information would you be interested in having access to these practices? What programmes have been proved to work best in your country?

7 *Transnational Relations*: How have you been affected in your organisation's work by developments outside the country (human rights demands, universal codes of ethics, practical interactions with corrections officials from other countries, personal experiences outside the country, programmes developed by other countries, new sentencing laws, political strife or war in your country or neighbouring countries)?

- Have those interactions been beneficial or harmful? What kind of external international influences are beneficial and which ones less so?
- How have international relationships with other countries or other political influences had an impact on correctional policy or practice in your country?

8 *Role of Corrections*:

- How do you think the public views corrections in your country/community?
- Is corrections viewed as a tool used to maintain the existing social order and power structure in your society?
- What levels of public support does the corrections service in your country have?

9 *General Assessments*: Are you basically satisfied or dissatisfied with developments in the field of corrections?

- What do you think of the relationship between sentencing laws and public opinion to the functioning of prisons, jails and community supervision?

- How do you view the release procedures in your country and do they contribute to or inhibit recidivism?
- What rehabilitative programmes could be offered, either in or out of prison or jail, that could decrease recidivism?
- How are intermediate sanctions (such as house arrest, ankle bracelets, rehabilitative programmes in the community, or intensive supervision, among others) in your country used, and how are they working or failing to work?
- Which intermediate sanctions would you increase or create, and why?
- How could changing the balance between intermediate sanctions affect prison and jail environments? Would that be an improvement?
- What are the developments you see as most likely to happen in next few years, and which developments would you prefer to see happening?
- What is most needed now to improve prisons, jails, community supervision, and the overall punishment process in your country?

Preparation for the Interview before the Interview

- Get a sense of how much time you are likely to have and what questions you will be able to ask during that time. No interview will enable you to ask all the questions you want, so it is best to choose your priorities based on whom you are interviewing.
- You should, if at all possible, record the interview by audiotape to aid you in writing the chapter. Seek permission of the correctional leader before recording the interview.
- You will have space for about 6,000–8,000 words (on average) when writing your interview. It is important to pick the most interesting information that you have obtained (in your opinion). Our top priorities are the officials' reflections on the changes experienced during their careers, how they evaluate these changes, and the interrelationship between theory and practice. We are also interested in developing insights into the person. Thus, these areas are high priorities for the interviews.

Instructions for Writing your Chapter

After the Interview:

1. Please write a short introduction to the actual interview. The introduction should:

    - Briefly describe the basic structure of corrections in your country. You have to be the judge of how much an informed reader is likely to know about the country and how much should be explained.

- Briefly describe the interview itself. Where and when was the interview conducted, how long did it take, was there one or multiple sittings, and how honest and open do you feel the discussion was? What was the demeanour of the interviewee?

2. For publication, edit the interview to bring out the most important discussion and answers. You will likely have much more information from your interview than we will have space for in the proposed book.
3. Write a short conclusion about your impression of the interview. What were the major themes? Briefly describe how accurate the leader's views were in accordance with known literature, without being overly critical about any lack of knowledge.
4. Write a glossary of terms or events mentioned in the interview a reader might not be familiar with. For example, if you interviewed a California correctional official and the *Plata* v. *Schwarzenegger* lawsuit was talked about, please define this lawsuit so that readers without knowledge of a country's specific terms and laws might be able to understand what is being referenced.
5. We have had two basic styles that are used to write up interviews. Both are acceptable, but we prefer the second style.
   - The first style is to simply transcribe the interviews – questions asked, answers given.
   - The second style, which requires more work, is to write short statements about the topic of a question and then insert long excerpts from the interviews. The main point is to have the voice and views of the leaders being interviewed, not your own.
6. Construct short biographies of yourself and the correctional leader who provided the interview. The biography should include information such as educational degree(s), experience in the corrections field, and any notable positions/honours bestowed. These biographies will be included in the book.
7. Send the completed interviews and biographies to Dilip Das (dilipkd@aol.com). The total interview, including the introduction, body of the interview, conclusion, and glossary should be approximately 6,000–8,000 words. Biographies should be 100–200 words.

Finally, each interview will be a book chapter which should be useable to teach students in a university/professional training class and/or as a book; it should be a source of knowledge and information to readers interested in corrections, including corrections practitioners, policy makers, trainers, researchers, academics in universities as well as teachers and trainees in corrections academies.

References

Annie E. Casey Foundation. (n.d.). Retrieved from www.aecf.org/
Audit of Department of Correctional Services. (2000). Correction Services. 3 April.
Besev, P. & Gajecki, M. (2009). *Predicting Offender Recidivism among Swedish Participants in the One-to-One CBT Programme.* Stockholm University, Psychological Institution. Retrieved from www.diva-portal.org/smash/get/diva2:222308/FULLTEXT01.pdf
Blakely, C. (2008). American criminal justice philosophy revisited. *Federal Probation*, 72(1), 43–47. Retrieved from https://saintleo.idm.oclc.org/login?url=http://search.ebscohost.com/login.aspx?direct=true&db=pbh&AN=36530724&site=ehost-live&scope=site
Boer, D. (2009). *Sex Offender Therapy Programme for Lithuanian Corrections (SeNAT).* Kalėjimų departamentas prie LR teisingumo ministerijos.
Boer, D. P., Hart, S. D., Kropp, P. R. & Webster, C. D. (1997). *Manual for the Sexual Violence Risk – 20: Professional Guidelines for Assessing Risk of Sexual Violence.* Vancouver, Canada: Mental Health, Law, & Policy Institute.
Bouzaglou, H. (2006). Unpacking the Jali Commission report. *Mail&Guardian*, 18 October. Retrieved from: https://mg.co.za/article/2006-10-18-unpacking-the-jali-commission-report.
Brasor, P. (2017). Media starts to focus on Japan's aging prison population. *Japan Times* Online, 28 January. Retrieved from: www.japantimes.co.jp/news/2017/01/28/national/media-national/media-starts-focus-japans-aging-prison-population/#.WV6HCFFLckJ
Byrne, J., Taxman, F. & Young, D. (2002). *Emerging Roles and Responsibilities in the Reentry Partnership Initiative: New Ways of Doing Business.* Washington, DC: National Institute of Justice.
Campbell Collaboration. (n.d.). Better evidence for a better world. Retrieved from: www.campbellcollaboration.org/
Cavadino, M. & Dignan, J. (2006). Penal policy and political economy. *Criminology & Criminal Justice*, 6(4), 435–456.
Česnienė, I. & Klimukienė, V. (2016). *Individualios kognityvinės – elgesio korekcijos programos "Tik tu ir aš" efektyvumo vertinimas* [Effectiveness of the one-to-one CBT programme]. Kalėjimų departamentas prie LR teisingumo ministerijos.
Cehlar, V. (2012). Evaluácia trestu povinnej práce a činnosti probačného a mediačného úradníka 'pred' a 'po' rozhodnutí súdu. *Justičná Revue*, 64(5), 701–706.

Chabalala, J. (2019). Investigations relating to prison officials, Bosasa complete – NPA. Retrieved from: https://mg.co.za/article/2019-01-19-investigations-relating-to-prison-officials-bosasa-complete-npa/

Coetzee, W., Loubser, J. C. & Krüger, W. (1995). Korrektiewe Dienste in Fokus [freely translated as: 'Correctional Service in Focus']. Johannesburg, South Africa: Hodder & Stoughton.

Comision Interamericana de Derechos Humanos (CIDH) (2013). *Informe de la Comision Interamericana de Derechos Humanos sobre la Situacion de las Personas Privadas de Libertad.* Tegucigalpa, Honduras: Organization of the American States and CIDH.

Daniel, L. (2018). South African prisons overpopulated and failing to address mental health issues. Retrieved from: www.thesouthafrican.com/south-african-prisons-overpopulated-mental-health/

Davis, L. M., Bozick, R., Steele, J., Saunders, J. & Miles, J. (2013). *Evaluating the Effectiveness of Correctional Education: A Meta-analysis of Programs that Provide Education to Incarcerated Adults.* Santa Monica, CA: RAND Corporation.

Department of Correctional Service. (2018). *Department of Correctional Service Annual Report for 2017/2018 Financial Year.* Republic of South Africa: Correctional Services, Department of Correctional Service.

Deslich, S. (2013). Telepsychiatry in correctional facilities: Using technology to improve access and decrease costs of mental health care in underserved populations. *Permanente Journal*, 17(3): 80–86. doi:10.7812/tpp/12–123

Dobryninas, A. & Sakalauskas, G. (2011). Country survey: Criminology, crime and criminal justice in Lithuania. *European Journal of Criminology*, 8(5): 421–434.

Dunoon, D. (2002). Rethinking leadership for the public sector. *Australian Journal of Public Administration, IPAA*, 61(3): 3–18.

Editorial Staff. (2018). 47 interesting facts about Nelson Mandela. Retrieved from: https://thefactfile.org/nelson-mandela-facts/

Fabelo, T., Arrigona, N., Thompson M. D., Clemens, A. & Marchbanks, M. P. (2015). *Closer to Home: An Analysis of the State and Local Impact of the Texas Juvenile Justice Reforms.* New York: The Council of State Governments.

Farrell, G. & Clark, K. (2004). *What Does the World Spend on Criminal Justice?* Helsinki, Finland: HEUNI.

Felix, J. (2018). SA's prison hell: crime, overcrowding, suicides and struggling staff. Retrieved from: www.iol.co.za/capeargus/news/sas-prison-hell-crime-overcrowding-suicides-and-struggling-staff-17449390

Foote, D. (1992). The benevolent paternalism of Japanese criminal justice. *California Law Review*, 80(2): 317–390.

Freedom House. (2015). *Freedom in the World 2015.* Washington, DC: Freedom House.

Fukuyama, F. (1995). *Trust: The Social Virtues and the Creation of Prosperity.* New York: Free Press.

Galeano B. I. E. & Tabora, E. A. (2015). *Tortura y TCID en Hondruas: En centros detencion policial, militar y centros penitenciarios 2002 a 2014.* Tegucigalpa, Honduras: CPTRT.

Garrard-Burnett, V. (1998). *Protestantism in Guatemala: Living in the New Jerusalem.* Austin, TX: University of Texas Press.

Gilligan, J. & Lee, B. (2005). The resolve to stop the violence project: Reducing violence in the community through a jail-based initiative. *Journal of Public Health*, 27(2): 143–148. doi:10.1093/pubmed/fdi011

Government of Japan. (2005). *Act on Penal Detention Facilities and Treatment of Inmates and Detainees* (Act No. 50 of 2005). Retrieved from: www.japaneselawtranslation.go.jp/law/detail_main?re=&vm=2&id=142

Government of Japan Ministry of Justice Youtube Channel. (n.d.). www.youtube.com/MOJchannel

Government of Japan, Prime Minister and His Cabinet. (n.d.) Ministerial meeting concerning measures against crime. Retrieved from: http://japan.kantei.go.jp/policy/index/crime/konkyo_e.html

Hammergren, L. (2009). Justicia y Seguridad Publica en Honduras. In *Estudio de Instituciones y Gobernabilidad*. Washington, DC: World Bank.

Hart, S. D., Cox, D. N. & Hare, R. D. (1995). *Manual for the Psychopathy Checklist: Screening Version*. Toronto: Multi Health Systems.

Home Office (2002). *Offender Assessment System: OASys Manual V2*. London: Home Office.

Hooley, D. (2010, 30 March). Evidence-based practices proven to lower recidivism. Retrieved 5 March 2019, from www.correctionsone.com/re-entry-and-recidivism/articles/2030030-6-evidence-based-practices-proven-to-lower-recidivism/

Huntington, S. P. (1991). *The Third Wave: Democratization in the Late Twentieth Century*. Norman, OK: University of Oklahoma Press.

Institute for Criminal Policy Research. (2019). *World Prison Brief: Japan*. Retrieved fron www.prisonstudies.org/country/japan

Japan Times Online. (2014). Ministry working to better situation of female inmates, 19 December. Retrieved from: www.japantimes.co.jp/news/2014/12/19/national/ministry-working-improve-situation-womens-prisons/#.WSgj_dwlEkI

Japan Times Online. (2016a). Prison rules close to first review since Meiji Era as recividism climbs, 31 December. Retrieved from: www.japantimes.co.jp/news/2016/12/31/national/crime-legal/justice-ministry-considering-review-treatment-prisoners-emphasis-rehabilitation/#.WV42ClFLckI

Japan Times Online. (2016b). Meiji Era brick prison in Nara set for new lease on life, 28 July. Retrieved from: www.japantimes.co.jp/news/2016/07/28/national/meiji-era-brick-prison-nara-set-new-lease-life/#.WSgg_twlEkJ

Japan Times Online. (2016c). Three courts mete out new partially suspended sentences in stimulant drug cases, 3 June. Retrieved from: www.japantimes.co.jp/news/2016/06/03/national/crime-legal/three-courts-trying-drug-cases-first-mete-new-partially-suspended-sentences/#.WV6ZgFFLckI

Johnson, D. (2007). Crime and punishment in contemporary Japan. *Crime and Justice*, 36(1): 371–423.

Klenowski, P., Bell, K. & Dodson, K. (2010). An empirical evaluation of juvenile awareness programs in the United States: Can juveniles be "scared straight"? *Journal of Offender Rehabilitation*, 49(4): 254–272.

Ko, S. J., Ford, J. D., Kassam-Adams, N., Berkowitz, S. J., Wilson, C., Wong, M., Brymer, M. J. & Layne, C. M. (2008). Creating trauma-informed systems: child welfare, education, first responders, health care, juvenile justice. *Professional Psychology: Research and Practice*, 39(4), 396. National Association of Counties (n.d.). Retrieved from www.naco.org/counties

Kropp, P. R., Hart, S. D. & Belfrage, H. (2005). *Brief Spousal Assault Form for the Evaluation of Risk (B-SAFER): User Manual.* Toronto: ProActive ReSolutions.

Kropp, P. R., Hart, S. D., Webster, C. D. & Eaves, D. (1999). *Manual for the Spousal Assault Risk Assessment (SARA) Guide* (3rd ed.). Toronto, Canada: Multi-Health Systems.

Lane, C. (2011). A view to kill. In J. McPhee & C. Rigolot (Eds.), *The Princeton Reader: Contemporary Essays by Writers and Journalists at Princeton University.* Princeton: Princeton University Press, pp. 241–246.

Lawson, C. (2015). Reforming Japanese corrections: Catalysts and conundrums. In L. Wolff, L. Nottage & K. Anderson (Eds.), *Who Rules Japan? Popular Participation in Japan's Legal Process.* Cheltenham, UK: Edward Elgar, pp. 128–163.

Lucko, P. (2010, 15 June). Prison system. Retrieved from Texas State Historical Association: https://tshaonline.org/handbook/online/articles/jjp03

Lulei, M. (2010). *Prevention in the Family. Transnational Criminology Manual.* Nijmegen, the Netherlands: Wolg Legal.

Lulei, M. (2011). *Sociálna práca v trestnej justícii a probácia* [Criminal Justice Social Work and Probation]. Nitra, Slovakia: UKF.

Lulei, M. (2013). *Komunitná sociálna práca s trestanými osobami. Komunitná sociálna práca: sociálna práca v komunite.* Bratislava, Slovakia: Iris.

Lurigio, A. (2016). Jails in the United States: The "old–new" frontier in American corrections. *Prison Journal,* 96(1): 3–9. doi:10.1177/0032885515605462

MacDonald, R. (2016, September). Prison corruption: The problem and some potential solutions [Scholarly project]. In *Columbia Law School Center for the Advancement of Public Integrity.* Retrieved from www.law.columbia.edu/sites/default/files/microsites/public-integrity/files/prison_corruption_-_capi_community_contribution_-_september_2016.pdf

Mačkinová, M., Mačkin, J. & Mačkinová, M. (2017). *Penitenciárna a postpenitenciárna starostlivos* [Penitentiary and post-penitentiary care]. Užgorod: RIK-U.

McCamey, W. & Carper, G. (1998). Social skills and police: An initial study. *Journal of Crime and Justice,* 21(1): 95–102. doi:10.1080/0735648x.1998.9721068

Ministry of Justice. (2007). *White Paper on Crime.* Retrieved from: http://hakusyo1.moj.go.jp/en/56/nfm/mokuji.html

Ministry of Justice. (2011). *Annual Statistical Report.* Slovakia: Ministerstvo vnútra Slovenskej republiky. Retrieved from: www.minv.sk/swift_data/source/policia/naka_opr/fsj/Vyrocna_sprava%20SJFP%202011.pdf

Ministry of Justice. (2016). *3 Challenges for Establishing the "Safest Country in the World".* Retrieved from: www.moj.go.jp/content/001181040.pdf

Ministry of Justice. (2017). *White Paper on Crime.* Retrieved from: http://hakusyo1.moj.go.jp/en/64/nfm/mokuji.html

Ministry of Justice. (2018). *Heisei 30-nenban hanzai hakusho* [White Paper on Crime]. Retrieved from: http://hakusyo1.moj.go.jp/jp/65/nfm/mokuji.html

MNP-CONAPREV. (2014). *Informe Annual a la Nacion.* Tegucigalpa, Honduras: MNP-CONAPREV.

Murray, J. & Farrington, D. (2008). The effects of parental imprisonment on children. *Crime and Justice,* 37(1): 133–206. doi:10.1086/520070

National Alliance on Mental Illness (NAMI). (n.d.). Retrieved from www.nami.org/learn-more/public-policy/jailing-people-with-mental-illness

Navarrete Calderon, C. (2006). Criminología: alcances, ciencia, disciplina y práctica social. In T. De Armos Fonticoba (Ed.), *Criminologia*.Havana, Cuba: Editorial Felix Varela, pp. 6–27.

Nelson Mandela Foundation. (2019). Nelson Mandela's prison numbers. Retrieved from: www.nelsonmandela.org/content/page/prison-timeline

Newman, G. R. (Ed.). (2010). *Crime and Punishment Around the World*. Santa Barbara, CA: ABC-CLIO.

Norris, B. (2015). Eduardo Enrique Gomez Garcia. In M. H. Hurley and D. K. Das (Eds.), *Interviews with Corrections Leaders around the World, Vol. 2*. Boca Raton, FL: CRC Press.

Norris, B. (2018). *Prison Bureaucracy in the US, Mexico, India, and Honduras*. Lanham, MD: Lexington Books.

Offutt, S. (2015). *New Centers of Global Evangelism in Latin America and Africa*. Cambridge University Press.

Paris, J. (2008). Why prisoners deserve health care. *AMA Journal of Ethics*, 10(2): 113–115. doi:10.1001/virtualmentor.2008.10.2.msoc1–0802

Peak, K. (2014). *Policing in America: Challenges and Best Practices* (8th ed.). Upper Saddle River, NJ: Prentice Hall.

Peak, K. J. & Giacomazzi, A. L. (2019). *Justice Administration: Police, Courts, and Corrections Management* (9th ed.). New York: Pearson.

Perez, O. J., la colaboración de Ana María Montoya, C., Montalvo, D. & A. Seligson, M. (April, 2013). Cultura politica de la democracia en Honduras y en las Americas, 2012: Hacia la igualdad de oportunidades. Tegucigalpa, Honduras: USAID. Retrieved from: www.vanderbilt.edu/lapop/honduras/Honduras_Country_Report_2012_V2_Revised_W.pdf

PEW Charitable Trust. (2016, 7 September). Use of electronic offender-tracking devices expands sharply. Retrieved from www.pewtrusts.org/~/media/assets/2016/10/use_of_electronic_offender_tracking_devices_expands_sharply.pdf

Priestley, P. (2008). *Tik tu ir aš: kognityvinė – elgesio programa* [The One-to-One CBT Programme]. Kalėjimų departamentas prie LR teisingumo ministerijos.

Prison Department under the Ministry of Justice of the Republic of Lithuania (2016). Retrieved from www.kaldep.lt/en/prison-department/

Ramseyer, M. & Rasmussen, E. (2001). Why is the Japanese conviction rate so high?". *Journal of Legal Studies*, 30(1): 53–88.

Roberts, J. (2009). Listening to the crime victim: Evaluating victim input at sentencing and parole. *Crime and Justice*, 38(1): 347–412. doi:10.1086/599203

Sakalauskas, G. (2012). Is there a need for probation law in Lithuania? In G. Švedas (Ed.), *Nepriklausomos Lietuvos teisė: praeitis, dabartis ir ateitis. Liber Amicorum profesoriui Jonui Prapiesčiui* (pp. 532–548). Vilnius, Lithuania: Vilniaus universiteto Teisės fakultetas.

Sakalauskas, G. & Jarutienė, L. (2015). *Probacijos veiksmingumo vertinimas* [Assessment of probation effectiveness]. Lietuvos teisės instituto mokslo tyrimai. Vilnius, Lithuania: Lietuvos teisės institutas.

Santana, R. & Romero, A. (2015). Politica Nacional Penitenciaria de Honduras. United Nations Development Program, PNUD.

Schmalleger, F. (2013). *Criminal Justice Today: An Introductory Text for the 21st Century* (12th ed). Boston, MA: Pearson.

Sekhotho, K. (2018). Correctional services: Prison overcrowding remains serious problem. Retrieved from: https://ewn.co.za/2018/08/23/correctional-services-prison-overcrowding-remains-serious-problem

Stober, P. (2016). South Africa: Violent crimes driven by poverty and unemployment. Retrieved from: https://gulfnews.com/world/africa/south-africa-violent-crimes-driven-by-poverty-and-unemployment-1.1897258

Sugiyama, T. (2016). Hikokinsha shogu saitei kijun kisoku kaisei ni tsuite [On the revision of the Standard Minimum Rules on the Treatment of Prisoners] *Keisei*, 127(3): 78–93.

Švedas, G. (2006). Baudžiamoji politika ir ją formuojantys veiksniai [Criminal policy and factors forming it]. *Teisė*, 59: 128–139.

Swank, D. (2003). Enforcing the unenforceable: Child support obligations of the incarcerated. *UC Davis Journal of Juvenile Law & Policy*, 7(61): 61–81. Retrieved from https://jjlp.law.ucdavis.edu/archives/vol-7-no-1/Unenforceable.pdf

Texas Department of Criminal Justice. (2014). *Texas Department of Criminal Justice*. Retrieved from www.tdcj.state.tx.us/index.html

Texas Department of Criminal Justice. (2016). *Annual Review 2015*. Hunstville, TX: Texas Department of Criminal Justice.

Texas State Prison Board. (2017). An inventory of records of the Texas prison system at the Texas State Archives, 1913–1933, 1943, undated. Retrieved from Texas State Archives and Library Commission: www.lib.utexas.edu/taro/tslac/20046/tsl-20046.html

Tocqueville, A. & Beaumont, G. (1833). *On the Penitentiary System in the United States, and Its Application in France; With an Appendix on Penal Colonies, and also Statistical Notes*. Tr. by Francis Lieber. Philadelphia, PA: Carey, Lea & Blanchard.

Torrey, E., Kennard, A., Eslinger, D., Lamb, R. & Pavle, J. (2010). *More Mentally Ill Persons Are in Jails and Prisons than Hospitals: A Survey of the States*. Arlington, VA: Treatment Advocacy Center.

Travis, J., Western, B. & Redburn, F. (2014). *The Growth of Incarceration in the United States: Exploring Causes and Consequences*. Washington, DC: National Academies Press.

Ungar, M. (2011). *Policing Democracy: Overcoming Obstacles to Citizen Security in Latin America*. Baltimore, MD: Johns Hopkins University Press.

United Nations. (2005). *Human Rights and Prisons: A Pocketbook of International Human Rights Standards for Prison Officials*. New York: United Nations.

United Nations (UN) General Assembly. (2016). *United Nations Standard Minimum Rules for the Treatment of Prisoners (the Nelson Mandela Rules)* January 2016, A/RES/70/175. Retrieved from: www.refworld.org/docid/5698a3a44.html

United Nations (UN) General Assembly. (2010). *United Nations for the Treatment of Women Prisoners and Non-Custodial Sanctions for Women Offenders (the Bangkok Rules)* December 2010. Retrieved from: www.penalreform.org/priorities/women-in-the-criminal-justice-system/bangkok-rules-2/

United States Census Bureau. (2016). Quick Facts: Texas. Retrieved from: http://www.census.gov/quickfacts/table/PST045215/48

United States Census Bureau QuickFacts: Cherokee County, South Carolina. (2017, July 1). Retrieved from www.census.gov/quickfacts/fact/table/cherokeecountysouthcarolina/PST045217

United States Court of Appeals Fifth Circuit. (1980, 20 November). *Ruiz v. Estelle*.

United States Customs and Immigration Enforcement. (2014). Retrieved from: www.ice.gov/about/overview/

United States Customs and Immigration Enforcement. (2013). *2011 Operations Manual ICE Performance-Based National Detention Standards (PBNDS)*. Retrieved from: www.ice.gov/detention-standards/2011/

United States, Department of State, Bureau of International Information Programs. (2004). *Outline of the U.S. Legal System*. Washington, DC: Bureau of International Information Programs, US Dept. of State.

UNODC. (2013). *Global Study on Homicide 2013*. Vienna: UNODC.

Van Zyl Smit, D. (1987). A comparative perspective on South African prison law and practice. *Criminal Justice and Ethics*, 6(2): 37–51.

Warren, R. K. (2008). *Evidence Based Practice to Reduce Recidivism: Implications for State Judiciaries*. Washington, DC: US Dept. of Justice, National Institute of Corrections.

Webster, C. D., Douglas, K. S., Eaves, D. & Hart, S. D. (2007). *HCR-20 Smurto rizikos įvertinimas (HCR-20: Assessing Risk for Violence, Version 2)*. Vilnius, Lithuania: Justitia.

Wenzel, M., Okimoto, T. G., Feather, N. T. & Platow, M. J. (2008). Retributive and restorative justice. *Law & Human Behavior (Springer Science & Business Media B.V.)*, 32(5): 375–389. https://doi-org.saintleo.idm.oclc.org/10.1007/s10979-007-9116-6

Woodward, R. L. (1999). *Central America: A Nation Divided*. New York: Oxford University Press.

World Prison Brief (2016). *World Prison Brief data: Lithuania*. Retrieved from https://prisonstudies.org/country/lithuania

Žukauskienė, R., Laurinavičius, A. & Singh, J. P. (2014). Violence risk assessment in Lithuania. *Journal of Psychiatry*, 17(4), 1–6.

Index

Abe, Shinzo 128
academia, working in 13, 17, 43, 58, 214, 215, 221
academic researchers *see* theory and practice
Act No. 93/2008 Coll. of Law (Slovak Republic) 24, 37
Act on Penal Detention Facilities and Treatment of Inmates and Detainees (Japan) 130
adjudication, juvenile crime in Texas 42, 59
Adopt a School programme 93
Affirmative Action 190, 191, 197, 199, 201, 205, 206–207, 211, 221
African Americans and Hispanics 46, 47, 54, 58
African National Congress (ANC) 182, 185, 187, 206; *see also* Police and Prisons Civil Rights Union (POPCRU)
aging prisoner population (Japan) 139, 217
Amarillo, Clements prison 63–64
American Correctional Association (ACA) 67, 81, 82
Anderson, Stephen 85–102, 221; career 88–89; corrections in the community 91–93, 95; evidence-based corrections 99; general assessments 100–101; lack of resources 98; medical care 97–98; mental health 95–97; overcrowding 94–95; overview 85–86; personal correctional philosophy 89–93; problems and successes experienced 94–98; role of corrections 99–100; theory and practice 98–99; transnational relations 99

Annie E. Casey Foundation 45–46, 59
Apartheid 182, 185, 186, 189, 211
Arizona State University, Lake Havasu branch 42
Arpaio, Sheriff Joe 76
assaults in prisons: decline in Japan 135; South Africa 208; YOP in Texas 75
autogobierno 109, 116, 121

Bangkok Rules see United Nations Rules for the Treatment of Women Prisoners and Non-Custodial Sanctions for Women Offenders
behaviour correctional programmes 18
big business, private corrections and detention 77
BJMP: Bureau of Jail Management and Penology (Philippines) 149–150, 151, 152, 153, 156, 160, 164; Modernization Law 154–155
boot camps 51, 64
Briscoe unit 64
BuCor: Bureau of Corrections (Philippines) 149, 150, 152, 163, 164
building design 132
Building Tender (Turnkey) 69, 82
Bureau of Classification (Texas) 64, 82

California, privatisation and 79–80
Campbell Collaboration 143, 148
careers: Anderson 88–89; comparative 214–215; Davila 62–68; Garcia Maradiag 109–110; Jitsawang 167–168; Latoza 151–153; Le Grange 183–185; Lulei 24–25; Mikėnaitė 12–13; Pirtle 43–44; Tomiyama 130–132
case/jail management (Phillipines) 153–157

242   Index

Central State Prison Farm, Sugarland, Texas *see* Central Unit
Central Unit 65
CETSP (Comision Especial de Transicion del Sistema Penitenciario) 121
changes experienced: comparative 215–216; Davila 68–69; Garcia Maradiag 110–112; Jitsawang 168–170; Latoza 153–157; Le Grange 185–189; Lulei 25–28; Mikėnaitė 13–14; Pirtle 44–49; Tomiyama 132–135
Cherokee County Detention Center (CCDC) 85–102; Facility Services and Programmes 87–88; five-pod environment 87
Child and Mother Home (Lithuania) 20
children, parental incarceration and 95
Christian core values 89
Civigenics 66
Clemens unit 63, 69, 74
client-contractor relations, private sector 78
Closer to Home (Report) 45, 59
Coastal Bend, Texas 66
Cognitive Behaviour Therapy 138, 148
Comayagua fire 105, 108, 117, 119
commissioned officers 150, 151–152
community: community corrections in South Africa 185, 191, 201, 202; corrections in Cherokee County 91–93; corrections officers links with 135–136; employment in 142–143; perception of inmates in Thailand 170; prison outreach to local 137, 145; social reintegration forum (SRF) 188
Community Education Centers 66
condenado 116, 121
conduct in need of supervision 42, 59
conquistadors 106
construction of new prisons (Honduras) 114
coping mechanisms (Phillipines) 156–157, 158–159
Correctional Services Act, 1991 (South Africa) 185, 186
Correctional Services Act 111 of 1998 (South Africa) 185, 193, 212
Correctional Treatment Policy Research Group (Japan) 141, 148
corrections officers: links with community 135–136; qualifications in Japan 130; resistance to change in Japan 133–134
corruption: DCS in South Africa 186, 206, 207; Phillipines 158–159, 163; workforce in Honduras 114
Cotulla, Texas 66
County Commissioners and County Judge, interference from 76
CPTRT: Centro de Prevencion, Tratamiento y Rehabilitacion de Victimas de Tortura (Honduras) 117, 118, 121
Criminal Law and in the Code of Criminal Procedure (Slovak Republic) 25
Criminal Procedure Act (South Africa) 185
cynology unit (Lithuania) 21

Dallas County Juvenile Justice Department 41–60
Dallas-Fort Worth area, human smuggling 56
Dangal ng Bayan Award 153, 164
Darrington unit 64
Davila, Adonay 61–84, 214, 215, 216; career 62–68; changes experienced 68–69; general assessments 76–80; overview 61; personal correctional philosophy 70–71; problems and successes experienced 71–74; theory and practice 74–75; transnational relations 80–82
Defensa Publica (Honduras) 107, 122
delinquent conduct, juvenile crime Texas 42, 59
demilitarisation, South Africa DCS 197–199
Department of Correctional Services (DCS) (South Africa) 182–212; demilitarisation of 197–199
Department of Corrections (Thailand) 166
Department of Juvenile Observation and Protection (Thailand) 166
Department of Prison Services (South Africa), establishment of 185
Department of Probation (Thailand) 166
Developing Offender Management in Corrections in Europe (DOMICE) 35, 38
digitalisation of inmate information 113

Index 243

DILG: Department of the Interior and Local Government (Philippines) 149–150, 151, 164
Diversion Courts/programmes 47, 51, 53, 54–55; evaluation of 55
doctors in prisons: Cherokee County 97–98; Japan 139, 146–147
Dominican Republic, model for Honduras 112, 116, 119, 219
drug crime: Dallas 44–45, 46–47; Japan 135, 137; Philippines 150, 155, 158, 162; stimulants addict programme 138; Texas 70, 71; Thailand 168, 169, 171, 174, 176
DSWD: Department of Social Welfare and Development (Philippines) 149, 164
Duke of Edinburgh Awards *see* President's Awards for Youth Empowerment
Duterte, Rodrigo 150, 155, 220

education 91–92, 100; detainee/inmates 50–51, 71, 210; inmates as auxiliary teachers 158; level of prison staff 131
educational and religious roots 88, 89, 90
educational opportunities, Slovak Republic 218
electronic monitoring (EM) 31, 32, 37, 51–52, 202, 210, 230
Emerald Correctional Management 65, 66, 80–81
Encinal, Texas 66
encomienda 106, 122
escape statistics 69, 114, 135
ESTEEM Court/programme 55, 59
EU: Lithuania 12, 13–14, 19; Slovak Republic 25, 215
European Economic Community (EEC) 117
European Organisation of Prison and Correctional Services (EuroPris) 19, 219
evidence-based corrections: Anderson 99; comparative 219; Garcia Maradiag 115–116; Jitsawang 173–174; Latoza 161; Le Grange 202–205; Lulei 35; Mikėnaitė 18–19; Phillipines 161; Pirtle 53–56; Tomiyama 141–143
evidence-based practice (Honduras) 120–121

evidence-based programmes (Japan) 138
external differentiation of prisons, Slovak Republic 23–24

families: behaviour correction in South Africa 202; community corrections in South Africa 201; electronic monitoring and 51–52; Family Visit Day Thailand 175
Federal Bureau of Prisons (BOP) 66, 82
female officials, South Africa 188
financial management 183–184
fire safety, Honduran prisons 117, 119
firearms 196
Florida State University 167
food management, Phillipines 155, 157, 158–159, 162
foreign prisoners: Japan 143; Thailand 174
funding: American privatisation model abroad 80–81; diagnostic plan in Honduras 116–117; Japan 135; lack of 98; Philippines overcrowding and 156, 159–160; South Africa 189; Texas 72, 97, 98
Fusina (National Inter-institutional Security Force) 118, 122

Galveston prison hospital 63
Gang Renunciation and Disassociation (GRAD) programme 75, 83
gangs: classifying members 69; culture in prison 71–72; Honduras affiliations 113, 119; Japan *yakuza* 135; Philippine *pangkat* 150, 160, 165; South Africa 187, 193–194; 13th Street gang 113, 122; 18th Street Gang 113, 121
Garcia Maradiag, Orlando 105–124, 214; career 109–110; changes experienced 110–112; evidence-based corrections 115–116; general assessments 117–119; overview 105–109; personal correctional philosophy 112–113; problems and successes experienced 113–115; theory and practice 115; transnational relations 116–117
gardening project, Lithuania 16, 218
general assessments: Anderson 100–101; comparative 220–222; Davila 76–80; Garcia Maradiag

117–119; Jitsawang 176; Latoza 163–164; Le Grange 206–211; Lulei 36–37; Mikėnaitė 21; Pirtle 57–58; Tomiyama 146–147
GEO, privatisation of prisons in Mississippi 79
Glenn Mills, Pennsylvania 45
global economic crisis of 2008 15
global positioning system monitoring (GPS) 87, 101, 102

Hare Psychopathy Checklist: Screening Version (PCL:SV) 18, 21
Haskell, Texas 65–66
healthcare in prisons 218; Phillipines 154; Slovak Republic 24; *see also* doctors in prisons; mental health
Henry Wade Detention Center 42
Hernandez, Juan Orlando 105, 109, 110
Historical, Clinical and Risk Management Scales-20 18, 21
Honduras 105–124, 215; criminal justice system 107; demographics 107; prison system 107–109; privatisation of prisons 80–81
human resource management 184, 192, 197, 199, 201; appointment of black people to higher ranks 190
human rights 1, 99, 100, 117, 157, 162, 193; Thailand 174
human smuggling/trafficking 56–57
Huntsville, Texas 61, 64, 72

Immigration and Customs Enforcement (ICE), US 62, 65, 66–67, 73, 82–83; Performance Based National Detention Standards (PBNDS) 67
immigration detainees 66–67
immigration detention centres/facilities 62, 215
Imperial State Prison Farm *see* Central Unit
indeterminate sentencing (Honduras) 112
individual case management systems, Lithuania 16, 218, 221
INFOP: Instituto Nacional de Formacion Profesional, National Institute of Professional Education 117, 122
inmates: change of characteristics in Thailand 168–169; classification of 24, 64, 113, 127, 158, 160, 163; idleness among 112–113; leased for labour 65; ownership of businesses in prison 113

Inmates in the Community programme 92
Intergovernmental Service Agreement (IGSA) 66, 76, 83
International Committee of the Red Cross (ICRC) 117, 159
international correctional standards 81–82
International Police Executive Symposium (IPES) 218, 224–225
internships 43
Ishikawa Island Workhouse 142
IWD: inmates welfare division (Philippines) 153–154

Jail Bureau (Philippines) 150, 151, 152, 153, 154, 158, 160, 161, 162, 163, 164
Jali Commission 187, 192–196, 206–207, 211, 212
Japan 127–148, 215, 217; current correctional standards 128–130; low incarceration rate 128; structure of prison system 127–128
Jitsawang, Nathee 166–177, 214, 220, 221; career 167–168; changes experienced 168–170; evidence-based corrections 173–174; general assessments 176; personal correctional philosophy 170–171; role of corrections 175; successes experienced 171; theory and practice 172–173; transnational relations 174
Justice, Crime Prevention and Security Cluster (JCPS) (South Africa) 187, 195, 212
juvenile system (Texas) 41–60; definition 42, 59; Juvenile Board 59

Kubols 156–157, 164

La Tamara prison (Honduras) 105, 108, 109, 110–111, 112, 113, 114, 117, 118–119, 122
Latoza, Randel 149–165, 214, 220, 221; career 151–153; changes experienced 153–157; evidence-based corrections 161; general assessments 163–164; personal correctional philosophy 157–158; problems and successes experienced 158–159; role of corrections 162; theory and practice 159–161; transnational relations 161–162

Law on Probation, Lithuania 14, 15, 18
Le Grange, Johan Ellis 181–212, 214; career 183–185; changes experienced 185–189; evidence-based corrections 202–205; general assessments 206–211; personal correctional philosophy 189–191; problems and successes experienced 191–200; role of corrections 206; theory and practice 201–202; transnational relations 205–206
leadership: importance in Japan 136; military *versus* civilian in Honduras 119–120; role of Warden in TDCJ 73–74
'Learning Centred Leadership' 223
Letot Centre 56, 59, 219–220
life skills 44, 202; Japan 137–138, 146, 217
Lithuania 9–21, 214, 215, 216, 217, 218, 219, 220, 221
Livingston, Texas 66
Livingston Codes 107
Lufkin, Texas 66
Lulei, Martin 23–38, 214, 220; career 24–25; changes experienced 25–28; evidence-based corrections 35; general assessments 36–37; overview 23–24; personal correctional philosophy 28–32; problems and successes experienced 32–33; theory and practice 33–35; transnational relations 36

Mandela, Nelson 182, 190, 211, 221; release of 185
Mandela Rules: United Nations Standard Minimum Rules for the Treatment of Prisoners 1, 143, 162, 166, 167, 177, 185
manpower, lack of 52
Matyag-Mata 159, 164
Mayores 150, 163, 164
medical care *see* healthcare in prisons
meditation programme, Thailand 173
mental health 63–64, 83, 87, 95–97, 182
Mexico 82
Middleton unit, Abilene (Texas) 64
Mikėnaitė, Živilė 9–22, 214, 220; career 12–13; changes experienced 13–14; evidence-based corrections 18–19; general assessments 21; personal correctional philosophy 14–15; problems and successes experienced 15–17; role of corrections 20; theory and practice 17–18; transnational relations 19–20
militarisation: DCS in South Africa 197–198; Honduras prison system 105, 110; public opinion in Honduras 117–118
Ministry of Justice Decree 368/2008 Coll. of Law (Slovak Republic) 24, 37
Ministry of Justice (Thailand) 166, 177
minority populations, arrest of 57–58
Mississippi, privatisation of prisons 79
MNP-CONAPREV: Comité Nacional de Prevencion Contra la Tortura 115–116, 117
Modernization Law of the BJMP 154–155

Nagoya Prison Scandal 128, 129, 130, 132–134, 138, 217
Nakamoto Group 62, 66–67
Nara Juvenile Prison 129, 131
National Autonomous University of Honduras (UNAH) 112, 115, 121
National Penitentiary Institute (Honduras) 105, 108, 109, 116, 118; creation of 110
NGOs 24–25, 27, 37, 114, 120, 145, 152, 154, 162, 185, 188, 204, 218; rehabilitation programmes (Phillipines) 154
NJMPTI: National Jail Management and Penology Training Institute 150–151, 165
Not In My Back Yard (NIMBY) 145, 148

one*carpeta* system (document/data management (Phillipines) 163
Optional Protocol to the Convention Against Torture 1
Organization of the American States (OAS) 117, 121
OTO individual cognitive behaviour correctional programme 18
outdoor exercise 143–144
over-representation of minorities 53, 57–58
overcrowding 213, 215–216, 220; Cherokee County Detention Center (CCDC) 88; Honduras 110–111, 119; Japan 129, 134–135; Phillipines 151, 153, 155–156; privatisation and 78, 79; South Africa 182, 185,

187, 191, 192, 194–195, 200, 201, 202, 204, 207, 208, 209; Texas 61, 68–69, 71, 87, 88, 94–95, 98; Thailand 168, 169, 171, 176
oversight, lack of in private prisons 77, 79

Pangkat 150, 160, 163, 165
paralegal units 153, 156
parental incarceration 95
parole 70–71, 80, 137, 185, 188, 191, 194–195, 201, 202, 204, 210, 220, 230
PD Training Centre (Lithuania) 19–20
penitentiary academy (Honduras) 111–112
Performance Based National Detention Standards (PDNDS) 67, 83
personal correctional philosophies: Anderson 89–91; comparative 216–217; Davila 70–71; Garcia Maradiag 112–113; Jitsawang 170–171; Latoza 157–158; Le Grange 189–191; Lulei 28–32; Mikėnaitė 14–15; Pirtle 49–51; Tomiyama 135–138
Philippine National Police Academy (PNPA) 150, 151, 152, 153
Philippines 149–165, 215–216; overview of correctional system 149–151
Pirtle, Dany W. 41–60, 214, 215, 220, 221; career 43–44; changes experienced 44–49; evidence-based corrections 53–56; general assessment 57–58; personal correctional philosophy 49–51; policies and program successes and failures 51–52; role of corrections 57; theory and practice 52–53; transnational relations 56–57
pistols, confiscation of in Honduras 114, 118
Police and Prisons Civil Rights Union (POPCRU) 187, 190, 197, 199–200, 201, 206–207
Port Isabel Detention Center (PIDC) 67, 83
post-prison programmes (Honduras) 113–114
PREA training 48, 59–60, 218
President's Awards for Youth Empowerment 203, 205
Preston Smith unit 64
prevention programmes 51

prison factories (Japan) 133, 136, 139
prison hospital 63
Prison Rape Elimination Act (PREA) 48, 59–60
Prison Services Act, 1959 (South Africa) 185
prison staffing levels 69
prison subculture 70
prison violence 63
private prisons 216; finance and 76–77; Japan 129; lack of oversight 77, 79; South Africa 207; Texas 61–62; Thailand 173
private sector 65–66; big business 77; client-contractor relations 78; flexibility 78; Private Finance Initiative Prison 148; rehabilitation programmes 73; saving money 77–78; staffing 78
privatisation, California 79–80
probation 14, 15, 18, 19, 24–25, 30–31, 37, 38, 48, 52, 53, 56, 201
probation officers 45–46; huge caseloads 58
problems and successes experienced: Anderson 94–98; comparative 217–218; Davila 71–74; Garcia Maradiag 113–115; Jitsawang 171; Latoza 158–159; Le Grange 191–200; Lulei 32–33; Mikėnaitė 15–17; Tomiyama 138–140
procesados 108, 113, 116, 122
Program for Aggressive Mentally Ill Offenders (PAMIO) 63–64, 83
psychometric tests 197
public opinion/perception 98, 102, 145; Thailand 175, 176
public sector, strengths of 78–79

Quezon City Jail 151, 155–156

recidivism 15, 70, 71, 91; Japan 128, 129; Phillipines 160
Reconstruction and Development Programme (RDP), South Africa 186
rehabilitation 70, 90; Japan 129, 136–137; President's Awards for Youth Empowerment 203; social reintegration forum (SRF) 188; South Africa 185, 202; Thailand 170
rehabilitation programmes 71–72, 92–93; Honduras 112–113; Phillipines 153–154; private sector and 73

Index 247

remand detainees, South Africa 187, 188
research 160–161; cooperation between researchers and practitioners 17; *see also* theory and practice
Residential Drug Treatment Programme (RDT) 44
restorative justice 203–204; victims and 94
'Rising Star Inmates Going to the Olympics' project 172–173
risk assessment/evaluation 17–18, 46–47, 54, 217, 219
Roach unit (Childress, Texas) 64
Robben Island 182
role of corrections: Anderson 99–100; comparative 220; Jitsawang 175; Latoza 162; Le Grange 206; Mikėnaitė 20; Phillipines 162; Pirtle 57; Tomiyama 145
Ruiz v. *Estelle* case 68–69, 83, 216

San Luis, Arizona 66
Scared Straight programmes 51, 93
schools 51, 92
security services, lax in South Africa 195
security technology and procedures (Honduras) 113
sentencing 29–30, 36, 86, 94, 112, 116, 137, 187; Thailand 170–171
sex offenders' programme 141, 142
sexual harassment and abuse of power 195
sexual violence 194
shock programmes 51, 93
Short Term Adolescent Residential Treatment programme (START) 44
SICA: Inter-American Integration System 117
Sierra Blanca, Texas 66, 80
Slovak Republic 23–38, 213, 214, 215, 216, 218, 219, 220, 221
social reintegration forum (SRF), South Africa 188–189
South Africa 179–212
South Carolina Department of Corrections (SCDoC) 86
spirituality/religion (Honduras) 112
sport 187, 203, 209–210
staff: assaults in YOP 75; change of mindset in Thailand 171; corrupt workforce Honduras 114; 'culture of lawlessness' in South Africa 194; Honduras prisons 111; morale and motivation in South Africa 187;

numbers in Honduras 118; pay and morale 89; Phillipines 154–155; prisoner to corrections officer ratio Japan 129–130; shortages in South Africa 187–188; training 130, 155, 216; turnover 49–50, 76, 217
State Jail programme, Texas 70
Strafvollzugsgesetz 144
Suzman, Helen 189

team building 202–203
technology: advances in 169; assisting with research in Thailand 173; linking of databases in South Africa 210
Telepsych 96–97
TESDA 158
Texas: Clemens unit 63; Dallas County Juvenile Justice Department 41–60; private prisons 216; State Jail programme 70
Texas Department of Criminal Justice (TDCJ) 61–84; Bureau of Classification 64; Gang Renunciation and Disassociation (GRAD) programme 75, 83; overview of prison system 61–62; prison management 73–74; staff turnover high 76; Youth Offender Programme (YOP) 83–84
Thailand 166–177, 213, 214, 215, 216, 217, 218, 219, 220, 221
theory and practice: Anderson 98–99; comparative 218–219; Davila 74–75; Garcia Maradiag 115; Jitsawang 172–173; Latoza 159–161; Le Grange 201–202; Mikėnaitė 17–18; Pirtle 52–53; South Africa 201–202; Tomiyama 140–141
Throughcare 129, 136–137, 147, 148
Tomiyama, Satoshi 127–148, 214, 215, 217, 220, 221; career 130–132; changes experienced 132–135; evidence-based corrections 141–143; general assessments 146–147; overview 127–130; personal correctional philosophy 135–138; problems and successes experienced 138–140; role of corrections 145; theory and practice 140–141; transnational relations 143–145
torture 117, 118, 193, 194
transnational relations: Anderson 99; comparative 219–220; Davila 80–82;

Garcia Maradiag 116–117; Japan 143–145; Jitsawang 174; Latoza 161–162; Le Grange 205–206; Lulei 36; Mikėnaitė 19–20; Phillipines 161–162; Pirtle 56–57; South Africa 205–206; Tomiyama 143–145
transparency, Honduras 114
trusty camps 63, 65, 84

ultra-maximum unit, South Africa 208–209
UN: Development Programme (UNDP) 117, 121; International Covenant on Civil and Political Rights 1, 144; Rules for the Treatment of Women Prisoners and Non-Custodial Sanctions for Women Offenders 166, 167, 176; Standard Minimum Rules for the Treatment of Prisoners (*see* Mandela Rules); Universal Declaration of Human Rights 162
unions 187, 192, 194, 202, 207
unit management, South Africa 204–205

victims: victim empowerment 203–204, 210; Victim Support Slovakia 24–25; Victim–offender dialogue (VOD) 188–189, 204; victims' rights 94
violence in prison 67–68
vocational training/programmes 50, 51, 69, 70, 72–73, 112, 142, 209–210

war on drugs 215–216, 220; Phillipines 150, 155, 162; US 94
'what works' 115, 120, 138, 141, 161, 231; *see also* evidence-based corrections
'White Commission' (South Africa) 186
White Paper on Corrections (South Africa) 187–188, 195–196, 212
Willacy Detention Center 66–67

Yakuza 133, 135
Youth Offender Program (YOP) 74–75, 83–84; *see also* juvenile system (Texas)

"Žalioji oazė" (Green Oasis) 16